WOOLMER ON CRICKET

Best Wishes

Bob Woolmer

WOOLMER ON CRICKET

Bob Woolmer
with Ivo Tennant

Virgin

First published in Great Britain in 2000 by
Virgin Publishing Ltd
Thames Wharf Studios
Rainville Road
London W6 9HA

A catalogue record for the book is available
from the British Library.

ISBN 1 85227 848 X

Bob Woolmer is represented worldwide by
MPC Entertainment, MPC House, 15/16
Maple Mews, Maida Vale, London NW6 5UZ.
Tel: 44 (0) 207 624 1184.
Fax: 44 (0) 207 624 4220.
Email: mpc@mpce.com

Check out Bob Woolmer's web site:
www.bobwoolmer.com

Typeset by TW Typesetting, Plymouth, Devon

Printed and bound in Great Britain by
Mackays of Chatham, Kent

Contents

Acknowledgements   vi

Foreword by Lord Cowdrey of Tonbridge   xii

Introduction by Professor Tim Noakes   xv

1 A Call from England   1

2 Cutting My Teeth   13

3 A Taste of Success   35

4 Taking the National Reins   61

5 Life with South Africa   87

6 The State of England   116

7 Whitewash   138

8 The Spectre of a New System   157

9 The 1999 World Cup   180

10 The Coaching Game   192

11 Final Thoughts   225

Index   249

Acknowledgements

Lord Cowdrey of Tonbridge was the first captain I played under in first-class cricket. He had been an absolute hero to me, along with players like Ted Dexter, Jim Laker and Fred Trueman, who as a kid I watched avidly on TV. To be part of Colin's plans for Kent was fantastic. I was also fortunate to live close to his house in Limpsfield, which made it possible for me to journey with him to away games during the county season. Not only was it a joy to travel in the luxury of a Jaguar, with the number plate MCC 307, but it proved to be a godsend. Colin's ability to impart knowledge was wonderful and to be able to listen to him talking about batting and cricket in general gave me a great kick-start to understanding this game. Once I had gained some confidence I would start to pump him with questions about all aspects of the sport, which was how my real cricket education started.

Advice initially had come from my father, who was responsible for my grip, stances and shot development, and then from Peter Hearne. As a seven year-old I learnt valuable lessons in my formative years, so important to any aspiring cricketer. I remember I could not glean enough at the time and spent hours practising, driving my mother mad as I drove ball after ball at the garage door. During Test matches I would be glued to the game on the family's first television set. The 40 minute lunch interval felt like an interminable time.

The encouragement and support of my mother and father was inestimable and it was because of the advice of them and people like Colin Cowdrey that in time I passed on my own knowledge to whoever I could. The support of so many others during my career, such as Bob Baraimian, headmaster of Holmewood House prep school, has made me immensely aware of the debt each cricketer has to the sport.

The five years of my life with the Proteas (I do wish I could have called them the Springboks) were the best and toughest of my career in cricket. I shared them with wonderful people. The players were on the whole fantastic to be with. We had our moments – of course we did – and they are documented in this book. The South African side in fact inspired me to write about my experiences, and to them I can only say a sincere thank you for all that they taught me and in my own small way I hope they will carry on communicating the real joy of the game. They owe me one thing, though! And that is to be the first side ever to win the World Cup on their home soil. We should have won it in England but who knows why we didn't?

I would also like to thank Corrie Van Zyl for the help and assistance he gave me towards the end of my time with South Africa and also to wish my successor, Graham Ford, all good luck in the job. He takes over at an interesting time in South African cricket and I do not envy him. He will have to be patient, understanding and also very firm. Already the side has suffered selection hoo-hahs, and Graham will have to be very diplomatic in his dealings.

It is, of course, amazing that cricket suffers the amount of politics that it does, and I hope the game will realise this before those people with hidden agendas shoot it in the foot. The love and passion for the game, on the whole, is enormous, for it has so much more to offer than any other game. I really get fed up with people in other sports crowing about their financial base and how much they are earning. Very soon football will blow a gasket and a number of clubs will fall by the wayside. The same can be said of the game of cricket, too, of that I am sure. But it will be the game itself that decides its future.

The number of people who spent thousands of pounds to follow England to South Africa for the recent tour amazed me. They followed a team that is continually pilloried by its press, because the former players who are in the fortunate position of being able to comment on the game do nothing but criticise them. I remember playing with those same individuals and listening to them saying, 'I hope I never knock the game when I am finished!' It is important for all of us to bring the game to the same pre-eminence it holds in Australia. They have continued to enjoy success because they are proud of their nation, they are proud of their players, and above all their players are proud to play for Australia.

South Africa have returned from the wilderness and have done fantastically well. Their cricketers are proud of their country. England must return to that state. The team should take a trip around Windsor Castle to see what the nation is all about. England has a greater sense of honour and heritage than any country, yet I get the impression that it's all taken for granted. New Zealand have a greater purpose now. Pakistan have passion and pride; India have lost theirs for a while. It is this passion that drives Australia. They have to be number one. Someone has to knock them off their perch, though – and soon.

The nine years that I spent coaching Warwickshire and South Africa have meant an enormous amount to me, but they have also meant a great sacrifice. My family and I have been apart more than we have been together in that time. I have had to earn a living and one cannot always choose where one lives or goes in life. I was fortunate to find out, after my playing career had finished, that coaching was my real niche in life, and here I have to thank Avendale, Varsity Old Boys and Boland for my initial opportunities. I realised that my true strength was in this field. Having discovered that, I moved quickly through the ranks. Again I was fortunate in that I gained experience before being thrust into the big time and on each occasion that experience was invaluable.

I once said that my ambitions were to coach successfully at county level, to write a book on coaching (*Skilful Cricket*) and to produce a video. Secretly I added that I wanted to coach an international side. I have achieved all that and so I now have to realign my ambitions. It is time to spread the word of cricket back into the schools. Back to the young, to show them the joys of the game and to provide them with every chance. My ambition now is to start a cricket and sports training centre, with state of the art technology to give all youngsters the opportunity to be the best, to make the most of their talent. I know there are hundreds of ex-cricketers with the same ambition. I hope that I can involve them, too.

In writing this book, I have been assisted by Ivo Tennant, who has put up with my grammatical errors and my habit of getting side-tracked on to another topic without finishing off the present one. He has patiently worked on a huge jigsaw. I am very grateful. The same goes for John Young of Young and Enterprising, who spent many hours researching episodes during my coaching career which made an impact on my life. John has been very methodical and persistent in his research. A big thank-you to Gill, my wife, who supplied me with coffee and over the five years of my tenure as South Africa's coach, cut out every single newspaper report available in the Western Cape and others that were sent to us and pasted them in the diary of events. Good or bad, the article went in and they make now for fascinating reading. Often what I read and the reality of what actually happened are, in my opinion, two entirely different things, but reading the reports has kick-started my mind into recalling what really happened. I am grateful to my sons, Dale and Russell, who gave up my computer at home to allow me to use it.

Two people have written very nice things about me for which I am very grateful. Colin Cowdrey has always been an inspiration, as I have mentioned. The other person I only came to meet after I became the South African coach. I can say without any hesitation that we have become firm friends and we share the same almost boyish enthusiasm and passion for the game. Professor Noakes, or Dr Noakes as he became known, has been brilliant. He and Morne Du Plessis set up the first sports science institute in South Africa to attempt to keep South African sport ahead or at least level with the rest of the world. The Prof. is a genius in his own field and recognised internationally as one of the top sports scientists. My relationship with him really started when we set up the medical committee and the cricket research committee, both now affiliated to the United Cricket Board. I asked him to research injuries and why they occurred and how they might be prevented. I always wanted the best eleven on the field. It took time for the medical committee to be accepted and we went through some rough patches when the captain and chairman of selectors became frustrated with a lack of progress. But now we are seeing the effects of the study and a gradual reduction in those injuries, despite the punishing schedules that are set for the players.

Over the last five years I have been moved by the calm and peace exuded by Jonty Rhodes, Andrew Hudson and Peter Pollock, and by the teachings of Ray McCauley. As yet I have not been able to come completely to terms with my own feelings on religion. There are still so many conflicts that worry me. I know that certain things have happened to me in times of deep despair that have been beyond human endeavour, and I would like to thank the Lord for the way he has supported me and for such a wonderful wife and family.

It was through Hansie Cronje and Ray McCauley that I met John Tyler, who, in conjunction with his company (Design Equity) has set me on an exciting new path towards starting my own cricket centre, which we are all hoping will provide sport for all communities. Sport that is both affordable and real, with the best coaching available to all. It is my strong desire to take the game (the modern and old) to as many young children as possible. South Africa is and will be a great starting point.

Through all the good and bad days, there has been one guiding inspiration: Gill. I suspect most women would have kicked me into touch given the amount of time I spent away from home. She has been simply wonderful. There are no words big enough or long enough to say what I mean. In fact as I write this introduction I am away in another hotel room, after another coaching course. We have promised each other a three-week holiday together, as we have never spent more than four days on our own for, I think, 13 years. In fact the only holiday I recall taking with Gill was in 1977 when we went to Corfu for two weeks before I joined Kerry Packer.

I dedicate this book to my wife and family, Gill, Dale and Russell, and to the memory of my parents who set me on my path. They are no longer with us now, but I shall remember them with affection for ever.

Foreword

Bob Woolmer has dedicated his whole life to the game of cricket. He has been enormously successful too, first with Kent and England as a player, then as manager-coach of Warwickshire and South Africa. I count myself lucky to have seen him put his foot on the lowest rung of the ladder and to have followed his meteoric career along its way.

We have several things in common. Both of us were born and spent our early years in India, driven on by 'cricket crazy' fathers. Settling back in England, we were lucky to enter schools that took real pride in all sports, but cricket in particular, so that our basic techniques were grounded securely at a younger age than most. Bob played every ball game on offer, as I did, and he was an outstanding schoolboy hockey player. This helped his fleetness of foot, sharpness of eye, suppleness of wrist and quickness of reaction – all essential when it comes to playing cricket well.

I was the Kent captain who welcomed the young Bob Woolmer to trials at the St Lawrence Ground, Canterbury. He presented himself wide-eyed and eager, ready to bat, bowl and field all day long, the most enthusiastic young cricketer you could wish to meet. Beneath the pleasant countenance lay a determination to learn every aspect of the game and drive himself to the top. His passion for the game was an inspiration, and this schoolboy enthusiasm has never left him.

Setting out as a slow off-spinner, he suddenly found he could swing the ball both ways. Much to his mentors' dismay, he put aside his natural gifts as a slow spinner with flight and took to running in at a brisk medium pace. It was his ability to swing the ball late and away from the bat that first won him a place in the Kent team. He was always a reliable fielder too, and his batting, in spite of his being put far too low in the order for his potential, came on in leaps and bounds.

He enjoyed some bowling triumphs, taking many notable scalps, but the effort he put into his bowling – Bob never did anything by halves – caused back strains, so he had to take things more cautiously. The batting took over, and he developed a high-quality technique. Gradually he forced his way up the batting order, even though Kent had great depth in batting, eventually establishing himself as a fine Kent batsman and a full England batsman in his own right, scoring three memorable hundreds against Australia.

Over the years he fell in love with cricket in South Africa, where he had spent many English winters. He was lucky enough to win a place in the Natal team in Durban alongside Barry Richards, one of the greatest batsmen of all time. Bob's particular strength is that he is a great observer and listener; his experiences with Barry Richards were to have a huge influence on his understanding of the art of batsmanship.

Durban also provided him with a lovely wife, Gill, and Bob took her off to Cape Town, where they have settled with their growing family. Cape Town, together with his links as a coach with Avendale Cricket Club, transformed his future in cricket. Bob has always been a good coach of the young, and he was to make a dramatic impact on the youngsters at the club, and they loved him for it.

Warwickshire were clever enough to appreciate his qualities and in 1991 he came to Edgbaston as cricket manager and coach. He played a key role in building a team which brought Warwickshire many triumphs. In turn, Dr Ali Bacher, the shrewdest of men, noted all this and marked Bob down as the man required to mastermind South African cricket and harness the abundant natural talent there. Bob returned to South Africa and has worked tirelessly, especially in terms of bringing black and coloured cricketers to the standard at which they can blend into first-class cricket on their own merits.

The key to all this success? Quite simply, Bob adores the game of cricket and takes enormous, genuine pleasure in helping keen young cricketers to realise their potential. He has been an assiduous student of the game, and is as knowledgeable about cricket as anyone I have met. Yet he is forever ready to learn, never a know-all bore. With him, there is no place for a 'broad brush' approach; he is deeply interested in the individual talent and style, suggesting and cajoling rather than laying down the law.

This book is an insight into Bob's way of thinking about the game: fresh ideas on old themes, forged over a long span. I commend it to every cricket lover. You will not be disappointed.

Lord Cowdrey of Tonbridge

January 2000

Introduction

One definition of a genius is someone who creates novel employment by doing precisely what he or she wishes. By that definition, Bob Woolmer does not qualify in this category. His profession, cricket coaching, has a long and venerable tradition not just in England, the land of his sport, but in many other cricket-playing nations around the globe. Bob is but one of many who have plied this historic trade. But if a genius is someone who redefines his trade, then he has a strong claim to the label.

The possibility that Bob was somehow different became apparent during the 1994 English season, the year in which Warwickshire, the county cricket team Woolmer had coached for four seasons, won three of the four domestic competitions. They also reached the final of the fourth competition, the NatWest Trophy. It was a unique achievement in the long history of English cricket, and it came at a most opportune time. The United Cricket Board of South Africa, searching for a new coach for the national cricket team, chose Bob in part on the strength of his achievements with Warwickshire, thus subjecting his coaching ability to the most intense scrutiny at the highest level of the game.

An analysis of his performance as coach of South Africa between 1994 and 1999 shows that within eighteen months of his appointment he had changed a team battered by defeat –

South Africa had suffered six consecutive one-day international losses on the Asian subcontinent – into one with the best one-day record between 1995 and 1999. In the 1998/99 season, his last as national coach, South Africa were voted International Cricket Team of the Year at India's CEAT Awards. In addition, Jacques Kallis, who had come to maturity under the tuition of Bob and Duncan Fletcher, was named International Young Cricketer and International Cricketer of the Year.

The achievements of the South African national team under Bob's coaching need also to be viewed from a historical perspective. South African rugby union has been a major international power for more than a century, but South African cricket has not enjoyed the same dominant international standing. This record was finally reversed only in the 1960s by the appearance of a uniquely talented South African team, the best in the world in 1970. But there was no opportunity to entrench this new-found dominance during the following two decades of isolation from international cricket.

In my view, history will judge it fortunate that Woolmer was the chosen influence during the crucial early period of South Africa's readmission to international cricket. For it was he, working alone and with little executive support, who showed South African cricket that the future, as in any human enterprise, belongs to those who are prepared continually to think ahead and to innovate. It is the only blueprint that can ensure continuing success and, ultimately, survival.

But history will also need to reconcile the success of Woolmer's team with the two outstanding blemishes on his international coaching career: the failure of his fancied South African teams to win the 1996 World Cup on the Asian subcontinent and the 1999 World Cup in England. The first can perhaps be excused as the performance of a young team still in the process of realising its true potential, but there was absolutely no defensible reason why the 1999 South Africans should have lost in England. The unpalatable truth remains that the team had actively to lose before Australia could win that tournament.

Perhaps the basis for that defeat will eventually be acknowledged. In my necessarily medical view, the foundation of any such shortcomings lies in the persisting failure to address, in a creative manner, the cancer of modern international cricket: the overwhelming emotional demands made on young men who must be away from their stable home environments repeatedly and for prolonged periods during their formative years. It is inconceivable to me how any player, more especially those who are more emotionally sensitive, can remain sane and be expected to perform consistently under those conditions. For the point is that victory for South Africa in the 1999 World Cup required more of the team in terms of performing consistently at crucial times during the tournament. In as much as that inability to sustain a high level of performance most likely resulted from an individual failure to cope with the ever-present emotional demands of modern international cricket, then controlling them remained beyond the influence of the coach.

Or perhaps South Africa really lost the 1999 World Cup because South African cricket never quite understood Bob or fully appreciated his special talents. In retrospect, it is notable that the early period of Bob's coaching tenure was characterised by a period of rapid innovation as his unusual ideas, readily embraced because there were no others, formed the basis for South Africa's success. But once a successful approach had been developed, there seemed to be a gradual regression into the false safety of conformity and predictability with a growing distrust of further innovation – an all-too-frequent feature of South African sport. And one from which, in the 1999 World Cup, only the unique genius of Lance Klusener, in particular, could almost come to the rescue.

The result of this lack of growth was that by the start of the tournament Australia had rapidly closed the previously large gap in performance between the two countries at one-day cricket; a growing distrust of change also meant that too few players played too many games, so the inevitable injuries occurred always at the most inopportune moments, as with Jacques Kallis before the first crucial game against Australia.

Or perhaps the lack of success in the World Cup resulted from a failure to attend to the necessary detail. For example, the use of the Woolmer-inspired earpiece would most likely have prevented the final tragic run-out in the tied semi-final against Australia. The earpiece would never have been detected in the opening game against India if more care had been taken to secure it invisibly inside the ear. On such details are success and glory denied in international competition.

One can only ever be as good as the working environment allows one to be. The unfortunate aspect to a truly innovative mind is that it will always produce ideas in advance of what is currently acceptable. And so I suggest that the final appreciation of Bob's value will come only in the fullness of time, as his profession begins to move along the path he has been the first to explore.

To understand why Bob chose that path requires an appreciation of the factors that have moulded his life as both cricketer and coach, for at the core of any revolutionary there must be at least three components: the desire and motivation for improvement; a nagging dissatisfaction; and the creative streak to visualise how change can best be effected. These conditions must be allied to a prodigious memory for detail and the ability to observe and recognise, especially the unusual. Bob's desire and creativity are most likely more established features of his personality; his dissatisfaction stems from his own experiences as an international cricketer.

In the introduction to Bob's first book, *Skilful Cricket*, Colin Cowdrey captured Woolmer's essential personal characteristics:

I have enjoyed watching Bob Woolmer's progress from an outstanding schoolboy cricketer to a fine all-rounder with Kent, working on his batting technique with such single-minded zeal as to win himself a place in the England team. Everyone admired his dedicated approach and enthusiasm for the game.

Bob Woolmer's strength was his determination to keep looking for ways in which he could adapt and improve his game, both as a bowler and batsman. He understands more than most players I have played with that you cannot afford to stand still; the game soon overtakes you if you are not alert to change.

The pivotal event in Woolmer's career occurred on the 1976 MCC tour of India when his batting performances deteriorated alarmingly. He recalls that he suddenly found it impossible to hit the ball off the square. The advice he received, that he should 'just hit the ball', he did not find particularly helpful. He learnt that if he were to succeed as an international cricketer, he would have to solve his own cricketing problems. Thus began his real education, and the two crucial determinants of Woolmer's success began to develop.

The first has been that, although he was an international cricketer, he has learnt his craft from the bottom up. He did not graduate directly from international cricketer to international coach, as is the norm; rather, he began his coaching career among Afrikaans schoolchildren in what was then known as the Transvaal province of South Africa, coaching children who neither spoke his language nor came from an established cricketing culture. The lessons he learnt there were crucial; as he would later say: 'If you cannot explain a concept to a ten-year-old schoolboy, then you cannot explain it to an international cricketer.'

The second determinant has been his willingness, nay compulsion, to learn from all who may have something to contribute. He is still the only coach who first approached me by saying, 'Tim, you know nothing about cricket and I know nothing about science. Thus we start on an equal footing. Teach me the science I need to know to become a better cricket coach and I will teach you the cricket to make you a better scientist.' So his approach was to surround himself with those whom he considered to be the experts in the disciplines he regarded as important: the physiotherapist, the sports scientist, the psychologist, the dietician, the sports technologist and the sports physician, among many others. In their presence he revealed the next crucial personal characteristic necessary for success: a genuine ability to listen to what they had to say. And then to apply their advice.

It takes a special wisdom and uncommon humility to recognise that which you do not know; to identify those who have such knowledge; actively to seek out their opinions and then to be unafraid of acknowledging their contribution. For at the very least this requires an ability to recognise one's own limitations; to treat all people as equals but at the same time to recognise and acknowledge each individual's special and unique characteristics. All are uncommon but essential features of the Woolmer personality and all are essential contributors to his success.

Yet while Bob is always open to the opinions and suggestions of others, he has no fear of his own opinion. Nor is that opinion ever sacrosanct. Life, he argues, is a learning curve; nothing is cast in stone and there is no paradigm that will not be shifted. Central to his philosophy is the conviction that there is rarely a single way to do anything – and if there is, have we found it? It is an approach any scientist would envy.

So did Bob keep his promise and teach me how to be a better scientist? I answered that question in a letter I wrote to him the day following the tied semi-final against Australia at Edgbaston on 17 June 1999. At that match I had sobbed openly and unashamedly the moment Lance Klusener had struck the boundary that tied the scores. My tears were of relief that now Bob's hard work and innovation would be rewarded; his vision and ability would be acknowledged; his frustration at being the maverick pathfinder would be momentarily forgotten. Those tears of joy became tears of sadness just a few deliveries later.

I composed the letter as I waited to board a connecting flight at Manchester airport. In it I wrote that, apart from many other things, he had taught me the narrowness of the margin between success and failure in international sport. The same fine line must surely exist in all our endeavours, yet it is only infrequently, as happened in the Edgbaston semi-final, that the narrowness of that edge is so starkly defined. Second, he had opened my eyes to the need for constant innovation. I had considered myself an innovative scientist but even I found it hard to match his relentless inquisitiveness. Nor, even with eyes wide open, could I match his observation skills and his ability to identify what is important in any cricketing situation. Perhaps, I wondered, I could become much more observant of the critical detail in my own profession.

Moreover, he had taught me the need for constant technological innovation. This was an idea quite foreign to me as both a doctor and, perhaps far more alarmingly, as a scientist. I had become accustomed to the usually passive role of accepting each new technology, largely by default. My simple approach was: If the technology is there, then let us use it as best we can. Bob taught me actively to search for the technology that would answer the scientific questions arousing my curiosity, not passively to await its development. It was this attitude that resulted in his being among the first to use video analysis in cricket coaching, and then to introduce South African cricket to the value of computerised game analysis. He remains one of the very few leading international coaches in cricket or rugby who realises that information technology will revolutionise sport beyond all our expectations in the next decade. My prediction is that if given supportive administrators of the kind he will find with Warwickshire, he will be one of the few to harness that technology to its optimum effect.

Finally, as a teacher, Bob taught me the policy, difficult in execution, of never dictating your opinion. Better by far to guide the thinking of one's students or cricketers, allowing them to arrive at their own conclusions. Perhaps the most profound question posed by C.L.R. James, author of what I consider to be the single most important cricketing book of all time, *Beyond a Boundary*, is: 'What do they know of cricket who only cricket know?' His point was that cricket is but the portal to a more boundless reality. Bob Woolmer has made the study of cricket his life's work, and in so choosing he has brought to those under his influence a greater appreciation of the complexity of the life that exists both within and beyond the cricket boundary. His example provides the cricketing paragon of how best to search, without limit of time or effort, for the ephemeral perfection of the well-lived life.

Tim Noakes MBChB, MD, FACSM

Professor of Exercise and Sports Science
at the University of Cape Town, South Africa

1 A Call from England

I ALWAYS WANTED TO COACH England. I was keen enough when I was with Kent and then Warwickshire in the 1980s and 1990s, but no offers were forthcoming. Instead, the United Cricket Board of South Africa, in whose country I had lived and worked during English winters since I was a young professional, employed me for five fulfilling and largely happy years. Yet when my contract with the UCB was coming towards an end in 1999, I was ready for a call from England.

I had shut the door on South Africa rather foolishly while we were touring Australia between November 1997 and January 1998. In my mutually agreed eighteen-month contract I had a clause stating that either party should give three months' notice of wanting to continue or part, which would provide a buffer for me if I wanted, or needed, to try to find another job. It also meant that I always knew what the UCB were thinking contractually, and as coach I always wanted to plan ahead anyway. January 1998 was the cut-off month of my current contract, so I pinned down Ali Bacher in the coffee shop of the Hilton Hotel in Sydney and asked him how he saw my future. We had just lost to Australia in Sydney and my relationship with Hansie Cronje was suffering because of conflicts over certain team policies – number of practice sessions, the quality and make-up of the fitness training, etc. In addition there had been rumours that

1

Hansie had asked the senior players if they were in favour of a switch to Eddie Barlow, the former South African batsman who once had been a candidate for my job and who was my biggest critic, so I was down in the dumps and in a negative mindset. The Doc probably was too.

I cannot substantiate these rumours, as during the tour I thought Hansie and I had got on well. The real sticking point was over the deployment of Paddy Upton, our physical trainer, and my use of the Sports Science Institute in Cape Town, which I admired and valued. Our practice facilities had generally been impressive and we were going to beat Pakistan in due course. We were having a lot of fun on the tour. Hansie and I had been clay-pigeon shooting together and the only problems we had were with Jacques Kallis, who had appendicitis, and Brian McMillan, who had a sore arm and whose wife, Denise, had to go into hospital for an operation. He flew home and missed the one-day matches.

Disappointing as these rumours were, they explain the decisions Bacher had come to make. During our discussion he said he felt that I should finish after the 1999 World Cup and that every coach had a time limit. He would recommend that to the board. I did not remonstrate, and asked him if there might be another role for me to play in South African cricket, and he said that certainly he would give it some thought, but he was unable to guarantee me anything. I had not yet received any offers from other countries and I did not feel as though I was on strong ground, but at least I had the opportunity to make plans for the forthcoming Test series against England and the West Indies, and, indeed, the World Cup. I wanted to identify the team that we could take into those phases.

One of the main criticisms levelled at me was that we did not meet enough in order to discuss future policies and strategies. It was only at the end of my time that Hansie, Peter Pollock (the chairman of selectors), Ali and I met to discuss plans in any detail. But I love working towards goals. I wish I had had someone pushing me as a player, identifying attainable goals and planning strategies. I captained Kent for only four games, three of which we won; we had Worcestershire nine wickets down when rain came in the fourth. The results are by the by, for the real fun was planning the downfall of each batsman when he came in. Having a plan for each session included how many wickets we should aim to take, how many runs we should score, how to dismiss a player, identifying the best batsman and how to bowl to him, and then, as Mike Brearley would have done, giving the bowler the confidence to bowl at the unsuspecting victim.

The point is that I like structure as well as looking to flair to win games. I came to agree with Ali's conclusion, but deep down I wanted to stay with South Africa. If I was supposed to be the best, then why ask me to stop? But I realised my time was up and that pressures behind the scenes must have led to this decision. These pressures came more to the foreground during our three-Test series with Pakistan in early 1998.

After a fine victory by 259 runs at Port Elizabeth in the third Test to square the series, Ali sat me down and questioned my coaching abilities. I had always said that if the players thought I was doing a poor job then I would stand down. Nevertheless, his remark during that meeting that the players had lost confidence in my coaching left me breathless. I asked who was saying that and he refused to tell me. 'How can I regain their confidence if I do not know what or to whom I was doing wrong?' I asked. I needed guidance from my immediate boss and I was getting fobbed off. I was obviously upset, and I asked Goolam Rajah, the team manager, to help me out. I asked him to go to every player to see if they had a gripe or if something was wrong. He could not come up with one name.

I believe the whole thing stemmed from Hansie not playing in the first Test of that series against Pakistan at the Wanderers in Johannesburg (he was recovering from a knee injury at the time) and the farce that occurred before that Test started. It was alleged that two of the Pakistan players had been mugged outside their hotel and they wanted to go home or at least have the match postponed. The police were at a loss to explain the mugging as there were no witnesses, despite there being any number of cameras and security staff in the Sandton area. The other strange thing about the mugging was that when the Pakistan team were invited to a cocktail party to meet the then Minister of Sport, Steve Tshwete, so that he could apologise to them, I saw Saqlain Mushtaq and Waqar Younis coming down in the lift, joking, and Waqar helping Saqlain to put on his neck brace when the lift got to the mezzanine floor.

Then came the rumours that they had been kicked out of Club 69 in Johannesburg for not paying for the services of its girls. Of course, rumours like this, if true, would wreck a Pakistan cricketer's career because the Muslim faith abhors whoring and drinking. After my visits to Pakistan, and having seen members of the team out and about, I can see there is a great deal of hypocrisy within the team. I know that a lot of cricketers enjoy a relaxing drink after a game – it relieves tension and makes for a more social spirit. Certain members of the Pakistan team enjoyed a drink but had to do so in a clandestine manner. To this day, the question of whether the players had been mugged or thrown out of a sex shop has not been answered, and for the purpose of international relations has been swept under the carpet.

The cost to the UCB of moving the game was in excess of a million rand (about £100,000). There was chaos for days, and it took the focus off a rain-reduced and drawn Test match in which both teams played some ill-disciplined cricket. Hansie watched this, and like the rest of us was disappointed. When reinstated for the next Test match in Durban, which we lost narrowly, he wanted a far stricter regime. In fact, Ali and Peter lectured the team on the disciplines required for Test match cricket. A similar chat took place later that year, in September, before the Commonwealth Games, and before we started our tournament in Bangladesh and series against the West Indies in November. The players were told in no uncertain terms that they were accountable for their performances, that it was a privilege, not a right, to play for their country and that they were far better than the results were showing.

There is always a balance to be struck between being accommodating and helpful and creating the type of discipline necessary for success. If a coach has to take on excessive disciplinary roles then he will become less able to do his real job of making individuals better cricketers. That may sound strange, because discipline is part of the job, but the key is to be able to make the player in question self-disciplined, especially in his cricket, and to make him realise he has responsibilities outside the game when he handles people and the media.

We went on to complete the most successful season in the history of South African cricket, but as I said, as the 1999 World Cup drew ever closer, I was ready for that call from England. And it came. David Lloyd had decided to stand down at the conclusion of the World Cup and I was, it was inferred, the England and Wales Cricket Board's preferred candidate.

The negotiations started after South Africa's tour of New Zealand in February and March 1999, when I arranged a strictly confidential meeting with Simon Pack, the international teams director of the ECB and the chairman's envoy, at my home in Cape Town. We had scheduled a week's full break for everyone during this period and I was duly visited by him on Tuesday, 13 April. Our discussions lasted the best part of three hours, during which time I made it clear I was an interested party as long as this was kept secret and did not interfere with South Africa's World Cup preparations. We spoke about team drills and what would be expected of me, and although I told him I wanted a holiday and was concerned about making an immediate switch to another country, I was left with the distinct impression that, although he was also going to see Duncan Fletcher on a separate trip, I was in demand.

What I knew for certain was that I wanted to have a break from international coaching because of the incessant travelling and the intensity of the work. Yet I was flattered to be wanted by England, for whom, after all, I had played Test cricket. Were they prepared to wait? Initially, yes, but the goalposts were soon changed, which led to huge complications.

At the time of Pack's visit, as I have said, South Africa were about to begin final preparations for the World Cup. Success in England – we were the pre-tournament favourites – would be the pinnacle of my career. I had not fulfilled my ability as a player and here was the very opportunity to atone for that as a coach. Coaching reputations are usually made because one's team is successful, and there was no doubt that as South Africa had won the Commonwealth Games tournament, the Bangladesh mini-tournament and had beaten the West Indies 5–0, my reputation, which had been somewhat tarnished after losing to England at Headingley the previous summer, had been restored. During the West Indies series England were in Australia; having defeated South Africa they were expected to give the Aussies a decent contest. That did not materialise, and immediately rumours had started that David Lloyd was going to resign at the end of the World Cup. My position was already clear: I would be leaving the South African side at the same time, this decision having been taken some eighteen months previously. I was up for grabs.

I was fortunate in having struck up a friendship with Michael Cohen, whose company in London, MPC Entertainment, handles many of the UK's top personalities, and who spends his winters in Cape Town. I immediately enjoyed his company and found him both charming and trustworthy. He was also a keen cricket fan, keen not least that I should take on the England job. At the time I was desperate for a complete break from the game. Michael was not so convinced and said that I should at least have a look at what England had to offer. In fact, throughout my chats with Pack, the one driving force keeping me truly interested in the position was Michael. He had so much confidence in my ability that it was almost frightening. The major problem I had was that I so wanted South Africa to win the World Cup, and did not want other considerations preventing me from concentrating on my goal. So I asked Michael – who lived in London, had friends in high places and knew what was going on – to represent me in my negotiations with the ECB. While the World Cup was on, he would keep in touch with Pack and hammer out the details on my behalf, reporting back as and when he had to.

Almost immediately after Pack had touched down and was back in his office, a newspaper reporter rang me about his visit. Bang went the confidentiality. I had to admit that I had been visited, and mayhem ensued. English radio, television and newspapers were full of the story – I even knocked soccer off the back page of the *Sun*! The trouble was that South Africa's arrival in England was imminent and I knew I would be besieged by questions. I had to knock the subject as hard as I could on the head. My team was already taking the mickey out of me: 'You can come to all the games except when we play England,' Shaun Pollock quipped, and the others chimed in. It was all good fun but I knew it had to be stopped.

At the first press conference in London, I said that I was flattered to be in the picture but would not be making any decisions until the World Cup was over for the sake of the South Africans. This applied to any other offers as well. I recognised that I was very fortunate that I would have a future after finishing with South Africa. The fact that by that time five countries and one county had spoken to me – New Zealand, who I had discussions with, Bangladesh, Pakistan and Sri Lanka as well as England and Warwickshire – was indeed flattering. I was also to see Dr Ali Bacher immediately after the tournament as there was still the possibility of a role for me in South Africa, perhaps as a coach to the black cricketers of the future. But my focus for now had to be on the World Cup and I wanted everyone to respect that.

I had been truthful when I said to Pack that I wanted a rest and that I did not think it was an ethical move to take England to play in South Africa having spent five years coaching them. Why try to destroy something that had taken five years to build up? It seemed pointless, and I was a bit miffed that the UCB had not yet tried to do something about deciding my future. If I was going to coach England, it would have to be from March/April 2000. I was assured that there would be no hurry, that the ECB wanted to ensure that they got the right man. There was also a possible conflict of interest as Dennis Amiss, Warwickshire's chief executive, was on one of the ECB's committees. He was keen to know what my plans were as he and his Warwickshire colleagues felt they had to tell their incumbent coach, Phil Neale, what his future prospects were. There was a chance that he would be considered for the England manager's job, which was probably going to be a full-time position.

The media began to press for answers. Every day I would pick up a newspaper and there would be a for-and-against article as to whether I would be suitable for the job. The pressure to make a decision was becoming too great. Eventually the ECB's stance that I did not have to make up my mind in a hurry was turned around with a proclamation that, as I had been adopted as a candidate, a decision by me was needed by 27 May, when the candidates were to be invited for interviews.

One of the offers Cohen had negotiated included a potential salary of £250,000 from Sri Lanka. In addition to this, flights would be provided for my family and a house in Colombo, which effectively would have doubled the package. Lloyd, apparently, had been paid £80,000, and Pack found it extraordinary that other countries were prepared to pay so much. He made it very clear to Cohen that he thought the ECB would not be prepared to match those offers. It is true that I vacillated a bit, but I was keen to see Lord MacLaurin of Knebworth, the chairman of the ECB. For one reason or another, this proved impossible. I found this strange, given that he had made his name by improving the fortunes of Tesco and would, presumably, have desired to see any candidate for a prominent position in the company as soon as possible. I wanted to tell him that if he could wait until the following March – in other words after England's tour to South Africa was over – I would take on the job.

When Michael Cohen telephoned Pack and said he wanted to discuss terms, he was informed that I had not yet been officially adopted as a candidate and that I would have to wait at least two weeks for confirmation, once a meeting of the ECB Management Advisory Committee comprising Brian Bolus, Ian MacLaurin, Tim Lamb, Simon Pack and Dennis Amiss had taken place. While the ECB were deciding whether or not to adopt me as a candidate, other countries were busy negotiating with Michael for my services and were prepared to wait until March 2000.

The World Cup by now was well under way. The ECB were filibustering. Eventually I was asked to attend a meeting in London in the same week as South Africa's World Cup semi-final against Australia, which put me in an impossible position. Bacher, Peter Pollock and Ray White (president of the UCB) had decreed, understandably enough, that the team should stay put in their Birmingham hotel. At a specially convened meeting with all the members of the management committee including Hansie Cronje, it was decided that I could not go for an interview with the ECB until after the World Cup. Eventually the ECB said they were prepared to wait until after the final, but by then it was too late for me.

Neither Michael nor I could believe that the ECB could be so unreasonable as to ask me to leave my South African team two days before the semi-final of the World Cup, a tournament for which we had prepared over the last five years, to spend a day in London being interviewed for a job coaching England. It was the final straw. My mind was made up. I had confided in Hansie Cronje, South Africa's captain, a couple of times and he was sympathetic and told me not to worry, that I should take the job and get paid as much as I could for it. But a few days before the semi-final against Australia, I decided enough was enough. I was far too emotionally involved with the team and I needed a proper break. I wanted to re-energise myself, although with hindsight I wish I had had a longer contract than just to the end of the World Cup. I would have liked to oversee the team through to the end of the 1999/2000 season while blooding a new coach during that time. It would have made a difference. I am sure that somewhere along the line all the speculation and indecision affected either myself or the players. I said no to England and felt bad about it, but I also reckoned that England needed someone to take over before New Zealand arrived for a tour after the World Cup. They desperately needed to bring continuity to the role David Lloyd had occupied.

This was the letter I sent to Michael Cohen, instructing him to inform the ECB that I was no longer in the running for the position:

14 June 1999

Re: England

Dear Michael,

After a lot of deliberation and discussion with my wife Gill and other advisers, I have come to the conclusion that it is in my best interests to say no to the England job. I know this is something that you do not want to hear after all the hard work you have put in. I am very grateful for everything that you have done and sincerely trust that this does not sully our relationship. Especially as I would very much like to entertain you in Cape Town.

I cannot carry on fooling myself that England is the job I crave. At the moment I need a prolonged break from the international hurly-burly and would prefer to pursue a career in coaching that leads me on to the path of my own academy in Cape Town, to further the aspirations of the disadvantaged societies in South Africa and do media work. I will continue to coach in the UK via Warwickshire for three more seasons and hopefully with your guidance enhance my cricketing aspirations. Let me say now that I do not rule out coaching England as an aspiration. But I do believe the timing to be wrong. It is a gut feeling and certainly in the short term I would prefer to spend quality time with my family. I would therefore like us to speak to

Simon Pack and withdraw formally my candidature for the England position as of today's date, and to make it clear that I do not want to waste the ECB's time by being overly hesitant. We can make a press statement in that regard immediately.

Michael, I do hope that you can understand my position on this matter and, as I said before, that it will not harm our friendship in any way.

Best wishes,

Bob

And there was another reason behind my decision. I had found Pack, an ex-Army officer, to be pleasant and solicitous, as had Cohen, but I discovered that not everybody wanted me. Brian Bolus, a former Nottinghamshire batsman who in our days in county cricket used to pad away every ball I bowled at him, had become an England selector during Ray Illingworth's regime and was now chairing the influential Management Advisory Committee. He clearly did not want me, made unattributed comments to the press and took exception to an agent dealing with the ECB on my behalf. It became clear to us that Pack did not get on with him. Michael became very frustrated with the shilly-shallying and vented his anger on Tim Lamb, the chief executive of the ECB, who was an old acquaintance, when they met at a floodlit match after the World Cup, telling him that the negotiations with the ECB were the most inept he had ever been involved in during thirty years of top-level business.

The day after South Africa were knocked out of the World Cup by Australia in one of the greatest of all one-day matches, Bacher and White met with Michael and myself at the Royal Gardens Hotel in Kensington. Ali was emphatic that he did not want me to coach another country and said that in future it would be stipulated in the contract of any successor of mine that he would not be entitled to coach another country immediately. Ali did not want valuable information to be utilised by our opponents. He said that we would meet again in Johannesburg to resolve my future with the UCB, and we did indeed do so. The upshot was that I was to work for him on a consultancy basis as by then I had decided to rejoin Warwickshire on a three-year contract.

But, as I said in my letter to Michael Cohen, I would still like to coach England at some point in the future. I have to say that I was staggered when the ECB appointed Duncan Fletcher to replace Lloyd only from the end of the domestic season, although I was certainly not surprised that they chose him. He and I shared similar coaching methods and I felt he was a very good choice, but at the end of the season? No way! I am afraid it showed in England's performances against New Zealand. One might say that Fletcher's presence would not have made that much difference, but the modern player is used to a coach and the captain's role has changed as a result. In addition, the England selectors had appointed a new captain. When Nasser Hussain was injured during that 1999 Test series, the absence of leadership showed.

The significance of the relationship between captain and coach is growing ever greater. I feel strongly that as long as a coach is learning and a captain is receptive, then a team can go forward; if they stagnate, the team will stagnate with them. I have been fortunate in my time to have had dealings with men of the calibre of Bacher and Pollock, Amiss and M.J.K. Smith, the former England captain who is now chairman of Warwickshire. I will always remember two things in particular with regard to M.J.K.: he taught me the phrase 'nothing is cast in stone' and that opinions should be listened to, and that no one has exclusive rights to cricket knowledge. I took these words to heart. As far as I am concerned, there is *never* any shortage of ideas around.

2 Cutting My Teeth

GIFTED SPORTSMEN DO NOT NECESSARILY make top-class coaches. This, I know, is a generalisation, and of course there are exceptions, but the reason I write this is because the top-class performer has achieved his success through natural instinct and timing while the lesser mortal needs longer to work on and improve those aspects. That is why Gary Sobers has never coached West Indies in a full-time capacity, why Mike Procter is better suited to being a selector and a commentator in South Africa, and why many of those who actually undertake this role at first-class level were thought of as average in ability in their playing days. These were old pros who knew a lot about the game but were confined to cutting and preparing the pitch and offering sage words of advice when prompted. They placed a handkerchief on a length and took the ball behind a solitary stump with bare hands. Their lives were lacking in glamour and appreciation.

Take Claude Lewis, the coach of my county, Kent, who oversaw the development of several individuals who played for England, including Alan Knott and Derek Underwood, two of the finest cricketers in the history of the game. He played, coached and finally scored for the county for sixty years, which was a remarkable achievement. His life was a fulfilling and happy one, but his career was not heralded.

Nowadays his profile, his status and, not least, his remuneration would be that much greater.

I would like to think that I have had something to do with the modern perception of the job as being more glamorous and scientific and carrying more influence. I was not as talented a cricketer as Procter, which perhaps is why I was able to empathise more than he did with less gifted players, but I did possess sufficient ability to play for my country and to be chosen for Kerry Packer's World Series, and I also knew what it was like to go in low in the order behind a bevy of Test stars, to be used as a second- or third-change bowler and to be regarded initially as a one-day specialist rather than an emerging talent. The benchmark for a really good Test cricketer is a batting average of 40. Mine was 33. I spent two years when I was at my peak as a batsman engaged in the World Series, and later, in 1982, when I could still have been playing for England, I joined the breakaway tour to South Africa under the captaincy of Graham Gooch. I regret neither of these moves, nor do I offer this as an excuse for not performing better, but, had I not been lured to join these banned organisations, and had I not succumbed to a back injury, I might have captained my county and country. Hence, when I retired shortly after my thirty-sixth birthday, there was much I still wanted to achieve in the game. Rather than leaving me dejected and lamenting my lot, my experiences as a player gave me the impetus to succeed as a coach.

My coaching style has always been very much on a team management basis, for I do not believe cricket can be run by a supremo. I believe in allowing people to develop their own roles within the team and giving them the leeway to do their own thing. That often brings the best out of an individual. I also believe there are basic principles that apply to all aspects of the game, yet there are different ways of playing. Some players like to restrict their shots while others like to use them all. There is more than one method of playing spin and seam, and it is the coach's duty to open the eyes of the player to find out what suits him. The player has to learn to take responsibility for his performance once he steps over the boundary rope, so preparation and advice are the key words for the coach.

It is often heard that if a player gets to a certain level he should not need technical help. Mike Brearley certainly thought along these lines. I firmly disagree. Certainly players in individual sports such as tennis and golf do not regard a request for help as a weakness, whereas I have the feeling many team players might. I can only say that I wish I had been lucky enough to have had someone working with me. One of the biggest regrets of my playing days was that I was unable at times to deal with a number of problems which I now help cricketers to overcome: the fear of failure, understanding why one plays the game and looking for the game within the game. Confidence is born of success and success is born of good technique, because without it one would be unable to deal with the problems cricket presents.

Good coaches will always leave a considerable mark on an emerging sportsman. When I joined the Kent staff, Colin Page, who looked after the second XI, influenced me considerably. He was a swing bowler turned off-spinner who would often recite the story that he was near a hundred wickets for the season and would never bowl again because an amateur down from Cambridge would take his place in the team during the university vacations. He was an autocratic coach who pushed youngsters hard to find out whether they were mentally strong enough to play professional cricket. Some very talented cricketers had to give up the game as a result. I was among many who thought at the time that he went too far, but I realise now that his approach was probably quite a good thing.

My career as a coach was largely shaped by my academic career – or lack of it. When I joined Kent, I had worked for ICI in High Holborn for eighteen months, a job which taught me about discipline and attention to detail. My father had organised it for me after I left school because my exam grades were not good enough for Loughborough College or a university. At the end of 1967, Kent CCC's manager Les Ames offered me a year's cricket on the Kent staff. Having agreed to that, it became clear ICI would not take me back again, so I had to find alternative winter work. Page told me there was money to be made from coaching abroad as well as in England, and that in the close season one could scrape together a decent living, so I took my coaching exams under the supervision of Harry Crabtree at the indoor school at Sevenoaks.

That winter, in addition to working at Holmewood House preparatory school just outside Tunbridge Wells – Bob Baraimian, the headmaster, was married to the daughter of the Kent president – I started my own cricket school by taking over the drill hall in Tunbridge Wells, bringing in enough money to provide netting and mats for two nets, which the council allowed me to put up. I ran a Christmas course, which made me £10 profit after deductions for expenses and encouraged me to stage another at Easter, which was infinitely more profitable and attracted greater numbers. I was assisted by Graham Johnson, who I was to play with for many years. This was the first of many such winter and Easter coaching courses I was to hold. It was very rewarding as players I coached went on to do well later on, and it gave me an insight into how to run a course and to deal with all kinds of parents and other individuals, let alone how to coach young cricketers.

Technically, I learnt from Colin Cowdrey, my captain when I first played for Kent in 1968. He would talk about technique all the time and he influenced me considerably when I became a coach. Colin told me never to be satisfied with what I had; he had taken that advice himself from Jack Hobbs, who had told him at the end of each year to assess his ability and if he felt he had weaknesses to ensure these became strengths by the following season. I was taught to play certain shots at certain times in my innings. For instance, trying to drive off the front or back foot against the new ball on the off side with the usual cordon of three slips and a gully was not something to do; Cowdrey's advice was to line up your off stump with the leg stump directly opposite you and play straight, leaving the ball alone early in an innings. He would try to make the bowler bowl at him. The Australians are marvellous at this. They walk to off stump and hit anything straight for four. They make the bowler bowl at the batsman and are not tempted by anything wide, forcing him to change his strategy. Later, I learnt from Brian Luckhurst, with whom I batted for Kent, and to a certain extent from Ken Barrington when he became England's tour manager. Alan Knott, too, possessed great knowledge and was revolutionary as well. He persuaded me that it was safer to hit into the spin than with it, advice that today would be seriously frowned upon.

There were also a number of coaches who would tell me to copy their approach. I prefer not to do that. I try to advise players I have coached to learn different elements of technique from different people, as I did, giving them options and letting the individual adapt his own style of play to the situation. What I dearly would have loved and needed throughout my career was someone to nag me into not getting out. Only recently I listened to Sir Donald Bradman being asked why he had averaged almost 100 in Test cricket and the next Australian batsman on the list achieved only 56. He said he did not know what the answer was but he could not understand why Allan Border kept losing his wicket. I thought about this remark for ages and realised that in county cricket there are times when a batsman does reach a stage of mediocrity. He thinks, Well, I've scored a century here so I don't mind if I get out. It is stupid thinking, because the next innings he might get an absolute snorter of a delivery or a bad decision. The batsman should be thinking in terms of a double century, not out, so that if the duck follows it will not have such an effect on his average. I was certainly one of the people who would think: Well, there's always tomorrow.

Barry Richards was one batsman who should never have been out, but he became bored. He admits that himself. He needed a challenge to rouse himself, such as when he made 190 for Natal against Rhodesia in a match I played in. In the first innings Robin Jackman had got him out lbw with one of his famous appeals. Barry was so annoyed that in the second innings he never let the ball hit his pads again. He was by some way the best batsman I have ever seen, but unfortunately he tired of county cricket and of course was unfortunate enough to play no more than four Tests for his country.

Even with players as good as Richards, coaching is important. Both he and Graeme Pollock were taught well in the crucial years between the ages of eleven and fifteen. The other extreme is someone like Geoffrey Boycott, not nearly as talented as Bradman, Richards or Pollock but who had the ability and the desire to score hundreds. He would be out more often because he was not so good a player, but he would never get himself out. My view is that the more you play, the more you learn, and the better you should become. Geoffrey benefited from this type of approach and so should English cricket. After the World Cup in 1999 I visited Trent Bridge to watch Nottinghamshire take on Derbyshire, and what I saw there after five years out of the domestic game in England was too many batsmen playing too many shots too early in the innings, and poor foot movement. This is partly due to the prevailing conditions in England, of course. Young cricketers need pace and bounce, Australian-type surfaces, and good nets. The ball must come on to the bat. Having said that, county cricket teaches people more about different pitches than anything else, so English cricket should be the best in the world, but other countries have caught it up and overtaken it.

One of the inherent difficulties in coaching is that the coach's experiences are the only ones he can ever talk about. If Javed Miandad tells me about certain conditions or players, it is second-hand information. I can only discuss pros and cons from my own perspective. Players are inevitably going to become bored with comments about how things were and how players played in the old days, so it is vital as a coach to be able to relate stories of other players and to realise that modern-day players prefer modern-day information. I used to keep a little black book on how I was out, how I got someone out and what happened during the match, yet this homework was considered stupid at the time and it was thrown out of the Kent dressing room by Alan Brown, the old fast bowler. I was told to use my brain instead.

I would always encourage a team, now, to use a diary. All eleven players should be looking to work out what to do if made captain – only they are not because they do not want the responsibility and would prefer to think about what they are going to do with their girlfriend that evening. By writing down something about the day's play that they have learnt, they will be more likely to take that on board and be able to deal with the situation if it occurs again. One such incident I specifically remember was bowling to Harry Pilling (5ft) and Clive Lloyd (6ft 4in). My length had to be spot-on otherwise the one drove what the other one cut! And there are certain details about certain grounds that should not be forgotten either, such as the effect of the wind at Port Elizabeth, renowned for freshening up the pitch. So keeping a diary is one sure way of learning and improving. Peter May once wrote that for every ball bowled there was an answer as a batsman; in other words, a batsman in good form and concentrating properly should be able to deal with any delivery sent down. The secret, of course, is always being able to be in 'good form'. Bowlers, however, will not enjoy May's statement: their skill is to get the batsman in two minds and then dismiss him. The nuances of the game are truly fascinating, and I have always found them so.

I had not necessarily intended to become a coach, although I enjoyed the coaching I did in England, which taught me much about my own game as well. My next step was to go to South Africa in 1970 and coach primary school boys. I had just won my county cap and Colin Cowdrey advised me to go abroad: 'Get some sun on your back' were his very words. He wanted me to play all year round to get stronger – the antithesis of the viewpoint today – and very kindly arranged a job for me with the Transvaal Cricket Union (TCU, now known as Gauteng). The thrust of the South African Cricket Union in those days was to take the game to the Afrikaans community, for rugby was their major sport, and particularly to promote the game in Afrikaans schools, so I was given a position as coach at Auckland Park Junior School, W.H. Geldenhuys, W.H. Coetzee Laer Skool (Lower School) and Southern Suburbs Primary School. I was very impressed with the almost fanatical discipline imposed on the children in these schools; as a result they learnt very quickly from me and I was happy and successful during this time. I was unable to play competitive cricket in South Africa because at that time they did not want overseas professionals in their leagues, but I managed to play some friendly games with the Auckland Park and Inanda country clubs.

That winter was my first experience of coaching teams, and it has stood me in good stead ever since, although as a green 22-year-old I did not understand apartheid. I remember going to the post office once and queuing behind black people for thirty minutes, and upon reaching the counter being told that I was at the wrong entrance. But I enjoyed working and playing in South Africa, and I went back in 1973 on a tour with Derrick Robins, who was a wonderful benefactor and had helped many players. I will always be grateful for his help. I also met Gill, my future wife, in Durban when I agreed to stay on and play for Natal and coach at Natal University. It was here that I was introduced to another wonderful bunch of people at the Kingsmead Mynahs, the coaching arm of the Natal Cricket Union. The head coach was one Barry Richards. As player-coach, I helped Natal University win the BP Cup, forging a strong relationship with the captain, John Bristow, who went on to captain the South Africa Universities side in 1976. I spent my next few winters playing in other countries, and in 1976/77 I toured with the MCC to India, Sri Lanka and Australia for the Centenary Test in Melbourne. Then came Packer.

My main involvement in the Republic started in 1981 when I took my wife and elder son, Dale, to see his grandparents in Tzaneen, the citrus farming area in the north-east of the country. Gill's father owned land there which produced avocado pears the size of footballs. On the plane going over I bumped into Stephen Jones, who was playing for Western Province. A week later I had a call from Eddie Barlow, then captaining Western Province, who wanted me to stay on and play for them. I did so on condition that I could coach a coloured club, or at least one in a less privileged area. The club chosen was Avendale, in Athlone on the Cape Flats, one of the few clubs to straddle the colour divide.

Rachid Varachia, president of the South African Cricket Board of Control (SACBOC – with the South African Council of Sport, or SACOS, the representative of coloured cricketers), had led a delegation to unite his organisation with the mainly white South African Cricket Union (SACU). Agreement had almost been completed when (so the story went) news was leaked that the Western Province Cricket Union with other white unions had drawn up two sets of fixture lists, one with coloureds and one without. SACBOC naturally saw this as a sign of mistrust, and vice-president Hassan Howa issued his clarion call of 'No normal sport in an abnormal society'. Any player that crossed the divide was thus immediately ostracised because the political struggle was more important than the sporting struggle. But the South African game had officially gone multi-racial in 1977 and I was keen to assist in the development of non-white cricketers.

Avendale was derived from the amalgamation of two non-white clubs (as they were called in those days), Avenirs and Ashtondale. The club played on three fields leased from Cape Town City Council, and I obtained equipment from funds donated by the Western Province Cricket Union and the club's president and benefactor, Mike Stakol, who was white and had a passion for non-racial cricket. Mike was not alone in having a social conscience, but his was better developed than most, and raising funds for Avendale was one way in which he could work against the apartheid system. Even though we were perceived to be joining the system of apartheid, we felt, naively maybe, that we were helping some of these people experience a better deal. One of the few ways in the late 1970s and 1980s for sportsmen to rid themselves of the stain of apartheid was to live together, work together and play together. Blacks and coloureds would then realise that not every white person was in support of the system.

When I first arrived, on 6 January 1981, Avendale had two self-made concrete nets with carpets on top. The netting was mottled and made of wire. When I batted on it, I found it to be shocking. I told the committee that if they wanted to produce good cricketers they had to do something about the surface, whereupon I was given a funny look. Stakol, though, realised we had to have grass nets. The standard of league cricket in South Africa was very high as there was no international cricket, and the only way I could see to improve the players' confidence was to raise their skill levels so that they could compete at a higher level. We had to upgrade the facilities.

Thanks to Mike Stakol's generosity we built a new pavilion, and had four concrete and carpet nets and four turf nets installed, which I helped prepare. We were fortunate, too, that we had sightscreens and a clubhouse, unlike a lot of other clubs. Bert Erickson, the club chairman, Stakol and myself formed a team and got a junior set-up going, providing children with facilities they could only dream about. I spent many hours preparing the pitch there, collecting subscriptions and even stocking the pub with beers and ordering pies for lunch. Club members would be coached in cricket and would help run these general functions, including hosting many touring sides. First-class English cricketers such as Christopher and Graham Cowdrey, Alan Igglesden, Paul Jarvis, Steve Marsh and David East, who used to come to me for coaching, came and helped with the coaching on Friday afternoons, when at times we would have in excess of 120 children.

From three sides in 1977 Avendale were running four or five times that number a decade later, but during the riots in the area, seven players left the club as a result of intimidation from youths who felt they should not be mixing with whites. The high school behind the nets, which was SACOS-oriented, refused to use the facilities, and on another occasion oil was thrown on one of the pitches. At one net session I ran, we could see trouble only 500 yards away. I turned to one of our African players and said: 'Behind every black cloud there is a silver lining'; he replied: 'Behind every black cloud there is a burning bus.' On another occasion a crowd with axes and knives on their way to a funeral took exception to a game that was in progress. Fortunately the last fielder into the clubhouse managed to bolt the door.

I felt passionately that I wanted to make an effective statement against apartheid, not least because my under-standing of it had changed immeasurably since the early 1970s because of episodes like these. On one occasion the gates at Western Province were blown up. On another night, the front door of our clubhouse had a limpet mine attached to it and its lower portions were blown to smithereens. I had also watched people I played with get thrown out of restaurants, because although we were desperate for everyone to share together in the cricketing experience we were constantly hamstrung by a number of intolerable apartheid laws. Derek Erickson, the chairman of Avendale's son who was representing Western Province Colts, stopped one day at a little roadside café to organise some hamburgers and Cokes for the team as they were in the midst of a nine-hour trip, and was told that black people would not be served. One of the white players smashed all the crockery, and everybody walked out. Then, during Mike Gatting's breakaway tour in 1989/90, Avendale was targeted as a club. We were playing a league game against Fishhoek and were told there would be a demonstration at the ground. I remember thinking that I wanted to talk to these protesters. Why us? I was struck dumb by the level of hatred. They started to have a go at me, and in the middle of the ensuing fracas I was arrested simply because I was on the field of play. A lot of arrests were made around the ground that day, but we refused to press charges.

The experience certainly made me realise the strength of people's feelings, but I was still politically naive. Andre Odendaal, a student and ANC activist, once criticised me for being mercenary and taking Avendale's 'white' money. Yet it was raised for all the right reasons, principally to help the coloured boys in the area. When I went there, we had three men's sides and no youth set-up; when I left nine years later the club had five and sometimes six men's sides and eleven junior age group sides, including sixteen boys who went on to play in the annual South African schools provincial cricket week, known as the Nuffield week. Around this time I was also helping John Passmore, a great benefactor of the underprivileged, with the cricket week he ran. This was with a view to selecting the best twelve black players for the John Passmore XI that would take part in the Nuffield week. Two Avendale boys also came to Sutton Valence School in Kent on scholarships, and a number to this day are playing in leagues in England as a result of the infrastructure of the club itself.

The philosophy of Basil Waterwich, the driving force of the Avendale club (along with Bert Erickson), was that the game could be a unifying force. They did not think you needed to become white for a day, which was one of the slogans that stopped others playing on Saturdays. I saw a great deal of talent over the years but little self-esteem or confidence, yet of all the coaching experiences I have had, Avendale was the most fulfilling, despite being hard work. And our achievements were recognised. Michael Owen-Smith wrote in the *Cape Times*:

In 1987 it had been arranged for the boys participating in Nuffield week to spend the day at the whites-only resort of Mazelspoort outside Bloemfontein, the Free State capital. Woolmer and his party of mixed races were given a substantial financial allowance for the day and were packed off to the nearest multi-racial homeland. [At the Thaba 'Nchu casino and hotel resort] they enjoyed infinitely superior facilities, but it did underline the problems Woolmer fought in those days.

This was not the age of development programmes and affirmative action. Financial support from the Western Province was minimal and it was always a battle to find funds for the array of professionals Woolmer brought from England to provide additional coaching and playing input.

What Woolmer and John Passmore achieved at Langa and Avendale was nonetheless huge, and it could have been a great deal bigger had the Western Province had a proper coaching structure in place. Woolmer, in fact, should have run the whole shooting match rather than having to cooperate with a director of coaching who achieved fame as an international rugby referee but had no worthwhile experience in cricket [Freek Burger – actually the director of development]. It remains incredible that Western Province could [subsequently] find no role for Woolmer anywhere in their structure, although it may not have been a bad thing because it led him to Boland, whence he became coach of South Africa.

Our set-up certainly benefited the local community. Dr Ali Bacher's drive to take the game into black areas did not begin until 1986. The John Passmore week, disbanded upon unity in 1992 because it was perceived to be racial, was, in my opinion, one of the best vehicles to bring black cricketers into a more advanced cricketing environment. To this day I am convinced the development of black cricketers was slowed down by this political move. An important means of advancing young cricketers was taken away, and the current development programme has not redressed this. In the current climate, I feel that new strategies – such as my proposed training centre in Cape Town – have to be evolved in order to satisfy political aspirations.

In 1984, Gill and I took the decision to emigrate to South Africa. My Test career was over anyway, I had already had a benefit, and in what turned out to be my final match for Kent, during Tunbridge Wells week, I had to be carried back to the pavilion from the crease with a back injury. One reason for going abroad was the climate, which would be more beneficial for my back ailment; another was to escape the English winters and lights being turned on at 3.30 in the afternoon. Besides, Gill had grown up in the Republic. The question was: what job should I do?

We plumped for Cape Town, where – for all the troubles emanating from apartheid, the violence spilling over from the townships and the Wild West-style shootings – Table Mountain is a wondrous spectacle and the climate is perfect. I gained a job in a Jewish denomination school, Herzlia High, whose departing headmaster, Mike Kessel, I had met in Natal. Things did not start propitiously. The incoming headmistress promptly told me, 'I don't know why you're here. We have a perfectly good staff to cope with the sport,' which contradicted totally the views of the governors.

I put up with this difference in philosophy for eighteen months. It was a frustrating experience: here was I, an ex-English Test cricketer taking the Under-15s, and only three people turned up. I decided to cancel the first two fixtures of the season in assembly the following morning, which prompted an outcry. I told the boys I could not pick teams if I did not know how good they were, and after that everyone turned up for practice. It was a worthwhile experience for me in how to motivate people.

I ran the hockey as well. The husband of one of the teachers in the middle school, Joel Cowan, learnt that I had played hockey in the UK and asked me to coach the varsity old boys club in addition to the school side. This in turn led to an association with Western Province Hockey, in particular with Keith Richardson, who ran the coaching committee. I had had some success with VOB/VOG, as they were known, and Keith contacted me to join in. This immediately enthused me and I started to take a number of courses run by the South African Hockey Association. Their director of coaching was a chap named Jock Coombes, and their coaching set-up was far superior to that in South African cricket at that time. It was very professionally run, and I was to glean a lot about coaching from the various courses I was sent on. I learnt, for instance, about what would be needed in terms of videos, psychology and different types of fitness training. Being involved in two sports was good for me in that

I learnt about how to coach in reverse, as it were: teaching the end product first, as one would if cheating on one of those puzzles with squiggly lines. I applied certain coaching techniques in hockey to cricket and vice versa, for the two were compatible in many ways. This had the effect of opening my mind to different and non-traditional methods.

A couple of years after we had emigrated, in October 1986, I received an offer from England. Christopher Cowdrey had become captain of Kent the year after I retired, and he, of course, had helped coach Avendale with me. The club was in truth becoming a bit of a nursery for Kent players, a fact which led to his telephone call. 'You're doing all this coaching of English players in South Africa,' he reasoned, 'so why don't you come to England and coach Kent?' The proposal was that I would captain the county's second XI and be with the first XI at weekends. I agreed to this for the 1987 season on a one-year contract.

Because I had been involved in hockey as well as cricket, I was very much a coach eager to enter a new era. I was particularly keen to try out new ideas, especially those relating to fitness. When the time came for me to go to England, I resigned from my post at Herzlia High. Although I would be coming back to South Africa in the English winter of 1987/88, I was hoping to be able to secure a job Western Province were creating, as a development officer in underprivileged areas. Because of my association with Avendale and John Passmore, I was keen to do this job and felt ideally suited to it. Before I left the country I discovered that I was a front-runner for the post, along with Freek Burger, a renowned rugby referee who had a job with the Ikapa town council as a sports officer in the Guguletu and other black areas, including Langa and Khayelitsha.

In England, I stayed with Chris Cowdrey at his house in Wincheap, parking my station wagon next to his BMW. One of the first problems I encountered, having got off the plane at Heathrow and gone straight to the old Hopper Levett indoor school, was an accident to Chris Penn, who while bowling put his foot through the floorboards. It was quite obvious that this facility was not good enough. Also, incessant rain prevented us from practising outdoors; the normal nets next to the Frank Woolley stand were continually under water. Because of my back injury I was limited in terms of what I could do on the field anyway – I could bowl a few off-spinners, field at slip or mid-off and bat at eleven in the order – but I could still coach.

County cricket certainly did not compare favourably to South Africa and Australia – in those countries the net facilities and weather are so much more conducive to getting players into form – but Kent at least were forward-looking. They had been the first county to make use of scientific evaluation in 1970, through the facilities at Kent University. It was the idea of Mike Denness, Graham Johnson and myself. Graham and I had been to South Africa and seen how well they trained there. The innovation was not too popular at the time, but it could be argued that this was why we were ahead of the pack in the 1970s. What I tried to do later was practise cricket skills in the morning and train in the afternoon, a reversal of normal practice. It was an obvious improvement as it meant that the players could practise their cricket skills without being so stiff that they could not move.

I set everyone at the club a questionnaire, which I felt was important to ascertain what the players were like and what they thought they might get out of the season. I knew several of the players very well, of course. Someone like Derek Underwood, a very senior player then in his last season, needed minimal assistance. He knew that you knew he could win a match on a wet pitch, and he thrived on pressure. He was as good as any left-arm spinner I have ever seen. He never went out of his comfort zone in terms of his own body, but was fortunate to have the type of body that did not break down. One reason for that was the fact that he had such a classical action, and he got himself fit by bowling and bowling. With Derek, it was a matter of tinkering with whatever was there: a no-ball problem, perhaps, or something to do with his rhythm.

Then I had to face my first personnel problem: the non-relationship between Christopher Cowdrey and Chris Tavare. One of the alleged reasons why Tavare lost the job as Kent captain was because he was an unenthusiastic leader of men. My view was that his role for England was very different to his role for Kent, and it certainly never rang true for me that he was boring and not stimulating. The decisions he made on the pitch – taking Derek Underwood off at a crucial period during the 1984 NatWest final, for instance (Tavare was accused of releasing the pressure on Middlesex that day when he took off Underwood with two overs of his twelve-over allowance left; indeed, when he came back for those last two overs, he was not the force he was, and Middlesex profited) – may well have sealed his fate after a vendetta was conducted against him that season. At the dinner after that final, days before any official announcement was to be made over his future, my wife and I overheard two committee members discussing the game and were shocked to hear Tavare would lose the captaincy to Christopher Cowdrey the next week – before the meeting to discuss such matters was due to convene.

The conversation turned out to be accurate, and the resentment Tavare felt was understandable. My experience of committees down the years, especially when dealing with players' futures, makes me feel this was not an unusual occurrence. A lot of conspirators are busy behind the scenes. Tavare was given a four-year contract, and by the time I arrived in 1987 there was very little, if any, communication between him and his captain. For someone in my position, this was completely untenable. Within a few days of being in England it was difficult not to notice the rift. If we were to be successful we had to bring the two senior players together, so I invited Tavare and his wife, Vanessa, who was particularly upset about her husband's demotion, to Cowdrey's house for a meeting to try to build a bridge, if not an immediate pontoon. The upshot was that we managed to get Tavare to contribute at team meetings, both tactically and technically, which is always very important for youngsters coming into the side. I believe we also managed to secure a truce.

I felt that Cowdrey should have taken over from Tavare in the normal order of things, but perhaps three or so years down the line. Tavare was a captain in the Brearley mould and he was very popular with the players. Cowdrey's more dynamic style of leadership would have fitted in nicely after a period under Tavare and would have kept Kent going forward. There were times when Cowdrey wanted a three-day game to finish in a day and a half, and there were times when his fielding positions reflected this. My view is that the coach should always be a sounding board for the captain, and I have applied this thinking to all my jobs, but there was some conflict between Cowdrey and myself. However, while I would sometimes question his ideas I tried to let him have his head, as the captain should have control. But it does make life difficult when coach and captain cannot agree on some of the methods. I tried to be an adviser, to give my point of view in as unbiased a way as possible, but in the end the captain has to take on to the field the team he is happy with.

Kent's problems evolved because too many youngsters came into the side too quickly. Richard Ellison, for instance, did not have the stamina to replace John Shepherd. Having started 1987 by winning the first three games, the first XI had a poor season, due in the main to severe injuries to our quick bowlers, several of whom were out for up to six weeks. Ellison was out for the whole season. The young second XI, though, including the likes of Vince Wells, Mark Ealham, Richard Davis, Graham Cowdrey, Simon Hinks and Nigel Llong, finished joint top of the table with Yorkshire, which was the successful part of my job that year. I worked particularly hard with Derek Aslett, who had lost his form. Here was someone who had taken on Malcolm Marshall, Sylvester Clarke and Wayne Daniel and had scored prolifically against them, but when I arrived at Canterbury he was right out of touch, having averaged 22 in 1986. One had to weigh up whether Derek's experience or Graham Cowdrey's youth was more important for Kent cricket. And were people like Hinks, who promised the world and never delivered, just clouding the issue? I helped improve Derek's average by seven points over the season, which over a wet summer was significant. Mark Benson also improved his average, by five points, Tavare by one point and Neil Taylor by nine points in a season of poor results.

The main reason I did not return to Kent for the 1988 season was that I was only offered a further one-year contract, which clearly indicated to me that the decision-makers did not have confidence in what I was doing. I was as a result wary of them; I knew that the only people who had questioned whether I could cope with returning to the club had been Colin Page and Brian Luckhurst, hitherto the manager but moved sideways when I arrived. The omens for a trouble-free year were not good.

Many things I have learnt in the game since have confirmed to me that this decision to leave was the right one. My belief is that the ideal administration of any club is one which incorporates former players from that club and businessmen with time to spare, and who can offer the necessary financial, legal or professional help and advice. One key area for any modern club is marketing – especially trying to raise finance to help the club survive and to provide an infrastructure that will advance it. My experience of a lot of clubs is that they have very well-meaning people who sit on committees but who are quite unable to give the amount of time and effort that is required. As a result, it is often almost impossible to get a decision out of that committee, and even when a decision is made the problem is not properly addressed. Examples of ineptness and faults being swept under the carpet litter the game. This is very frustrating, and I daresay this sense of frustration is caused in part by not being able to afford the most skilled professionals, especially in the marketing areas, as well as through having to cope internally with an inordinate amount of professional jealousy.

I have been fortunate that during my coaching career I have been involved with two of the best administrations one could work for. Warwickshire, with Dennis Amiss, M.J.K. Smith and, in particular, the vice-chairman of the club, Tony

Cross, allowed the captain, coach and cricket committee to run their operation without interruption; South Africa, too, gave the captain and coach as much support as they could hope for, although I will admit that there have been times when I wanted to go in a certain direction with South Africa but was stymied, a case in point being my seeming obsession with video statistics and analysis: I was asked not to be so keen on this being the panacea for all ills and to concentrate instead on the basics of coaching. I have also been lucky to have had the opportunity of listening to a lot of lectures on team building and team interaction. I really believe that administrators should attend such seminars and lectures as well. I reckon that would go at least some way towards ridding clubs of 'them and us' situations, which can be so destructive.

And there was certainly such a situation at Kent. The one element that always worried me about the club was the split between those educated at public schools and those educated at state schools. At functions, there was an obvious divide. One of the reasons Kent has not progressed is the influence of the 'Band of Brothers', as they were dubbed, the club formed by Lord Harris. I was brought up by Page to watch out for them; in fact, all the old pros in the Kent side told stories about the Band of Brothers. The standard joke was that during every Canterbury week they would all be rolled out of winter storage, unwrapped and installed in their canvas deckchairs – and it was often difficult to tell which of them were alive or dead. I felt strongly that if I had been at Tonbridge School (my parents wanted me to go, but could not afford it) I would have had an easier life at Kent, although the Band of Brothers influence was less significant when Les Ames was in charge in the 1960s and 1970s. He was the best cricket manager I have ever come across because he would not take nonsense from anybody. His retirement, and the fact that I had joined Packer, were not to my benefit. After I had signed up to World Series cricket, E.W. Swanton, journalist turned committee man, did not talk to me for three years.

During that season with Kent there was an episode which seemed to me to encapsulate this parochial type of outlook within English cricket. When play started at Canterbury I used to watch for half an hour and then go for a run down the Nackington Road past the hospital. On one occasion I went wearing loud orange running shorts – loud, that is, by the standards of the time – and a Kent T-shirt. As I ran back to the ground, Derek Aslett was walking over to have a net. He shouted to me to feed the bowling machine for him. I said, 'Dressed like this?' He replied that nobody was going to notice, but little did he know! For an hour I fed the machine for him, then showered and went down to lunch. By the time the next committee meeting came round, there was a full note from E.W. Swanton complaining about my attire while coaching. I apologised and tried to explain the set of circumstances that had led to it, saying it would not happen again. In later years, I always ensured I coached in shorts – white ones – and later still I gave up trying to explain to the South African team sponsors that we should practise in whites. Things had changed, but the orange-shorts objection showed the type of thinking that existed, and probably still exists in Kent cricket – and English cricket.

Professional sport now demands professional attitudes, and it is better to strive for innovation than to stand still. The difference in attitude when I went to Warwickshire was incredible. Even my wife noticed how much more tolerant the committee were. In all walks of life people talk behind your back, but at Edgbaston more individuals were prepared to say things to your face. There was far less sarcasm in the dressing room, too. I also noticed how much more integrated players were abroad, in Boland in particular. Warwickshire's team spirit was much stronger: everyone got on the same bus and let the driver drive. With Kent, there was always a fight over the destination. Political lobbying was at its height at Kent CCC during my time there, but nevertheless it was a wonderful place to play cricket, on a lovely ground before a receptive public.

Kent finished that 1987 season well down the Championship table and did not excel in any of the one-day competitions. Had I in fact returned too soon to the county with whom I had spent my entire career in England? I certainly felt that the stretch of time away from home had come too soon after we had emigrated. It was with regret that I left, because I never enjoy giving up on a challenge, but I decided it was best for me to make more of a nest in South Africa before returning to any sort of cricket management. Although my experiences at Kent certainly made me better equipped for dealing with the varied individuals who make up a cricket club, it was still clear to me that I needed more experience in handling people. I felt competent enough technically to help players, but what I needed was to be able to deal effectively with committee men. In order to be a successful coach you have to be able to gain the confidence of the players and maintain good relationships with those with whom you are discussing their futures. Aligning yourself with the players all the time means you do not gain the confidence of the committee, and vice versa. A coach has to be rational with both parties, but finding some middle ground and occupying it is very difficult.

I had long been immersed in the game and its history, in technique and in the application of technique. I had the advantage of having played cricket at the highest level, and now of having coached a county side. What I still had to find out when I went back to South Africa, however, was how top-class cricketers would take to my coaching methods in what was an evolving art.

3 A Taste of Success

I N THE WINTER OF 1987, I was officially interviewed for the position of Western Province cricket co-ordinator. Freek Burger, who is now in charge of coaching and appointing all the rugby referees in the country, was given the job. He was a nice enough person, but this was a shattering experience for me. The officers of the Western Province Cricket Association could not comprehend what I had already achieved in the game in South Africa. To this day, and no doubt for the foreseeable future, I find it very difficult to enthuse about Western Province administrators.

I was conscious of the fact that I had no future with Kent, mainly because of the difficult nature of club politics there, but then the Western Province Hockey Association came to me with a proposal to raise funds to start hockey in the 'black' areas. In order to do this and run Avendale at the same time, I was sponsored by a company called Cape Underwear, a lingerie chain which was part of the clothing company Seardel. It was owned by Aaron Searle, a friend of Mike Stakol and also a supporter of colour initiatives in sport. The tenability of my financial position depended on such sponsorship. I was getting up at 6.30 a.m. on dark Saturdays, driving into the townships, picking up black hockey players, driving them to a ground, dropping them off, going back and picking up the next team, and so on. Quite often they had three or four games every Saturday morning. In those days there was still two-year national service, and I used the Western Province Defence Force (sports division) to help coach and umpire the games; I was little more than a taxi driver. The games would be staggered through the morning, so I would catch maybe half an hour at most of each one. I was working a six-day week just to earn enough money to keep my children at school.

I felt abandoned by the WPCA, and in particular by Fritz Bing, its president, and Eric Saxon and Chris Schutte on the general committee. To this day I do not know or understand why I was ostracised, as the game has always been my passion. I do not possess great religious faith, but I am sure God helped me through this difficult period in my career. I was working from Monday to Friday as a hockey coach and fund-raiser and on Saturdays operating as a taxi driver and coach, having helped cut and roll the fields as well. The pressures on my family life in Cape Town became increasingly intolerable.

In order to supplement my salary at the end of the 1980s, I took on some additional work. Jannie Momberg, now an ANC politician, Eddie Barlow and Stephen Jones were the three main movers trying to take Boland, essentially a wine farming district spread over a huge region of the western Cape and one of the most beautiful areas in the world, into the Castle Cup, the A section of domestic competition at that time. Boland had changed from being a subsidiary of Western Province in 1981 to separate union status, but the standard of cricket at Boland was not high and they played in the B section, or Bowl competition, along with Border, Eastern Transvaal, North Western Transvaal and Griqualand West. When they were refused entrance to the Castle Cup and the better-quality opposition provided by Western Province, Eastern Province, Transvaal, Northern Transvaal, Orange Free State and Natal, despite having won the Bowl competition, Momberg and Jones left in high dudgeon. Boland had a R250,000 (about £50,000) overdraft. Kevin Bridgens, who had played a few games for Western Province but had moved to Boland, was then enlisted as chief executive, and he tried to find a local coach to help with preparations. I accepted on the basis of going twice a week for R1,500 (about £300) a month, whereas Graham Barlow, formerly of Middlesex, wanted a full contract that they could not afford.

My first experience of Boland was arriving at the SFW nets in Stellenbosch to find that they had not been put up, the pitches had not been rolled and there were no balls to practise with. Bridgens arrived half an hour late with the practice balls, which was not a great example to set. The next day I watered the pitches and got the groundstaff to roll them. The organisation was, to say the least, archaic, but all of us got stuck in, which was a wonderful experience.

One of the first objectives was to set out goals in terms of Boland's future. Apart from killing the overdraft in Boland's case, it is very important for any coach/management to have clear short- to long-term strategies. The Bowl was the obvious target, and we had to make plans as to how to achieve it. Without money, players had to be found from within the Boland league system. Languishing at the bottom of the Western Province league was Stellenbosch University. In my experience, university cricket tended to throw up a lot of good youngsters, especially in South Africa. Stellenbosch was no exception to that general rule, and we realised we had to persuade the South African Cricket Union that we needed Stellenbosch University, which geographically lay inside Boland's border, as a Boland league club. This would take some time, as we had to break down a number of political barriers, not only in the Western Province cricketing administration, but at the university itself, whose rugby sides were staunchly Western Province.

The second objective was to ensure we had our own ground with decent practice facilities available to all – and within reach of all. Again, Stellenbosch University was the ideal venue, so it became imperative that negotiations took place. In the interim we were to base ourselves at Brackenfell, another Boland league cricket club, half an hour from Cape Town. The club and the municipality went out of their way to give us what we wanted; unfortunately, the practice facilities fell short of first-class status and the square accommodated only three pitches, which made playing provincial and local cricket problematical. The municipality, however, built new offices above the sightscreen for Boland and upgraded the nets as best they could. These were good times.

Brackenfell was a temporary step on the way forward. It was now important to look at the playing staff and to see where and how we could improve the general standard of the individuals. This meant watching a lot of cricket around Boland; often it would mean driving for an hour before reaching a match. I was also co-opted on to the management committee dealing with all these problems, and was very pleased as a result to see the game from a different perspective. I remember well the discussions and plans that were formulated at these meetings, from the first team through to the development programme. It was a key time in my cricketing education. It is very important to have a thorough and well-grounded overview of all aspects of the game, and my experiences on the Boland committee would stand me in really good stead for the future as I was dealing with a wide variety of cricketing projects and problems on top of the coaching: pitch maintenance; the laying of artificial surfaces on new grounds; kit provision for underprivileged schools and clubs; finance management within clubs; coaching courses for school teachers and club cricketers; and development of a blueprint for the game throughout the disadvantaged communities, to name but a selection.

Due to the enormous distances involved in overseeing Boland, area committees had to be formed to run the programmes themselves. The Boland development committee would put together a format and the area committees would follow where they could or adapt it as they could. An area committee comprised a chairman (a prominent town person), a high school representative, a junior school representative and a club representative, plus, it was hoped, an experienced coach whose job it would be to run courses for children with the help of other qualified coaches in order to foster and improve the game in the country areas. These area committees and this blueprint are now fully operational. Boland has the highest representation of players of colour in its provincial team.

I spent four years in the B section, and the moment Boland gained promotion to the A section at the end of the 1992/93 season, everything changed dramatically. Having had four years on the management committee, I was removed and told that I must concentrate on the cricket. Yet when it came to the selection of the playing staff, I had no input whatsoever and I was not even consulted over the choice of captain. I was astonished that after four years of successful labour any ideas I had were no longer needed. The captain selected was Terence Lazard, who had been a regular in the Western Province team for five or six seasons until Allan Donald hit him on the head – 'cleaned him up' in the South African vernacular – in Bloemfontein when he refused to bat in a helmet. Confidence levels inevitably suffer after a blow to the head, and in his last season for Western Province Lazard averaged 11 with the bat. His place in the team was therefore in jeopardy. He was still, however, a very fine player against average bowling and the decision to get him to play for Boland was the correct one, but he would switch provinces only on the condition that he was made captain. But if he was captaincy material, why had he not been considered for Western Province?

With Lazard came Kenny Jackson, an average batsman but full of confidence and with tremendous grit. John Commins, a class performer, also came, along with Faiek Davids. All four were fringe Western Province players on account of poor form and the fact that they had to compete there with a very good batting line-up including Gary Kirsten, Daryll Cullinan and Brian McMillan, with talented youngsters like Jacques Kallis, Hylton Ackerman and Herschelle Gibbs pushing for places. Of the four players, Lazard and Commins were to average in excess of 40, Jackson played one or two fine innings but disappointed, and Davids never played again as he turned up to practice only once – to tell me he could not come to practice. The job as coach for that first year in the A section was to prove my toughest challenge thus far. The attitude of the former Western Province players towards the Boland cricketers was that they were country bumpkins who knew nothing about the game. The perception was that Boland was still very much in the sticks. This had to be broken down, but doing so became harder as the season progressed and matches were lost.

I can categorically state that Terence Lazard was the worst captain I have ever had to deal with, either as a player or a coach. In fact – and he knows this – I recommended to the Boland management committee that Commins should replace him as early as the second month of the season. I even prepared a seven-page document on why Lazard should hand over the role. Naturally, this caused some resentment between us, but I felt it incumbent on me to be honest, to act in the best interests of Boland. At no stage did I feel any animosity towards Terence; in fact I spent hours throwing balls to him and working with him on his game. I had a lot of time for him as a person off the field, but his captaincy in terms of field placings, bowling changes, man-management, batting orders, etc. was very poor. Furthermore, his relationship with our overseas player, Phillip DeFreitas, who also averaged 40 with the bat – and 21 with the ball – was to deteriorate to such a degree that the two players nearly came to blows on the field at Port Elizabeth at the end of the season. Experiences like this teach you so much about the game. There were many days when I pored over potential solutions to the differences between myself and Terence. His views on cricket forced me look at myself to see where I was going wrong and made me lose confidence in my judgement. As a coach you cannot afford to lose sight of basic cricketing principles, and this was the first time in my career that mine had been challenged so forthrightly. I have always felt able to get on, and understand, other people's views on the game, and I regard this as one of my strengths, but as I said, there is usually a positive side to such an episode: my experiences would be invaluable in the 1994 season in England, when my coaching beliefs would be tested once again, by Brian Lara.

The committee told me they had total faith in their captain and in their coach. Because of the statement I had made about Lazard's shortcomings, we were obviously at arm's length. But it was mainly off the field that Boland was having its major problems, some of which were already festering as a result of the appointment of Henry Paulse, a schoolmaster who became president/chairman but who knew little about the game. Ted Wicht, the chairman of selectors, who was then seventy, was the only person who knew what the game was all about. Decision-making was, as a result, often cloudy. There were various administrative hoo-hahs which did not make matters easy. I was once asked, for instance, to collect some tracksuits for the team, but when I arrived I discovered they had not even been made yet.

Another gaffe which caused a lot of petty argument came when I, as coach-manager, was given pre-booked air tickets for a Friday day–night game against Natal. Unfortunately, a number of the players selected for the game were not on the booking list. In fact, the list of those to travel against those actually selected to play was only about fifty per cent accurate – which, incidentally, would have caused a lot of unnecessary grief in the event of a plane crash or other accident. We duly played the game against Natal, and I announced, after checking one of the tickets, that we were leaving on the 1000 hours flight to Cape Town, but when we reached the airport the next morning I was informed that one of the players had been booked on the 0730 flight. In addition to that, the flight we were all supposed to be on was fully booked, and unless we took the one remaining business-class flight we would have to wait until 1600. I offered that possibility to the players, and asked if anyone should have gone back early, but I got no reply, so I paid the extra to upgrade and we all flew back home.

When we got to Cape Town, I was approached by Colin Dettmer, our opening bat, who told me that Anwell Newman, our other opening bowler, should have gone back earlier but had been told by another player, Omar Henry, not to be stupid, that 'you can't play a club game after a night game', or words to that effect. I went straight to Stellenbosch to watch my side play, then the following Monday I turned up at the office as usual, only to be told by Kevin Bridgens that I was in hot water with a Mr Hamilton, chairman of the Van Der Stel cricket club. Now Mr Hamilton's son, Gavin, kept wicket for Van Der Stel, and like a good doting father he had always wanted to know why Gavin was not selected for Boland, and was convinced that I had a bias towards the university players as I was their coach. Mr Hamilton had written a letter accusing me of deliberately preventing Anwell Newman, a Van Der Stel player, from getting on the early flight from Natal, and thus preventing Van Der Stel from winning; that I was an obnoxious coach, a know-it-all and a disgrace to the Boland Cricket Board.

The real facts were that the Boland Board, Bridgens and Newman had known about the Van Der Stel game and the request for Newman to be back early, but Newman's ticket was in the name of Michael Cann, who was not even selected for the Natal game. Yet despite the clear administrative nature of this bungled episode, it was my name that was mud and Bridgens, who regularly made errors like this, who got off scot-free. Bridgens even had the temerity to tell me that I should have checked the tickets carefully before leaving! I sometimes wonder what goes through these people's heads when they act so irrationally, fuelled by their petty jealousies. My relationship with Bridgens and Henry Paulse continued on its ever-deteriorating way; indeed, to this day Paulse runs Boland with, I believe, the ineptitude of someone who has no clue how to run a cricket side whatsoever. Hylton Ackerman Sr, who has coached at Boland for the best part of five years, has also now been hounded out.

The new Paarl ground at Boland, originally the Boland Bank Park, is one of the most beautiful grounds in the world, but the tale of its construction is also like a script for a *Fawlty Towers* series, and the playing surface to this day leaves much to be desired. Until more cricket expertise and people with innovative minds help make Boland a vibrant cricketing fraternity, they will struggle to survive in the ever-competitive climate of South African cricket. Teams such as Griqualand West, having been promoted to the A section more recently, have raced past them. It is a sorry state of affairs.

From 1991 to 1994 I had the pleasure of coaching arguably the best bunch of cricketers one could wish to meet, and who, by 1994, had become the team of the 1990s. The position of coach at Warwickshire was up for grabs at the end of the 1990 season. Dennis Amiss, my old England colleague who was to become the club's chief executive, contacted me in South Africa to ask if I would be at all interested in applying. The timing, just like his cover drives, was immaculate. My time with the Western Province Hockey Association, trying to raise money and introduce hockey to the townships, was about up. This was sad as I had had a lot of input and had managed to make a difference: the council, for instance, had just put down our first Astroturf pitch in Cape Town. It was also sad because I have always been fond of my hockey, and my sons play it to this day, but Warwickshire's offer, as I said, came as a godsend, because with my association with the WPHA dying a natural death, a major proportion of my income would have been eradicated. My involvement with Boland was only part-time, and I am not sure what I would have done in the off-season, although I had decided, long-term, to set up my own coaching school. I knew that, like all business ventures, this would have been a risk, but it was not as if I had been earning a fortune anyway. So I filled out the CV and questionnaire, sent it off, and in due course was selected.

Warwickshire were christened 'the Bears' by Bob Cottam. I was to take over from him after an acrimonious period at the club during which both he and Bob Evans, a local solicitor and chairman of the club, had had to resign after a disagreement with the committee. Cottam left to become the new England bowling coach. I was never made totally aware of what happened, but quite frankly it had nothing to do with me.

In the middle of March 1991 I arrived at a cold and bleak Heathrow to be met by Amiss, who was at that time chairman of the cricket committee. During that season I was invited to a box at the Priory Tennis Club owned by Midlands Travel, the firm that Andy Moles, the Warwickshire opening bat, was working for in the winter months. In those days, cell (as they are referred to in South Africa) or mobile phones were fairly new and the club had furnished me with one so I was easily contactable. I was watching a match involving the French tennis player Mary Pierce when it went off. Without any thought I picked it up and answered it. Andy Lloyd was on the other end, and we began to discuss an injury to Allan Donald. I was deeply engrossed in the conversation when suddenly, and most embarrassingly, the umpire on the court shouted: 'Would the man with the mobile phone please be quiet as we are frankly not interested whether Allan Donald will or will not be playing cricket in the next match!'

Before the season started, Andy Lloyd was on a golf tour with Derrick Robins in Cape Town and he arranged to meet me at my home to discuss the team and our roles within it. This meeting took place at home over some magnificent steak Gill had prepared. We drank Nederburg Cabernet Sauvignon with it and talked at length about Warwickshire cricket. It was an excellent get-together, and Andy showed a genuine love for his team and made some perceptive comments about his players.

On my first evening, Dennis told me that some of the players would be up for a net, and asked me to have a look at them. I agreed, and that first day as coach in charge of Warwickshire was a typical English spring day, misty and slightly damp without being wet, extremely cold if you had just come from a Cape Town summer and very grey, with a low ceiling of cloud hovering over Birmingham. I addressed the staff, saying that I was here to help and to learn as much about them as they were to learn from me. I said that if success was what they yearned for and really wanted, then success they would get, but it would take as much effort from them as from me, or indeed anyone at the club. We then had a general conversation about going to Trinidad for our pre-season tour, and also about what we were going to do after the meeting.

The players changed and we jogged and stretched, doing some ball drills and finishing off with some short twenty-metre sprints. As we were coming to the end of this, a large, rotund man came walking across the field from the groundsman's hut. It was quite a purposeful walk. We were at that point as far as it is possible to be from his abode in the bottom right-hand corner of the ground. We had cut up the ground slightly as a result of our exertions, but the damage was superficial and the grass would recover in good time. As this guy reached us, he shouted: 'What the f*** do you think you are doing?' I presumed this irate figure was Andy Atkinson, the Warwickshire groundsman, so I went over to him and said: 'Hi, my name is Bob Woolmer and we were just doing some sprints.' 'I know who the f*** you are,' he exploded. 'Why didn't you ask my permission to use the ground, or at least ask if it was fit, and why couldn't you use the colts ground?' The tirade continued in this manner. I backed off and sent the team back in to change and go home, apologised and said it would not happen again. I thought that would knock the problem on its head. Wrong! 'You f***ing coaches are all the same! You think you can just do what you like! I've got a Test match here in July [this was March, don't forget] and I'll be lucky if the ground recovers in time.' Boy, did I catch a mouthful.

That evening I popped around to see Dennis and Gill Amiss to discuss my first day, and at some stage I mentioned to Dennis that we were not allowed to use the main ground for exercise and fielding. His reply was: 'Of course you can – that's what it's there for.' The upshot of this conversation was a bit of a row behind the scenes, and I was told that in future I must go through the chief executive (the late David Heath) if I wanted to speak to the groundsman. Nothing like making an early impression.

Andy Atkinson later went to work at Newlands in Cape Town, and then the Wanderers in Johannesburg, and is now a pitch consultant in South Africa. He did not forget our first encounter, for not much later, when I was doing some radio commentary and went to look at the pitch at Newlands, he came over and said to me: 'Who let you on to the field? You're not at Edgbaston now.' He also said that I was the only international coach with a one hundred per cent record – in the sense of played seven, lost seven (as my record at that particular time was). And it all stemmed from that first day at Edgbaston. While Andy was in charge of the ground at Warwickshire, my input into the type of surface desired (when I was asked for my thoughts, that is) was, 'Just a good cricket wicket please, Andy.' The Atkinson tale illustrates well how easily people can get upset over minor things in the game. Andy was quite rightly proud of his work, and he was an excellent groundsman, but he went on to demonstrate that dealing with people really was not his forte by falling out with Keith Fletcher at Essex and Duncan Fletcher in Cape Town. This was a great shame, as people with Andy's expertise are sorely needed in the game.

Despite this unexpected ending to my first session with the players, it had been a good one. I was particularly impressed by a left-hand batsman named Roger Twose. I was told that he was a struggling second XI player, that the club was not sure he was going to make it. My first impressions were that he looked organised and would indeed make the grade, but I kept silent as I had only just started. I was nervous when I met my new charges. As with all the jobs I had had before, I seriously wondered whether or not I was up to it. As I did at Kent in 1987, I sent each player a questionnaire, seeking an insight into their thinking, ambitions and goals. Their answers would also give me, as I was to find out later, some ammunition when times were tense between coach and player.

But it was in Trinidad on the pre-season tour that I really got to know the Warwickshire players, and to understand what made them tick. It soon became abundantly clear to me in which direction I had to start from a coaching perspective. As in any sport, one soon finds out that each player has a level of selfishness in him – the nature of cricket is such that some selfishness is necessary. It is important, for example, not to throw one's wicket away at certain stages of the game. It is also important to understand that at times one has to take a risk. There are three Jewish sayings in this respect that I was taught by my good friend Mike Stakol, who was, let it not be forgotten, a marvellous businessman: If you are not for yourself, who will be for you? If you are only for yourself, what are you? If not now, when? It is possible to interpret these three sayings slightly differently, of course, but to me they epitomise the game of cricket: do not throw your wicket away; always want the ball in the field; practise hard for your own reward; never shy away from a bowling spell; help your team-mate and in that way the team will do better; spend a little extra time on something if you have to; be part of your team so that it becomes part of you. And whatever you are like, you can change. If you want to practise, do not say, 'I will do it tomorrow,' for as we all know tomorrow never comes. I really live by these sayings; I believe in them deeply. The use of the notorious earpieces in South Africa's opening World Cup fixture in 1999 was a case in point. Two minutes before the start against India we decided: If not now, when?

Warwickshire's first game in Trinidad was against Clarke Road United down in the south of the island. We had to play on matting, which was a problem because a lot of our players had not brought flat shoes with them and had to play in spikes. Partly as a result of this, we played spin really badly that day. At one point Neil Smith, coming down the pitch, got his spikes caught in the matting and was stumped while lying prostrate on the ground. The evening's celebrations were rounded off with a singsong, the Clarke Road United captain singing to Andy Lloyd: 'Captain, your ship is sinking!'

We were billeted in a largish house – three in a bedroom in some cases – which turned out to be a wonderful environment for team discussions. The youngsters were sent down the road to get rotis (curried pancakes) and beers, and early on that tour we started what was to become a team ritual over the next four years: a cricket meeting in which we discussed how we would approach aspects of forthcoming games. One would have expected professional cricketers to do this all the time, but one of the most noticeable traits in modern English county teams is the lack of real professionalism. My recollection of the dressing room in my days with Kent was that the players were still there at ten o'clock at night listening to the likes of Alan Brown and Alan Dixon holding forth on the game; by 1991, the groundstaff at Edgbaston would have been put out if we had not cleared the ground an hour after the game.

It is a disease that is common to a greater or lesser extent to all counties. The opposition coming in and sharing a beer, or meeting in the bar and being able to congratulate, commiserate or to meet and make friends is not an integral part of the game any more. This harder approach was something we introduced with the South African team during my tenure. There is no hanging about any more; the team bus leaves an hour after the close of play so that we have time to reflect on the day's play. Also, because players get to the ground so much earlier than they used to, staying behind after play has lost its appeal as the day becomes too long.

At Warwickshire, after that good tour of Trinidad, we quickly fell into a cohesive and professional routine, and I started to apply some of my new ideas (although I cannot take credit for all the innovations at the club; Warwickshire was well stocked with forward-thinking players). In order to achieve a better understanding with Warwickshire's players, at a pre-season training camp I arranged lectures by prominent sports specialists in physiology and psychology, and started a process I hoped would educate them into self-determination from a fitness perspective. And certainly we began to improve. I brought out to South Africa in the close season various young players, not all of them from Warwickshire, who I felt needed the exposure of being away from home in order to expand their knowledge of cricket. It also gave me the opportunity to work one on one with a number of English pros in Cape Town. Those who came to those nets at Avendale included Dominic Ostler, Graeme Welch, Keith Piper, Dougie Brown, Ashley Giles, Chris Adams (then of Derbyshire), Neil Burns, Vince Wells, Paul Jarvis and David East, in addition to the Kent players I had coached previously. As well as learning themselves, they were all instrumental in helping coach hundreds of youngsters who flocked to the junior nets and themselves went away (I hope) better players.

The injuries the Warwickshire players began to suffer from in 1991 also led me to the offices of Professor Tim Noakes, the foremost sports scientist in the world, who lived in Cape Town. He was head of the Department of Exercise and Sports Science at the university. I wanted to seek his opinion on whether bowling made a cricketer fitter or more tired, and thereby more susceptible to injury. He gave me an immediate response but put the ball straight back in my court. Yes, of course exercise made a human body fitter, but he felt a bowler could easily become fatigued, or might even have a bad action, and that they were causes of breakdowns, and he also reminded me that, of course, certain types of bowling could not raise the heart-rate above the norms considered to improve fitness.

We were not to pursue this conversation until much later when Tim helped me run the South African national side, but while I was with Warwickshire I fortunately had an ally in Dermot Reeve. After I had sent out the questionnaires to the players, Dermot's had come back accompanied by a three-page letter which outlined a number of ideas he had that he felt would help Warwickshire. Dermot had been doing some research himself into fitness, in Perth in Australia. He had spoken to a number of exercise specialists there and had this theory that anaerobic training was the way forward for cricketers. Anaerobic training is a mixture of speed and stamina. A 400-metre run is anaerobic in that you run as fast as you can until you are completely out of breath, then rest and do it again. I remember the Western Province hockey team doing twelve of these every night before we went to the inter-provincial tournament in Durban. In 1988, Natal was the only province to have Astroturf, and that meant playing at a higher pace for much longer – hence the 400-metre sprints. In those days I was still able to try a few myself, but needless to say I did not last the course.

Partly as a result of Dermot's obvious enthusiasm for the game and how it could be improved, he immediately intrigued me. I knew he was a 'bits-and-pieces' player who had come from Sussex, and whose main attribute was the ability to swing the ball (at no great pace); he was also a batsman who was known for tenacity rather than style. Imran Khan, his former Sussex team-mate whom he impersonates so well, did not rate him, but Dermot made himself into a good cricketer. When I saw him bowl for the first time, I was struck by the awkwardness of his run-up. Even his delivery was more like a discus thrower's than a pie chucker's, to use Rodney Marsh's famous term describing some of our bowlers, but it was easy to see that he had what cricketers call a 'golden arm' in that he was able to take wickets and break partnerships. The key, I think, was his tremendous confidence in his ability, and, as unkind as I have been about his action, I can honestly say that he deserved to represent England in one-day cricket, which was considered his forte. When he took over as captain after Andy Lloyd, he quickly demonstrated his undoubted knowledge of the game. He was certainly the best one-day captain I have come across. He would learn about man-management, as we all would, and his innovations were sometimes a lot of fun. The controversy he caused when he pioneered the use of the reverse sweep to destroy spinners in 1993 in the one-day game was ongoing; I would have hated to be a member of the opposition when he was batting or setting fields.

Quite often sides come up with irritating players who can put the opposition on the back foot just by being a pain on the field. Warwickshire were fortunate to have two: Dermot and Roger Twose, as the latter gained in confidence. This practice is commonly known as sledging, and on occasions it can be a useful method of destroying a batsman's concentration. Probably one of the funniest comments I have heard came from the wicketkeeper Geoff Humpage. A young batsman came out to the middle for Oxford University and took a minute and a half to take guard, airing a very plummy accent in the process. He took a final look around the field, settled down to wait for the bowler, lifted his bat high as the bowler approached the crease and had his middle stump knocked three yards back. He stood there disbelievingly for a long time, so Geoff came up, replaced the stump and said, 'Can I get your dog for you to help you find the way back to the pavilion?'

Warwickshire had good seasons in 1991 and 1992, finishing well up the championship table and twice reaching the semi-finals of the NatWest Trophy. Allan Donald underlined what a top professional he had become by running 400-metre sprints on his days off. This showed just how much he wanted to achieve in the game. Dermot Reeve's first season as captain followed in 1993, one of the most traumatic from the point of view of injuries. Our attack had comprised Gladstone Small, a wonderful bowler on his day but who, like all of us, was ageing and suffering from various niggles; the mercurial and impossible Paul Smith; the up-and-coming Dougie Brown and Graeme Welch; Dermot himself; and Neil Smith and Paul Booth as spinners. The lynchpin of our attack, though, was Tim Munton, a wonderful bowler in English conditions, a tireless workhorse and, in the words of Andy Lloyd, someone who never gets injured. Alas, Tim did pick up an injury, as did all our bowlers, although we seemed to be able to nurse him through eight overs on a Sunday. We finished a very disappointing fourteenth in the Championship as we just could not bowl out our opponents, but through excellent one-day cricket, and in particular as a result of the determined and innovative captaincy of Dermot, we reached the final of the NatWest Trophy.

This final was one of the two great limited-overs games I have been involved in, the other being South Africa's frantic World Cup semi-final in 1999 against Australia. We played

Sussex and fielded first, normally a great advantage in September, but the pitch and the conditions favoured the batsmen. Our injured fast bowlers suffered: Munton went for 70, which was unheard of, and Sussex piled up a huge total of 321 in 60 overs. This would be a winning total at least nine times out of every ten games, and at 24 for 2 it already looked as though it was all over for us. But then Paul Smith took on the Sussex attack and scored a marvellous 60, and Asif Din, in partnership with Dermot Reeve, played one of the great one-day innings, amassing 104 runs in the process. The two of them reverse-swept, ran cheeky singles, struck outrageous blows and amazingly brought the innings to a situation where we needed just one to win off the last ball. Twose sliced the ball over the packed infield, we ran two and the ball disappeared into the crowd in the gloaming. Warwickshire had won an unbelievable game.

That victory gave us the most wonderful lesson, namely that in cricket it is possible to win from any position. That is why the game is always worth fostering and persevering with, for it is far more important than the bickering and backstabbing that is often caused by professional jealousy. If we had lost that final it would have been generally thought that Warwickshire had had a dreadful season. Of course we had to remind ourselves that we had finished fourteenth in the Championship, but we could be proud of the fact that we had worked strategically for weeks nursing those injuries to enable us to reach Lord's and win that game.

As well as morale-boosting wins like that, Warwickshire's tours during my tenure as coach – starting with that trip to Trinidad in 1991 – were, I felt, very much part of the reason why the team improved so dramatically. In 1992 and 1993 we went to South Africa, to Avendale, whose facilities, I felt, were as impressive as any club's in the world. But Warwickshire's greatest successes came after a tour to Zimbabwe in 1994. At Harare, in particular, we were treated to some of the best batting conditions anyone could wish for, and for that we were indebted to Trevor Penney's father, who organised the pitches. We also adopted slightly different methods of practice, and as a result had a wonderful tour. It was good timing in many respects, because our new overseas player was just about to join us – a small West Indian called Brian Lara.

My initial encounter with Lara was on his first day at Edgbaston when he attended a press conference. Dermot Reeve gave him his county cap, and I was very impressed with how maturely he handled the occasion. I knew he was a fine player, and I had been lucky enough to catch some highlights of a memorable double hundred he had scored against Australia at the SCG in January 1993. He had been my recommendation to the committee the year before as our overseas player, and although we had eventually gone for Dermot's first choice, Manoj Prabhakar, Brian was at Edgbaston now. That day I also met his agent. I had always felt that it was important to put the player's sport first and making money second, but during the 1994 season there were times when I felt the very opposite occurred.

Brian arrived at Edgbaston in prime form, of course, fêted as a national hero after his recent world record Test score of 375, made against England in Antigua, eclipsing the total of that other West Indian national hero Gary Sobers, who generously came on to the pitch to hug Lara after he struck the decisive boundary. Fortunately we had signed Lara just two days before this epic innings; one can only imagine how the price would have rocketed had it all taken place a week later. Still, I am certain that during his first season at Warwickshire he made a tremendous amount of money. When, against Durham on 7 June, he broke the second world batting record with his amazing 501 not out, he was stunned by the amount of media attention he attracted, and was to continue attracting. For once, English cricket was big news.

During these emotionally and physically demanding times Brian was usually polite and erudite, but as time passed he became reclusive and much harder to get hold of. Early in the season he practised spasmodically, which to a certain extent was understandable as he had just come back from a hard Test series and was already demonstrably in good form, but he was also reticent about attending team practices. And there were occasions when he arrived at the ground as the game was starting. The habit of most teams is to arrive one and a quarter hours before play is due to begin, leaving time for a light practice with stretches and some catching to hone the skills before eleven o'clock. Brian took part in perhaps only a fifth of these sessions during the season, and I know Dermot and a number of the other players were upset that he did not take more interest in that part of the game.

I held a different view. I thought that pushing Brian over relatively minor issues such as time-keeping would be counter-productive. After all, he continued to score runs through all this, at the same time being put under outrageous pressure by his agents to make a bit of money (sorry – a lot of money). So long as the rest of the team remained supportive of each other and encouraged Brian when he played, then that, I felt, was all that needed to be done. I wrestled with the problem daily, though, as I still had my doubts at the time as to whether or not this was the right approach.

I was encouraged in my belief by the positive effect Brian was having on the batsmen. He would help them out and boost their confidence in the middle, and during one match against Middlesex at Lord's he gathered the top six batsmen together under the Compton stand and talked for half an hour about responsibility, building an innings and why they should not throw their wickets away. So although he was unpopular for his lack of commitment off the field, he was thoroughly committed to the team's success on it. Dermot, who holds the stage well himself, was put out that Brian became too much the focus of attention, and there were a number of occasions when he and I differed as to how Brian should be treated. Dermot often talked about the situation in terms of my letting him down – I wrestled with that little proposition well. I am a firm believer in giving the captain full support, so effectively what I was doing by counselling caution, if not a hands-off policy, in terms of our treatment of Brian was going against the grain. However, in Tim Munton and Gladstone

Small I had two allies. One kept the team focused and the other kept Brian in touch with the team. And all the while Brian scored runs – more than 2,000 in the season.

During this 1994 season Dermot picked up a groin and hip injury and played mainly in the one-day fixtures. This, of course, meant his relationship with Brian became that much more difficult. Dermot was prone to criticising Brian for picking and choosing his games, but now there was scope for similar accusations by Lara. I stood in the middle and juggled the balls. During this period our chief executive, Dennis Amiss, was of immense help, intervening in situations, for instance, in which Brian felt I was being unfair.

The first sign of real trouble was when Brian, under pressure to score a century in the Middlesex game I have just mentioned to achieve his seventh in a row and create a record, was dismissed fairly early on in the first innings. I suppose deep down he was very disappointed. Rain had interfered with the game – the first day had been washed out completely – and Middlesex, who were chasing a target, began very slowly and were soon behind the run rate. Dermot decided to experiment with Brian's occasional leg-spinners, but he was expensive and failed to take a wicket, and at tea Middlesex were 100 without loss needing a further 120. As they edged closer to victory Brian became disillusioned with the game's progress and walked off the field, claiming he had a knee problem. He came to me and told me that this was why English cricket was rubbish, and that in the Caribbean the game was never played in this way. I was very disappointed that he had walked off, and more disappointed still with his attitude. I told him that because of the vagaries of the English weather, Championship games would on occasion need to be resolved through runs being given away. I tried to explain it was better to make a game of it and lose when trying to win, but nothing would convince him.

Meanwhile, out in the middle we started to take wickets. Middlesex finished nine wickets down and eleven runs short, and I recorded in the Warwickshire CCC annual that 'coming back from a precarious position and nearly winning the game set new confidence levels'. I could understand Brian's resentment of that type of cricket, for it does seem a rather false way of playing the game, but I am a firm believer that cricket has to provide results and must entertain, keeping up with other sports while maintaining its unique identity. Brian, however, remained far from convinced. It was the first time I recognised what strong views he held on cricket.

Top sportsmen are very rarely 'nice' people, by which I mean they are rarely easy-going or laid back. Even David Gower, for all the relaxed aura he has about him, was tough and driven. Such players want success and have a clear vision of what it is going to take to get it. I believe we all learnt a lot about Brian in 1994, yet a few years later he was to return to Warwickshire and have a disappointing season as captain. Such problems normally occur when people do not wish to immerse themselves in a different working environment. Too often cricketers and cricket administrators are so far apart in their thinking that it is no wonder problems crop up. Brian Lara's problems stemmed from not being able to thrash out differences of opinion with Dermot, yet both had brilliant cricketing minds. It was a simple clash of egos. Had we managed to bring these two minds closer together, we might have had an awesome combination. All four trophies in 1994 would definitely have been feasible.

Another unfortunate example of the difficulties that occurred took place at Northampton. Gill and the boys had just come over for the school holidays and I had been granted permission to spend three days with them. We had decided to take a barge trip from Stratford to Evesham and back. It was a wonderful three days in fantastic weather. We met Andy Lloyd at a local pub and shared a bottle of wine on board, discussing Lara and Reeve and how I should handle them. I was raring to go when I drove to Northampton for the Sunday game, only to find that Brian did not want to play and that Dermot had called him a prima donna on the field during the Championship game. Brian had walked off, and their relationship was at an all-time low. To make matters worse, the television cameras were there.

In his first innings in the Championship game Brian had scored 190 against a bowling attack that included Curtly Ambrose, but he had taken a knock on the head. Then Allan Jones, the umpire, had disallowed a catch at the wicket during Northamptonshire's first innings, ruling that the ball had reached Keith Piper on the bounce. Brian had said something to him along the lines of 'How can you see from there?' Dermot had quite rightly tried to calm him down, but the situation culminated in his calling Brian a prima donna and Brian walking off complaining about a sore head – an all-too-sudden ailment. When I arrived, he was sleeping under the table in the dressing room. I had a long chat in the physio's room with both Dermot and Brian, and eventually I decided I had resolved the problem. At least I thought I had.

Lara then played against Northamptonshire, only to declare he would not be able to take his place in the next match against Lancashire as he had a sore knee. Where had that particular ailment come from? I had spoken to Brian earlier about who he felt was the best bowler in world cricket and he had said Wasim Akram, so, like all suspicious coaches, I wondered whether he was ducking out of playing. I tried to put that thought out of my head, reasoning that he must be tired, and I was also concerned that if Brian did have a knee problem then it should be looked at. When I suggested this to him, he was very short with me and just said that I did not trust him. Eventually he brought me a doctor's note from a gynaecologist in Berkshire! Obviously I still wanted him to see a club specialist so I referred the matter to Dennis Amiss, who, after a long chat with Brian, allowed him the match off against Lancashire. My mother always said to me that things happen for a reason, and Warwickshire, without their star batsman, went on to beat a powerful Lancashire side, Roger Twose playing a magnificent innings against Wasim Akram on a deteriorating pitch. The belief in the team's abilities gathered pace. Winning was possible without Brian Lara.

I suppose one could argue that if we had been more sensitive to the pressures Brian was under, we would have given him the time off and put more faith in our own players anyway. Lara, of course, was a magnificent performer. His batting was almost flawless and overall his effect on the side was positive. His ability to score at a run a ball showed him to be almost Bradmanesque in his ability. Through judicious handling and with some luck, we were able to convince Brian that he should keep going in what is the toughest arena in the world to motivate yourself for, given that it can be seven days' cricket a week. It is a tribute to his character that he kept going.

The impetus we needed for a really successful season was the Benson & Hedges Trophy win on 9 July at Lord's. The toss was vital that day, we won it, and beat Worcestershire's total of 170 off their allotted 55 overs with some ten overs to spare. We had been dubious about our ability to bowl out opponents in the Championship without Allan Donald, and felt this would be a real handicap, yet we actually clinched the Championship by bowling out Hampshire at Edgbaston after they were 100 for 1 at lunch. Our next challenge was the NatWest Trophy, for three trophies out of three. The toss is certainly all-important on an early September morning, but this time Worcestershire won it, and chose to have a bowl. Although we struggled to 89 for 3, the advent of rain meant we had to start again on the Sunday. Our total of 223, of which Lara made 81, was, alas, not enough. Graeme Hick (93 not out) and Tom Moody (88 not out) batted magnificently, and we lost the match by eight wickets. Our final challenge was to overcome Gloucestershire at Bristol on 13 September to win the Sunday League, and we did not make a propitious start. The scoreboard read 3 for 3 at one stage without a run off the bat, then Courtney Walsh dropped a sitter at mid-wicket off Trevor Penney. In partnership first with Brian and then with Dermot, Trevor made sufficient runs to give us a reasonable total to defend of nearly 200. We then bowled superbly to win the game. It rankled that we were described as a workmanlike team of average players lifted by the performances of Lara. We only lost four times in five and a half months – how average is that? Brian was undoubtedly the catalyst for our success, but you do not win anything as a one-man band. As with Manchester United's Treble of 1998/99, it was a season none of us is likely to experience again.

And now, of course, after five years away from Edgbaston, I am back. I knew when I re-signed for Warwickshire at the conclusion of the World Cup in 1999 that the staff I inherited would be rather different in make-up from the one I had left in 1994, but one person I was depending on was Tim Munton, who had been such an effective performer. We had become close friends, so it came as a shock when I received a telephone call from him that autumn to say that he might have to leave the club. This had much to do, he said, with a breakdown in communication. I was concerned that he should stay; I had certainly hoped he would at least assist me as coach. He had bought a property in Cape Town with the proceeds of his benefit and came over to do some business (he works for a travel company), so I arranged for him to have dinner at my house.

Tim and I chatted for over five hours, and try as I might I could not change his mind. He was adamant that although he loved Warwickshire and was grateful for all that they had done for him, he felt that his input was not what it was and that certain members of the cricket committee were after him, or at least did not respect him. Obviously, having not been involved with the club for five years, I found it impossible to know both sides of the story. It certainly seemed from what I had heard that Tim had a case and that there should be a meeting with the chairman and the general committee. This was a difficult position for me to be in, not least given our friendship. I could understand that Tim's injury record had not been good and that there was some anxiety as to whether he could make it through another season, yet I knew that even when he was injured he could have a positive effect on the team and the club. I wondered what had gone wrong. Tim was always a frank and straight-talking person and I was amazed that the two parties had not been able to get together to iron out any dispute. He was widely respected as a person and had always been a great communicator.

Not having Tim as one of my senior players will undoubtedly make life harder for a while during my second tenure at the club. It will be a priority of mine to find that type of person again in the dressing room.

4 Taking the National Reins

I WAS THOROUGHLY IMMERSED in what was going on in the middle during Warwickshire's final Sunday League game against Gloucestershire when two reporters rushed up to me and said: 'Have you heard the news?' I had not heard anything. 'Mike Procter's been given the sack by South Africa and they tell us you are in line for the job.' That moment was genuinely the first inkling I had that there would be any change in the position of South Africa's coach. I had heard on the cricket grapevine that all was not well, but a sacking was quite different news. I certainly had not been contacted by anyone.

The celebrations that night were plentiful, but sleep was fitful. The following morning Dr Ali Bacher, the chief executive of the United Cricket Board of South Africa, tracked me down at the team's hotel and asked if we could talk. I said I was in the foyer and had been up all night, so he suggested I went to my room. He asked if I would be interested in being interviewed next Friday for the position of national coach. It was not the hardest of questions to answer. I had hoped that I might be employed by England at a junior level; instead, Phil Neale of Northamptonshire, who ironically was to take over from me at Warwickshire, had been appointed as

Under-19 manager/coach and I was overlooked. I was disappointed as I felt that over the past four seasons I had achieved a lot with Warwickshire; certainly Dermot Reeve, who had been in and out of the England side, felt that my ideas on the game and my management style were far ahead of anything England had experienced.

I was ambitious. I had made a conscious decision that I wanted to take coaching to a different level and had set out to coach an international side, to study the great players and to pass on as much knowledge as I could. I felt that there were better ways to prepare, better ways to get fit, better methods of training, and perhaps the only way to put these ideas into practice was in Test cricket. I had no hesitation in agreeing to go to the meeting, and I decided there and then that I must get back to South Africa as soon as I could.

There were obviously one or two things to clear up before my departure. Dennis Amiss, who had been responsible for bringing me back into the game in England, already knew about South Africa's approach. In an effort to keep me at Edgbaston he offered me a further three years on my contract in addition to the following year, but said that if I was given the South Africa job then the club would not stand in my way. Such was the attitude of the club that they not only accepted I was going to leave, they even encouraged me and realised it was a big step forward for me. Later, they were to make me an honorary life member, which touched me deeply. In contrast, Kent, for whom I had played for nineteen seasons, had virtually ignored me. At the same time I had been fighting – that is the only word I can use to describe it – with Boland. Henry Paulse and Kevin Bridgens had seen fit to take away my sponsored car and reduce my salary without giving me any reason at all. It was extremely mystifying, and very disappointing after all I had achieved with them, so once again the timing of a call to a new job was good.

Owing to my success with Warwickshire and that particular battle with Paulse and Bridgens, I had intended to resign my coaching position with Boland. As I have said, I could not stand the underhand ways of a number of people in cricket there. If they did not want me, why could they not just say so? The difference in the two managements I dealt with at Edgbaston and Boland was astounding. Warwickshire were a very well-run outfit. There was none of the griping and backstabbing one encountered at other clubs. If you did not like the way people carried on, you got up and said so. Spending time speculating about what other people are saying and constantly looking over your shoulder and as a result not concentrating on your job is far from ideal. Success in cricket comes not from listening to such individuals but through being hard on oneself without running oneself down.

But it was still a surprise to me that South Africa had even bothered to ask me for an interview. The other two candidates were Duncan Fletcher, who played for Rhodesia in the 1980s, and the ubiquitous Eddie Barlow, the former South African all-rounder who had not yet found a proper niche for himself. As it turned out, I travelled from the airport building in Cape Town to the UCB offices in Johannesburg with Eddie. I always found him to be a tremendous enthusiast, yet I have never spent a more dispiriting two hours. He said he could not understand why he had to go for an interview; they knew his track record and they should act on it. He then immediately contradicted himself by saying, bizarrely, that he had only come for the interview because he did not actually want the job but would prefer life on his farm. He was just going to tell the selection committee where to go. It was, to say the least, a somewhat confusing car ride from the airport to the UCB offices.

Listening to Eddie Barlow, I was briefly reminded of myself when I was at school. I remember being desperate for the captaincy in my last year in the first XI, when the system was organised by vote. I was already captain of the hockey team at the time, and was nominated for the cricket captaincy, but in a very weak moment I decided not to take it. Magnanimously, I suggested that someone else should do the job to spread the load of responsibility, despite the fact it was a position I dearly wanted. I captained Kent Schools and the Association of Kent Cricket Clubs Under-19s, as well as the Tonbridge & Tunbridge Wells district of the AKCC, so I had my fair share of captaincy, but the position I really wanted I let go. Rather like Eddie, I did so because there was a fear that I might not be appointed. It was disappointing, though, that during my tenure as South Africa's coach Eddie was allowed to help me only occasionally. Perhaps that is the wrong way of putting it, though. Perhaps he had no inclination to help me out – he certainly wrote some pretty vitriolic articles in the press during my time as coach.

The interviews were scheduled for 23 September 1994, and the announcement was to be made the following day, which was good as I had arranged to go to the North-West province in Potchesfroom to run a coaching course with their provincial side. That afternoon I received a telephone call from Ali saying that I had the job and that he would be announcing it the next day at a press conference in Johannesburg. I immediately telephoned Gill and she told me that Ali had already told her. There was a distinct note of joy in her voice.

The next few days were frantic. The first thing that went through my mind was elation, and then, as always, huge doubt over whether I really could do the job. Such doubt has always been inherent in me – although after it recedes, the ideas start to flow – but one could hardly blame me for being nervous. Taking over an international side as a coach is not the easiest job in the world. Every coach knows that he is likely to have a honeymoon period, followed by what might be called a reality period and – he hopes – a growth period. This is invariably followed by a questioning period, which comes when the team is not successful. During this period he has to learn to deal with all types of media, with disappointment, success, professional jealousy and, above all, with the players and the different ways in which they cope with it. There is little in the way of guidance through all these periods; you stand or fall on your own merits. But I would say the biggest obstacle that faced me initially was whether an Engelsman ('Englishman' in Afrikaans) could make an impression or be able to gain the confidence of the South

African public, although I did have an advantage in that I had been coming to South Africa since 1970, playing cricket here and assisting various provinces in their efforts to encourage the playing of cricket in the Afrikaans and black communities.

Nonetheless, it was a brave decision by Ali Bacher to hand me the reins. I had first met him when I was representing Natal under the captaincy of Barry Richards against his Transvaal side in the 1973/74 season. He was justly renowned for being the only captain of South Africa to lead his country to a whitewash in a Test series against, of all countries, Australia, in 1969/70. The Australians would argue that they had just undertaken a demanding tour of India and that Garth McKenzie, their outstanding fast bowler, was ill, but the reality was that the South African side of that era was awesome. Richards, Barlow, Bacher, G. Pollock, Irvine, Bland, Lindsay, Lance, Procter, P. Pollock, Trimborn and Traicos would have been capable of beating the outstanding West Indies sides of the 1970s and 1980s. Ali led them very well and his reputation as a motivator of men was probably born then.

He was a Test-class, rather than a world-class, batsman, an on-side player of note with a closed face of the bat and closed grip. Anyone who bowled on his legs was cannon fodder. In that Natal v. Transvaal game, Barry Richards devised the strategy of a predominantly leg-side field and asked me to bowl round the wicket at Bacher's legs. This was intended to frustrate him, and there was no doubt that it worked. After three overs I sensed he was not happy. 'You are more negative than Trevor Bailey,' he eventually chirped. (Bailey, incidentally, was a hero of mine.) I replied: 'Are you that old that you played against him?' Ali took exception to this remark, and instead of playing me cautiously and seeing me off tried to flick the next delivery over long leg. Instead, he tickled the ball down the leg-side and was caught behind by Tich Smith, the Natal wicketkeeper. It was a lesson in keeping one's cool and, from the bowler's viewpoint, making a strategy work.

I remember on another occasion Ali, in his capacity as a medic, prescribing me some Indocid suppositories to rid me of a back pain. In fact, I often turned to Ali for advice, and sometimes he turned to me. During that period I was, of course, working alongside the Western Province Hockey Association in addition to assisting John Passmore and Avendale, having been shunned by the Western Province Cricket Association, so I saw mini-cricket grow at an enormous rate. It was especially popular within the primary schools. I was in charge of Pinelands, and we were one of the first areas to have a complete mix of backgrounds: Xhosa, coloured and white South Africans. Upon returning to international cricket, Ali handed over the running of development (including mini-cricket) to Khaya Majola – a left-handed batsman who had played for the African team against Natal in 1976 and who was then overseeing amateur cricket – and Hussain Ayob – a former fast bowler who worked with Majola as director of coaching – but he made sure the development programme was initiated elsewhere, enabling Kenya, Zimbabwe and Bangladesh to gain one-day international status and, in the case of Zimbabwe, Test status.

Every now and then Ali would sound me out about the possibility of my filling a coaching role in South African cricket. In August 1994 he had approached me via Dennis Amiss to see if I was available to head up South Africa's first cricket academy, sited in Johannesburg, which was to be sponsored by the paints company Plascon. I declined this offer because of the difficulty of uprooting the family, and we all wanted to stay in Cape Town anyway. Ten years before that a similar situation had occurred. Ali had wanted me to take over the position of director of coaching in South Africa, which was then under the umbrella of the Rembrandt group. I was interviewed by a member of that company at the Dorchester Hotel in London. Again the post was based in Johannesburg, a city with which Gill was familiar having been to school in Pretoria, but by then I had had the offer of a job in Cape Town and was reluctant to go to Johannesburg and live there. Ali was not overly happy with me when I turned it down.

Our relationship, however, developed after my appointment as South Africa's coach. Ali, again, was supportive most of the time, allowing Peter Pollock, Hansie Cronje and myself a fair amount of freedom. Difficulties did occur, however, when political issues came to the fore and Ali decided to adhere to the wishes of the politicians over speeding up the integration of black and coloured cricketers into the Test and provincial teams. In my opinion, he let them take too much control of cricket. While it was important to encourage black cricketers, they had to be good enough to play at the highest level. As a result of the policy condoned by Ali the best players in the country have been put under unnecessary pressure because of political concerns. They are feeling the expectancy of the nation and their freedom of expression is being stifled. Ali may well have gone down a dangerous route, one that I fear will cause great concern in South Africa.

Should one man have such an influence over the game in South Africa? This is a question I have often been asked by people around the world when talking about the game's most publicised administrator. Ali does indeed have enormous power in South African cricket. There is no doubt in my mind that he needed that power early on in order to move the mountains he has moved, and his development programme is a wonderful legacy. However, I felt Ali was unable to give sufficient freedom to his employees in terms of each person's job specification. I know, for example, that Imtiaz Patel, who many thought was being groomed to replace Ali when he moves on to oversee the World Cup in South Africa in 2003, resigned as director of professional cricket because he felt unable to achieve anything without reporting to Ali all the time. My own experiences have been similar in some respects. What always perturbed me was Ali's tendency to listen to Hansie Cronje when he went to see him, rather than calling me in as well. More might have been achieved if the three of us had got together as opposed to my having to hear stories second-hand. It can never be understated how vital an aspect of management communication is.

One matter over which we were never in agreement was taking wives and girlfriends on tour. When I was a youngster and playing cricket, I did not want the hassle of girlfriends floating around. My focus was on the cricket. If you got fixed up every now and again on tour, that was a bonus. Even when Gill and I were married she did not come to every game, and why should she? One does not see the bank manager's wife in the office with him. But my views on the subject were shaped by my experiences with the Kerry Packer organisation, where three people were assigned to look after the women who attended the cricket; all administration, travelling, shopping and ticket allocations were undertaken by them. Their well-being was considered vital to the happiness of the men, and hence the success of the cricket, and indeed the husbands continued with their cricket regardless and there were very few, if any, problems. I distinctly remember my first discussions with Ali and Hansie on this subject and the look of dismay when I said I was totally in favour of wives and girlfriends travelling. Having fought as hard as I could, though, I eventually gave up, but I refused to act like a schoolmaster and smack the boys' bottoms. In my opinion team discipline should come from team members.

A more modern outlook is required to contend with the pressures on relationships today. The constant excuse that the presence of wives on tour leads to poor performances is really not a good one. Some players improve by as much as forty per cent on the resumption of their marriage and family life when they return from tour. On South Africa's last two tours to England certain rules were made and changed and rehashed, but they did not work. The wives and girlfriends went over, found jobs and accommodation and arrived at the ground to watch their husbands and boyfriends play. Telling them they were not supposed to be there was ridiculous and intolerable. Roll on men who are tolerant of women in cricket! Saying we lost to England in 1998 because of the presence of women, as some did, is on a par with the excuse 'The sun got in my eyes, sir.'

Going to India for a long tour is always the toughest assignment. The conditions there test even the most patient of people, and when South Africa travelled there at the end of 1996 the UCB did very well in recognising that fact, allowing wives and girlfriends to come on tour and giving players an allowance based on a points system per games played. This was fine, but when management was accorded the same treatment I started to question the idea.

Consider this simple example. Gary Kirsten, then in prime form and a vital cog in our team, had met and fallen in love with Debbie Cassidy, who was in the middle of her studies to become a schoolteacher. She was a fantastic influence on Gary, who had changed from being a real party animal to a quiet and studious character. His cricket reflected this change: he was dependable and hard-working, someone who recognised that he had been given a gift and was prepared to work at it. As he had accumulated a lot of Test match points, he received the full R10,000 (about £2,000) tour allowance. Yet the coach and the manager, each of whom had been married for twenty or more years and had children, were offered half that (consider also that the management's bonuses were far inferior to those of the players).

It was not difficult to foresee a problem with that system. I could not afford to take my wife and family to India. If Gill came, then my boys would have to as well, for we could not leave them at home. What with that and school terms, we were unable to be together as much as we would have liked. It could be argued that I knew what I was getting myself into when I picked my job, and I do not have a problem with that. However, I have always believed that time put in should be rewarded. That is not to say that the UCB have not been generous in other ways, but they were inconsistent and dogmatic. Ali once said to me, flat out: 'We are not going to pay for your children.' I told him that was fair enough, but giving me the full allowance that a senior player received would have made it easier for *me* to pay for my children. I actually believe that Ali was working for the best for the players, but I sometimes wonder if he went about it properly.

I know that the same problem has dogged most touring teams, although the Australians are an exception because they learnt directly from the Packer years. I just hope that cricket's administrators learn from these experiences, as this will be an ever-increasing problem in a modern society where the expectations of married couples are as high as the divorce rates. I do not envy Ali his job as chief executive officer of a major cricketing country; as a coach I watch the various witch-hunts and backstabbing that go on with horror. The game is under pressure, fighting a battle with a lot of other sports for the attention of the public and its youth, so the sooner we help each other and try to avoid shooting ourselves in the foot the better.

It was interesting to note that the itinerary of South Africa's tour to India in February 2000 was cut in length to just a month, incorporating only two Tests and five one-day internationals. Why? Because the South African team would have been decimated by withdrawals because of length of time away from loved ones in a harsh environment. India is a place where a team should consider, for instance, taking its own chef, especially as spicy food is really the only food that is cooked well and a lot of Western dishes are prepared in strange oils. It is the same for Indians touring the West. They live on spicy food, and it is difficult to get the real thing away from home. For our visit to Pakistan in 1997 we took with us 500 kilos of pasta, biscuits, sponsor's beer and sweets, as well as 200 videos and various electronic games. One might say we are pampering the players too much, and perhaps we are, yet obtaining an edge is the key. Beating India in India is a dream of many countries and is still very difficult to achieve. There are still a lot of areas that need attention if teams are to be more successful travelling abroad and it is no wonder that countries at home have such a big advantage. Management means finding out what individuals need, what they can have and what they have to put up with. Australia always seem to create that balance. When they go to a country they become part of it. We did that in Pakistan in 1997 and came away victorious, but we were still a long way away from getting everything right. Touring has been going on for years yet there always seems to be a divergence of opinion on how one should go about it. The key is to find out how to get the best out of each player without upsetting the others, which in turn means greater communication, more flexibility but also attention to team discipline.

Despite all the pressures both of us had to face, in all my dealings with Ali I maintained a high respect for him and what he had achieved. And the feeling must have been mutual because, as I said, it was a brave decision to hand me the job of national coach of South Africa. When I took up my appointment, Kepler Wessels was South Africa's captain. The influence of senior players on a cricket side is always of the utmost importance, and when I took over as coach there was a distinct lack of such figures. Owing to the consequences of apartheid, the likes of Jimmy Cook, Clive Rice and Peter Kirsten were only finding their feet in international cricket. The last South African side to appear in Test cricket had featured players long since departed from the scene. Peter Pollock, Mike Procter, Eddie Barlow and Barry Richards could only relate their experiences from the late 1960s and 1970. There was nothing wrong with that, of course, but the generation gap was there, and it was unbridgeable. The South African team culture had to be rekindled. The only player who had any worthwhile Test match experience, with Australia, was Kepler Wessels, and his influence on the rebirth of the team would be enormous. His courage and mental toughness were of inestimable value to the new South African side.

The first thing I did with Kepler was discuss the roles that we would play and discover his feelings about the game. It transpired that we had similar thoughts, and our meeting went well. The team to travel to Pakistan in October 1994 for the limited-overs Wills Triangular Series had been selected before my appointment so I had to work with those players – not that I was complaining, as they were obviously in the selectors' eyes the best available. One who might possibly have made a difference, though, was Adrian Kuiper, but a shoulder operation put him out of the tour before it was due to start.

There was a two-day camp at the Wanderers before we flew to Pakistan. I was extremely nervous at our first team meeting, but I managed to put across one or two of my philosophies on the game. I do remember declaring: 'We are all in this together.' I was not trying to eschew responsibility, simply explaining that if we wanted success we had to work hard for one another and help one another. I could not be a good coach, I reckoned, unless the players in question wanted me to be one. In other words, communication was imperative. In Pakistan we were to be pitted against Australia – about to become, if not already, the best team in the world – and, of course, Pakistan, the 1992 world champions. We were going to be playing on pitches totally foreign to anything most of our squad had ever encountered and in a country whose culture was far removed from that in South Africa.

We lost our first game to Australia by just six runs. They were in the middle of a Test series and were therefore more accustomed to conditions on the subcontinent, whereas we had only just arrived. South Africa had also just lost their last five one-day internationals and had left England on a downward spiral. My job was to rebuild the confidence of the players and to start winning, but while we were in Pakistan the downward spiral got steeper.

One positive aspect to the tour was the realisation that despite the brown, dry and grassless pitches in Pakistan, a finger spinner does not obtain the turn and bounce one might expect. Pakistan's strength lay in their fast bowlers Wasim Akram and Waqar Younis, in tandem with the wrist spin of Mushtaq Ahmed. For all his undoubted ability, Saqlain Mushtaq, Pakistan's pre-eminent off-spinner, has not been as successful there as he has in England. The all-rounders Azhar Mahmood and Abdul Razzaq have also emphasised that spinners in Pakistan are less of a threat than is popularly imagined.

That 1994 tour to Pakistan was frustrating for reasons other than the fact that we were on the wrong end of a 6–0 hiding. For instance, the back-up statistics I had been used to receiving when with Warwickshire were no longer available. We were assigned local scorers who more often than not sat on the opposite side of the ground and were never available to give me the type of breakdown I wanted as a coach. It was after this tour that I started to investigate the possibility of a computer scoring program I could carry around with me on a laptop, and at the same time use it to communicate with my family, write reports, listen to music etc. I was introduced to Compaq, who generously donated the first computer, and eventually I was shown a fairly straightforward scoring program devised by Frikkie Botha from the Northern Transvaal. After some practice, I started using it in earnest just before the 1996 World Cup.

My interest in this aspect of coaching was triggered again when we toured Australia in 1997/98. Unfortunately the timing of this renewal of interest was awry because I was told that I should stick to the basics of coaching and not see this machine as the be all and end all. My enthusiasm had been fired by discovery of the fact that match analysis could be made easier by a day's play being condensed into just 55 minutes. Each player's game profile could be extracted with one click of a mouse, and employing such a system would make it much simpler to organise motivational tapes and highlight the opposition's weaknesses. My dream was to have a dossier of dismissals for all players in Test match cricket, at the touch of a button to be able to tell the bowlers where the best area to bowl would be and what types of pitches these batsmen liked to bat on.

Although my enthusiasm was blunted, there was still hope. We were eventually able to get a local version of this system up and running, and with regular usage it should be able to make major improvements. I am so glad to hear that Graham Ford, my successor as coach of South Africa, now has two systems available in the dressing room for the coach and players, although negotiations with the CSIR are on-going. It is a wonderful boon for a coach to have this technology. I believe that eventually a control centre will be set up whose job it is to take a video feed via satellite from every international played. Operators will be able to provide relevant statistics not only to the coach but individual players on their own laptops in the hotel room via the Internet. Such a facility will also allow them to download the day's play and to study and analyse their own dismissals/innings as well as that of their opposition, thereby having a clearer view of what they are doing. If they have a problem, they will be able to send the video clip to their personal coaching guru for suggestions. The mind boggles every time I learn something new about computer technology, and I really do get excited about what might be achieved if we could persuade Bill Gates to get directly involved.

There is still much territory in the game of cricket to be visited and studied by science. The basics of the game will always remain constant, but I am sure that by careful use of technology we can improve performance, which after all is what a coach should be trying to do. I am keen to pursue my ideas, and I know Warwickshire will be able to benefit from them during my second spell at Edgbaston.

But these concerns were not at the forefront of my mind at the end of 1994. The 6–0 thrashing during that first visit to Pakistan quite naturally led me to believe that we needed to try a different approach in the one-day game. From winning three out of four trophies two months before with Warwickshire, every time I met the press now I was being asked if each defeat meant I was under increasing pressure as a coach. Our original plan in the limited-overs game under the captaincy of Kepler Wessels was to try to score at least 220 and then pound away with a better-than-average seam attack to keep the opposition in check, but, as I said, our experiences in Pakistan made us think again. I called a meeting at the end of the tour to discuss areas of our game we could improve. In some ways this was successful, but in other ways it tended towards divisiveness. Hansie Cronje, who had had an outstanding tour, was keen to bring about change, yet he received minimal support. Most of the team were in awe of Kepler and what he had achieved, but change was essential.

With the help of the selectors – in addition to Peter Pollock, these comprised Rushdie Magiet (now convenor of selectors), S.K. Reddy, Garth Le Roux and Clive Rice – Hansie Cronje was named captain at the age of 25, the youngest ever captain of South Africa, and we made a fresh start. We decided that we would encourage players to utilise their flair, and to be prepared to take risks. We also set down certain prerequisites – we called them one-day disciplines – a vision to be shared by all the players. We had a team session in which we wrote down a number of such disciplines and added to them as and when we needed to. For one-day cricket this started life as a three-page booklet; by the time I left the team we had included enough points to fill eight pages. Over the years, adhering to these disciplines made us into the best one-day side in the world.

Cronje was captain for most of my time as coach of South Africa and he soon earned the respect of the players under him. An interesting question once asked of me was: How does Hansie maintain his muscular Christianity on the cricket field? He is as hard a man in the middle as anyone I have seen, for competitiveness is also very much part of his personality. I believe he is handling both better as he becomes more mature. His faith was certainly a help through the difficult periods we endured when the government put us under pressure over having players of colour in the team. I believed that he would see the good in what I was trying to do, and that I had no hidden agendas. There were times when I thought I could not trust him, but always his beliefs led me to reckon that he would not let me down, and ultimately I found that to be the case. One of the most bitter articles I have ever read came from the pen of a Cape Town journalist claiming he had inside knowledge that Hansie could not trust me to get his upper order in form for the World Cup in 1999. What that journalist failed to realise was exactly how much work went in on a daily basis with those players. Three coaches were working as hard as they could to help them perform to their potential, yet this one guy had the audacity to criticise what we were doing from 6,000 miles away.

Hansie is one of the best captains South Africa has had and will ever have. Naturally there will be people who knock him and he will not win every game, but that is international cricket for you. An eighty per cent record of success in one-day cricket and an increasing ratio of triumphs to losses in Test matches might result in his being regarded as South Africa's best ever captain. Certainly a more dedicated, determined and passionate team man you will not find.

He benefited greatly from Kepler's influence early on. It was Kepler who emphasised the work ethic, he who gave the team belief. Everything he had picked up from playing for Australia was transferred to the South African team. This was exactly what was needed at the time, but winning matches can sometimes create a psychological state of mind that manifests itself in an intransigence of thought, a laager mentality which, interestingly enough and for historical reasons, is often felt to be a failing of Afrikaaners. The changes in the fielding restrictions in one-day cricket, the introduction of night games and other new rules meant that South Africa needed a different strategy. We needed variety, and we needed the best possible spinner in South Africa to be included in our squad, so we turned to Pat Symcox.

When I took over in 1994 as coach from Mike Procter, the side to tour Pakistan had already been selected and Pat had not been included. The three spinners were Clive Eksteen, Tim Shaw and Derek Crookes. Derek was young and inexperienced, Tim had a wonderful domestic one-day record and Clive was generally recognised as the best spinner in South African cricket. A policy of an all-seam attack was very much to the fore, with the likes of Donald, Schultz, De Villiers, Pringle, Matthews and Simons on the scene. There was little room for a spinner, but Pat was introduced and he came to symbolise our success in one-day cricket. Pat had been near retirement only a few months earlier, but had kept playing for Natal. I feel that, along with Hansie and Peter Pollock, I was responsible for resurrecting Pat's career. He was a mature cricketer, but in the international arena he needed guidance and confidence. We discussed field placings, methods of attack, control of line and length and differences in his action. For example, coming round the wicket and getting close to the stumps is never easy for an off-spinner, but Jim Laker had discovered an effective method, I had learnt it, and I suggested it to Pat. Inexorably, if carefully, we changed tactics: less seam, more spin.

Hansie was also very much involved in this, as a captain always has to be at one with his bowlers, especially when it comes to setting field placings for a spinner. In the one-day game it is much easier to set fields as there is a limitation on the leg-side, and for the first fifteen overs. Pat was a strong competitor throughout his all-too-brief international career, and at his peak was prepared to bowl at any time. Only at the end, when reputations and averages became the motivating force, did he err on the defensive side, often talking himself out of bowling in certain situations – understandable, but quite frustrating. In Test match cricket, he was often not the same force. I believed he was not patient enough, always looking for wickets too soon. He was also hampered by the state of South Africa's pitches and selection policies which certainly favoured seam bowlers, not to mention, at a later date, the emergence of Paul Adams.

Pat's batting, however, was a godsend. Modern cricket demands batting in depth, with upper orders constantly under great pressure from very fit and very fast bowlers. Pat's incredible innings of 81 and 55, followed by taking three wickets for just eight runs, against Pakistan in Faisalabad on another tour at the end of 1997 won us a Test. It is worth remembering that game because, as a result of a drawn first Test in Rawalpindi and a very strange draw through rain intervention in Sheikapura, we had gone to Faisalabad on a pitch likely to produce a positive result. Pat came to the wicket in the second innings with South Africa in serious trouble. At the start of his innings he played back to Mushtaq and missed a straight ball, but by an amazing quirk of fate it went between middle and off stump without dislodging the bail. Pat went on to add vital runs with his partners for the last two wickets, and Pakistan crumbled. We won the series

1–0, in the process becoming the first side to beat them in their own country for some time.

Confidence is a strange phenomenon. As Pat's grew he became an integral part of our one-day set-up. His return to one-day cricket came against New Zealand and Pakistan in the 1994/95 series in South Africa. He did well, and was selected to tour New Zealand in February and March 1995 during their centenary season. He made himself into a very fine one-day player with the confidence in his own ability to bowl the ball in the right place and bat with guts, power and determination. But as I said, his Test record is not what it should be owing to a combination of unresponsive surfaces, lack of opportunities to bowl and a certain amount of reluctance to develop a different line.

Pat was always a vibrant tourist, if not always the most diplomatic. There are certain countries where it is almost impossible to move around because of the number of cricket fans. Playing in India, for instance, was unbelievable. A constant throng of twenty to thirty people was pushing and shoving and demanding autographs. It became intolerable, and Pat did not always handle it well. Patience as a spinner is paramount, but this was a department in which he was probably lacking, although his desire to make quick inroads on the field provided the team with an element that is vital to success, if utilised properly. His prime job was to unsettle the opposition, which he achieved by always being in their faces. This was the case in particular with the Sri Lankan captain Arjuna Ranatunga, who rather invited comment, it has to be said, by obtaining a food sponsor for his bat. Ranatunga carried a little more weight than a modern professional sportsman should carry, and Pat was never shy to point that fact out to him. The Sri Lankan did not take at all kindly to this and complained to Ali, who asked me to have a word with Pat, whose response was unprintable. Needless to say, I never passed it on. I believe cricket is richer for the odd comment on the field, although I do not like, and would discourage, the kind of insults the Australians subjected me to in 1975.

Pat also made his own luck, not least during that Test match at Faisalabad when the ball went through his stumps, and on another occasion I remember when he was caught in front of an unlocked gate at Perth, the fielder's momentum taking him back into the crowd and giving Pat a six instead. In general it was good to have him around. If he had had more sustained confidence and possibly a touch more skill he would have had a permanent place in the side, although he will probably feel that South Africa's political direction prevented him from playing longer and more often. The necessity for the inclusion of players of colour did mean that Paul Adams was pushed to the fore, although it could easily be argued that he was there on merit, for his Test bowling strike rate is only four points short of Shane Warne's, who is without doubt the best leg-spinner in the history of the game, a bowler who unfortunately would often save his best for Tests against South Africa.

Fear of failure increases with age and, of course, weight of criticism. A spinner has to rely on his guile as his art is becoming harder and harder. Pitches tend to be flatter, and bats, at 2lb 10oz or more, heavier. Fortunately Pat played cricket for all the right reasons. His departure from the South African squad just before the World Cup in 1999 was disappointing but understandable, and Pat, I think, will look back on his brief career in international cricket with a lot of joy and no little pride because he achieved a lot.

One of Pat's hobbies is to collect cricket books whenever he can, and he is slowly putting together a formidable library. In this quest for artefacts he had a soul-mate (and room-mate) in that other great bowler in South Africa's cause, Fanie De Villiers. In Bangladesh I remember Pat plundering the shipbuilders' scrapyard, and Fanie nearly flew home from Pakistan on the carpets he acquired there. Allan Border once said that De Villiers would be the first person he would pencil in for a combined Australia/South Africa team. Like most swing bowlers, his genuine strength was his away-swinger. He did not really bowl an in-swinger as his action was too round-arm, but he had a ball that angled in and an excellent variation in pace which all swing bowlers need. He also had

a conventional slower ball that used to finish off Sachin
Tendulkar in the one-day game more often than not.

My abiding memory of Fanie off the field is of him cycling a
rickshaw down the lanes of India. He was always a man for the
ultimate challenge in life. Even when he had retired, he was
parachuting into the Wanderers and sitting at the top of the
floodlights at Centurion Park raising money for charity. If ever
there was a better team man, one more crucial to South
Africa's re-emergence in international cricket, I would like to
meet him. He was intensely critical of his fellow players and
sometimes unfairly so, but because he was so honest it never
seemed to matter. He now commentates and does a lot of guest
speaking around South Africa, for he will always be liked by all.
He has a lovely family and is devoted to them. His daughter,
Sunee, suffers from a hearing disorder, and he continually
raises money for the charity that helps children unfortunate
enough to have been born with it. He always called me 'Boss'
and gave me the utmost respect, and for that I am grateful.
During those early days when I needed the support of the
senior players, Fanie was always the first to help.

South Africa had the players for success, and it was my job
to mould them into a winning outfit. The first team meeting
that actually brought about an improvement in our game was
an impromptu fines gathering following a Test defeat at the
hands of New Zealand at the Wanderers, after our trip to
Pakistan. (Fines-gathering meetings, by the way, do not have
anything to do with the cricketing side of things. There are a
variety of special awards about which only team members
know; the outside world I am sure would like to find out what
they are, but the code of secrecy is strong. Those who have
played professional team sports will know exactly what I am
talking about.) Castle Lager, our sponsors, always ensured
that we had a bucket of beers delivered to the dressing room
at the end of the day's play, but, amazingly, the players
hardly ever touched them. On this occasion, however,
everything was drunk. A similar fines meeting in Faisalabad
had also ensured that our stock of beers was drained (there
are times in a cricket team's life when it is good to drown

your sorrows). On this occasion Jonty Rhodes acted as the catalyst, and the upshot of it was twofold: the players went away with a renewed determination to re-establish South African cricket, and a genuine bonding of the team seemed to have taken place in that short time. It is sometimes amazing how little things can make a big difference.

We next met in Cape Town in December 1994 for the start of the Mandela Trophy, a quadrangular tournament with Pakistan, Sri Lanka and New Zealand. For that tournament we included two new players in our team: Mike Rindel, a left-handed batsman from Northern Transvaal who was as free-scoring as one could wish for, and Dave Callaghan, a hard-hitting all-rounder. Both these players would have a huge impact on the team's performance. Also introduced, along with Pat Symcox, was a different approach towards batting orders. Flexibility was now the key. Ways and means of unsettling the opposition became a part of our game. At the same time, though, defining roles for our players was important. They had to feel comfortable about what was happening – but not so comfortable that they would relax. There are certain cricketers who want a nice easy life; they know where they are going to bat and field, and that is that, but in one-day cricket it is better for responsibilities to be chopped and changed and shared out where possible, though I have since realised that although this can be done on a good pitch, it is not so simple when the ball is moving around.

On two occasions during that Mandela Trophy tournament we used 'pinch-hitters' for the first time: Rindel opened with Gary Kirsten at the Wanderers, and with Callaghan at Centurion Park. Both times the experiment came off. This ploy was often criticised, but we knew there would be occasions when it would be worth trying. In the 1999 World Cup in England it was almost impossible to bring it off against the Duke ball, which moved around a lot more, so we opted to have a pinch-hitter who was more of a batsman than is customarily the case going in at number three. Eventually we decided to put the pinch-hitter in around the thirty-fifth over, which worked really well: Lance Klusener had a wonderful tournament. Flexibility is definitely needed at all levels of cricket.

In the middle of that successful Mandela Trophy tournament, we achieved the unlikely feat of coming back from behind to win the three-Test series against New Zealand. At Durban, the team improved dramatically on a difficult pitch. A Test in Durban was always a sticking-point with the media as each time we had played there we had left out the spinner and included five seamers. Only once has a spinner done well in Durban, and that was in 1998 when Mushtaq Ahmed bowled us out in the second innings leaving us 29 runs short of victory. Matches there have usually turned on vital runs scored down the order – Allan Donald in particular has had considerable success with the bat in Durban. On this occasion he was not playing, but Fanie De Villiers carried the attack magnificently and helped put on a vital 44 runs for the last wicket, giving us a valuable overall lead of 41 runs in a low-scoring Test. It was a tremendous advantage. Some splendid bowling by Fanie and some hostility from Brian McMillan during New Zealand's second innings meant that South Africa were left needing 150 to win. The eventual eight-wicket victory, plus the two victories in the one-day matches, did wonders for our confidence.

Not long after that I was faced with my first challenge in terms of bolstering an individual's self-esteem. There was only one player who was really struggling through this period and that was Andrew Hudson, long thought of as the best technical player in the country. If something odd is going to happen in a game of cricket, he is the sort of player, unfortunately, who will suffer as a result. At the Wanderers against New Zealand he nicked the ball to the wicketkeeper, Adam Parore, and just walked off. It was quite clear to those of us on the boundary that the ball had bounced before reaching Parore, but Andrew was so trusting that he departed. He was also involved in some infamous run-outs when often he would sacrifice himself. I remember Ali Bacher saying to me that Andrew was vital to the team and that we had to get him into form. He suffered from the rigours of pressure, and I did indeed have a long talk with him in my hotel room on behalf of the selectors, telling him that we needed him to perform as he was one of our best players, that we could not go on supporting him if he looked impressive but kept getting out.

These were harsh words, for he was opening our batting, but his response was to score a magnificent hundred, albeit benefiting from the fortune of being dropped first ball. It is always worth remembering that luck plays a vital part in the game. Even the great Sir Donald Bradman emphasised this. Andrew was one of the most devastating players of quick bowling, especially in the one-day game, that I have ever seen. I will never forget one shot he executed off the bowling of Waqar Younis at Sharjah, pulling a ball just short of a good length for a flat six over wide mid-on. Incredible. For all his ability against pace, though, he suffered from an inability to play spin – in particular, off-spin. This undoubtedly shortened his Test career.

Andrew was one of the nicest men you could wish to meet on the cricket circuit, so it was a tremendous shame that he did not play for South Africa for longer. He was a devout reborn Christian, and he convened a bible study class which a number of the players regularly attended. This was good for the squad: I was greatly helped in having players who were always looking to assist their team-mates because they had a far broader and more ethically sound outlook on life. It was occasionally a subject for a bit of mickey-taking – I remember Mark Ramprakash sledging Jonty Rhodes once by saying that lions (i.e. England players) eat Christians, although he was very apologetic later and said that it was a comment made in the heat of the moment – but the depth of the team's beliefs meant they did not harbour a grudge.

Our fortunes generally picked up as the 1994/95 season progressed. Hansie proved to be a very positive captain on the field, although I remember Sir Richard Hadlee giving him some stick from the commentary box during the series against New Zealand. As a squad, we were even starting to feel a little cocky. At the end of the international season

Hansie went to England and played for Leicestershire, and learnt a lot about his own game. It is amazing how many people denigrate county cricket; it seems to have a marvellous effect on overseas players, almost like a finishing school.

The off-season gave me time to reflect on my role as coach and South Africa's achievements to date, and also to plan for England's forthcoming tour, starting in October 1995. We held a mid-year camp, which all the players attended. They were all on contracts and I felt it was vital they should be told how fit they needed to be, and that I made sure they were focused on what we had to achieve up to the beginning of a season which would comprise a short tour of Zimbabwe, our first five-Test series against England, and the World Cup. Personally, I was feeling good. I had just been given a fillip in the shape of an eighteen-month extension to my contract with effect from after the World Cup. I was happy with this for obvious reasons, but also because it was always my intention to have long- as well as short-term goals.

It was important, for example, to get to know our reserve strength and try to decide who our players of the future would be. The South African Academy was now in its inaugural year, and Bacher had organised a tour to Sri Lanka for the Under-24s for August. As well as a good opportunity to have a look at our up-and-coming cricketers, we wanted to use the tour to give more experience to Jonty Rhodes, about whose technique we were having doubts.

Jonty had many attributes: he was a fine hockey player who used to get into the thick of things in the goalmouth area, he had devastating speed over twenty yards, a low centre of gravity which gave him incredible mobility, a tremendous eye (although I did not believe he watched the ball hard enough), a true competitive edge and a wonderful work ethic, but he was terribly fidgety at the crease and came hard at the ball both defensively and when attacking. His shots in front of the wicket looked decidedly insecure; consequently, he tended to work everything square and look to sweep all the time. Unfortunately, when you play at the highest level a lack of technique finds you out very quickly. This is a fact. I have seen many technically poor players survive at provincial and county level but fail to make the step up. Bowlers in Test match cricket have to be far more disciplined, and so effective is the analysis of opposing batsmen these days that bowlers will relentlessly probe any perceived weakness.

I played with John Snow, Alan Knott and Keith Fletcher, all of whom were very sharp at spotting a weakness and exposing it, but the Australians are the masters at this discipline. With modern video and computer technology, a batsman's strengths and weaknesses can be analysed, his flaws identified, and tactics and strategies devised to frustrate him and then get him out. Obviously this is more easily accomplished on certain surfaces, and certainly it works both ways as batsmen can study bowlers and work out methods to counter their slings and arrows, but that is the beauty of the game. In South Africa, as I have mentioned, we are steadily building a database of all opposing batsmen, and soon, given that television shows all the cricket in the world as it happens, we will be able to have incredibly detailed profiles of all the players we are about to face. David Leadbetter, the great golf guru, once said there was golf instruction before video (BV) and after video (AV), and that there was no comparison between the value of the two. Cricket, too, falls into this category, as do a number of other sports. But all this excellent preparation comes to naught if the player (a) is not skilled enough, and (b) does not want to adapt. Jonty, fortunately, was keen to work on his game. I started to chart where Jonty hit the ball. I knew this would be a time-consuming job, but I also knew it would probably be worth it.

In the end we decided not to send Jonty on the Under-24 tour, preferring instead to fill the spare place with a promising young cricketer, and we did indeed take a fantastic bunch of young cricketers, some of whom have graduated to the national team – players of the calibre of Adam Bacher, Gerry Liebenberg, Jacques Kallis, Shaun Pollock, Lance

Klusener, Nicky Boje, Roger Telemachus and Dale Benkenstein, who took over the captaincy. What a wonderful leader
he is going to be. In my opinion, assuming he makes his way
in the South African side, he should succeed Hansie Cronje.
I think the pressure would be too much for Pollock, who is
such a wonderful all-round cricketer that he should be
allowed to continue to concentrate on that.

That Under-24 tour was a fantastic experience for all of us.
We won all the representative matches and drew the one-day
series. There were some amusing moments, too. We had
arrived via Singapore, which had already confused Kallis,
who thought it was part of Sri Lanka. Having reached our
hotel, the Taj Samudra, a lovely place, the boys were very
taken with the motorised rickshaws, the 'tuk tuks'. We then
decided to take a run of about three kilometres to get rid of
some our jet lag. This appealed to Paddy Upton, our exercise
specialist, and off we went – or at least the players did while
I stayed behind. Sri Lanka is incredibly humid and oppressive
at this time of year, and as the players were running along
the beachfront, Adam Bacher turned to Upton and said: 'Gee,
it's hot. I can hardly breathe. What altitude are we at?' This
comment, and many others during that trip, resulted in the
bestowing of a Polly the Parrot award for the most ridiculous
comment of the week. In fact there were so many I think we
might have awarded it daily. I certainly remember Kallis,
after bowling ten overs on the trot, saying as the drinks
trolley arrived in the middle, 'Thank God! Some more petrol
for my radiator.'

The standard of these young South Africans was very high,
even in the face of poor umpiring. The partisan nature of the
crowds also provided them with a stern test. I remember one
terrific innings of 168 by Gerry Liebenberg during one of the
one-dayers; when he was eventually out, he returned to the
pavilion to no applause at all from a sizeable crowd. Their
maturity and skill shone through regardless, so much so that
there could be no complacency from the senior players. The
future for South Africa looked bright indeed.

5 Life with South Africa

I F SOUTH AFRICA HAD A BEVY of good players, fitness was the key to allow them to dominate in their chosen sport. Fitness would always weigh heavily on my mind throughout my career. There would be many lessons learnt during the years, but the most common would be that injuries will occur and that adequate back-up is essential. Prevention of injury and rehabilitation became a paramount goal. I believe I made significant progress in this respect while I was with South Africa, but it is still only scratching the surface. There is no doubt that Bobby Simpson was correct when he said that modern lifestyles are far more sedentary and that youngsters of today have to be indoctrinated with the fact that training in specifics is a prerequisite to becoming a top sportsman. Of course there will be the odd exception to this rule, but fewer and fewer, I suspect, as the game advances.

I believe that South Africa was the first national side to appoint a full-time exercise specialist in Paddy Upton in order to make training methods more professional. My belief was that centrally contracted players should pass a health and fitness test on an annual basis. Such a system has a two-fold advantage: it cuts out those who seek to remain in the comfort zone, and it may well identify an injury a player might be quietly suffering from. Every game has its demands, and cricket is as demanding as most.

Paddy Upton was asked at the training camp to run a variety of tests on the players to ascertain what their fitness levels were. These tests began at the Rand Afrikaans University in Johannesburg and involved a bleep test, a five-kilometre run, strength tests, eye tests, coordination tests and much more. It was very involved and was designed to give Hansie and I a good idea of how players were progressing, especially if they were injured, and to allow the contracts committee a chance to see how the players responded to being selected to play for their country. The tests steadily became more sophisticated, and were eventually moved to the Sports Science Institute in Cape Town, the brainchild of Professor Tim Noakes and Morne Du Plessis, the ex-Springbok number eight.

I have always believed, from the early days of my playing career, that cricket should always look to find better ways of achieving and sustaining fitness, making better use of the ground-breaking work that has gone into improving athletes around the world. This was especially the case in 1995, because I could envisage a rapid escalation in the number of international one-day games and Test matches. It was also important that medical management was constantly reviewed and updated. I had two allies in this respect: Noakes and Craig Smith. Smith, our physiotherapist, needed motivating when I arrived, as well as some assistance because people were blaming him for not diagnosing injuries properly. If Allan Donald was not fit, someone had to take the blame, and it was usually Craig, but he understood the importance of physical fitness and rehabilitation and was soon doing an excellent job. I still wanted to tighten everything up, though. I wanted a centre for the players where they could be assessed by Professor Noakes, and then for them to be sent to the best man available to deal with whatever injury they were suffering from. The Sports Science Institute would speed up the testing procedure so that the guys who were away from home a lot already could spend less of their time involved in these matters. I also wanted a facility that could study injuries to see if they could be prevented, and a further facility that Upton could use for his administration. So for me, the SSI was a godsend.

I did not know at the time, of course, that I would eventually be on the receiving end of a backlash over the institute and its methods from, of all people, my own captain, although I was of course aware that the institute would not initially have much of a clue about the game of cricket and that what I wanted to achieve would take time. Even Upton was less than enamoured with my using the SSI, saying that he could do just as good a job and that it would cost the UCB less. The chairman of selectors also had his doubts about the merits of the project, and eventually I had to cut back on the usage of this facility, but I still feel that the authorities in South Africa need to fully utilise whatever expertise they have in their country. Unfortunately there is some competition between Johannesburg and Cape Town, and I dare say there are scientists who believe Noakes is not the ideal person for this task. What I do know is that I am right about the importance of keeping up with change in all fields; to this day Noakes rewrites his *The Lore of Running* almost on a daily basis as further discoveries about sports science are made.

In the end I came to the conclusion that I had to take the blame for things turning sour as I had not put my case strongly enough. I should have done more homework. I had just tried to institute this set-up with the South African side when it was considered unnecessary. Upton was excellent to start with, but found that there was too much time between matchdays and possible fitness days, and he felt that rest was more important for the survival of the players. I will not argue with that sentiment, but it needs to be remembered that modern itineraries at international level require individuals strong in body and mind. Being an active man, Upton began to find his task boring. He was also prone to take his role as social secretary too seriously, and often led the binge that followed success. He eventually left by mutual agreement.

By the time Paddy Upton lost favour with the team, however, he had already set up structures that allowed local fitness trainers to look after the players, and I or the UCB had simply to trust that the players would get fit and ready for the national programme, although we did appoint Justin Durandt of the SSI to liaise with all the local/provincial trainers in order to keep some control over the process. But I often found it depressing, that what I thought stimulating and innovative others found a threat to their equilibrium. In my opinion the South African team could have achieved so much more had I been given support over such matters.

Pat Riley, in a book called *The Winner Within*, called this attitude 'the disease of me'. There was always going to come a time, in other words, when my ways would be questioned. One of the criticisms levelled at me was that the players never had any feedback. This was not the case. Certainly by the final year of the institute's involvement each player had a clear idea of where he stood. The real effect of the tests was to make sure the players realised what state they were in and what their responsibilities were; with that aspect out of the way we could concentrate on the skills of the game whenever we took part in a competition or a practice session. In Hansie Cronje we had the fittest captain in world cricket by some way, so it was disappointing that he was not one hundred per cent behind the initiative. The upshot of it was that I feel we achieved only seventy per cent of what we might have managed.

Credibility is vital as a coach. Every now and then things go wrong, and while there is obviously no way of pleasing everyone, one must always have contingency plans, ways of coping with the fall-out, so I had also been toying with the idea of sports psychologists to help the team. I have read a lot about psychology in sport, books by American baseball and basketball coaches, and picked up their helpful one-liners. A number of the South African players had individuals they went to talk to, and I had dabbled while at Warwickshire with the work of Dr Ian Cockerill from Birmingham University. I had also talked at length with Clinton Gahweiler, resident psychologist at the SSI, and I had used Hylton Calder while at Boland. Cricket clubs always claim they are impoverished when anything new is mooted, but I believe every cricket coach – indeed, any coach in any walk of life – should do a basic course in understanding sports psychology. I believe the player of today needs a lot more support than the player of yesteryear did. Modern society is far more complex, there is more money in the game and the media involvement at Test level has increased hugely.

During my time with South Africa we were never able to identify one individual who could really help, simply because the majority had no concept of what it is like to play cricket in a Test match arena. One of our team psychologists was particularly recommended by the Plascon Academy, but he made a gaffe during the 1995/96 season when, with England 240 for 4 at Centurion Park, he called everyone together and said that at some time that morning we would be batting. I thought this was a great start. He looked as though he was going to motivate the bowlers to roll over the opposition in one session, but he then added that he wanted all the batsmen to visualise hitting the balls on fire. This faintly ridiculous statement destroyed his credibility in the seconds it took him to say it. Perhaps the greatest 'brain doctor' I have met was Mike Brearley, whom I played under for England. He was able to hold the attention of the players because of his experience as a player and captain, and as someone who is deeply sensitive to the pressures of Test cricket. Sports psychology is in its infancy, as is cricket psychology, and in the latter's case it is more easily practised by those who have spent time in the Test match cauldron. There is no substitute for relevant experience.

Communication is always a key word for a coach who is trying to get across what he means. It was certainly a key element with the South African team. A case in point was when Daryll Cullinan played in Australia in 1997/98. On a previous visit, he had been a victim of the sledgers. The Australians obviously recognised that he was a very good player, but that he was suspect temperamentally, and they laid into him. By the time of this, his second tour, Daryll must have been apprehensive about this. I was aware of it, but I had no idea just how he was feeling. I only found out well into the middle of the tour that Daryll had gone to Ali Bacher and had expressed doubts about touring Australia and, indeed, his ability to handle Shane Warne. I attempted as best I could to play down the whole confrontation, but when we played in Melbourne and Daryll walked out to bat, I could not believe the change in mood. Not just from the Australians' body language – which reminded me of a pack of dogs spotting a squirrel in the woods – but from the crowd's involvement as well. And then I understood the magnitude of the problem. I felt it was too late to help, and that even if I had had time I certainly did not have the skills to change things round. As Daryll approached the crease the noise was unbelievable, from both players and the crowd. Daryll was greeted by Shane Warne with the words, 'I have been waiting four years for you.' Daryll replied, 'Well it looks as though you've spent the time eating.' Yet the pressure must have been intolerable.

I was confronted by a vulture-like press after the game and was asked whether I thought Daryll was under a psychological cloud when facing Warne. There was no doubting that was the case, but my immediate task was to try and diffuse the situation, so I said, 'If he is, then it is our job to help him clear the clouds away.' Unfortunately this came out in the press as 'Bob Woolmer says Daryll Cullinan is under a psychological cloud'. Daryll must have received a fax about it and was pretty upset. When he confronted me, I told him my side of the story, but it was too late and the damage had been done. What is more, I only learnt this some two tours later when, in discussion with Daryll before a Test in New Zealand, he brought up the issue again.

Despite avoidable problems such as this, the worth of a sports psychologist is still being debated. Some cricketers and administrators remain sceptical. I remember Peter Pollock once saying to me that the presence of too many advisers means too many people for the players to blame, and they are wise words. But by making people available even on a part-time basis for as long as a player feels that they are necessary is worth doing, because there is an enormous amount of expertise available out there that is worth tapping. It is important, though, that choices are made wisely. I believe any adviser needs to have a certain knowledge of the game to be able to lift players out of depression to a level where they can perform; after that, it is up to the player. Facing Allan Donald on a pitch of uneven bounce requires sheer courage and a high degree of skill, and there is little anyone can do to help after a certain point.

But the real question to ask of any promising young player these days is: Will he be able to handle success and wealth? I look at Brian Lara, for instance, and wonder whether he was advised correctly at the beginning of his career. Certainly his reputation now hangs by a thread, yet he is one of the nicest people you could wish to meet in cricket. If he has problems, it is because the demands on his time are too high. During the 1994 season he would often wander into the dressing room at Edgbaston at a late hour and, with an apology, put his pads on and go and score a run-a-ball hundred. No preparation, no stretching, nothing. This kind of success in a player therefore complicates my role, for as a coach I keep stressing that stretching and correct preparation are vital before a game.

Although a strong work ethic remains the best way to achieve success, it is not everything: we prepared fantastically well in general for the 1999 World Cup and still could not excel. Whenever I or any other player has had a good day the chances are we have been in excellent shape mentally, in what we call the 'zone'. It could also be called 'deep concentration', and I have known it referred to as the 'bubble'. It is a state of mind which seems to put everything into perspective – slowly. Facing a bowler of Donald's pace, for example, the batsman's focus can be on what might happen: might I get hurt; I hope the hospital is a nice place; I hope the brain surgeon is good. I jest, but the point is that relaxation and watching the ball are the keys to making runs; letting the instincts take over, trusting in your technique, and not worrying about time. I often equate it with living in a white room, a narrow room where only you and the ball exist and everything happens in slow-motion. This is how I remember my eight-hour innings against Australia in 1975 at the Oval, for instance. When I played club cricket at the end of my career in Cape Town I found I could simulate the zone very easily, although obviously at that level there were fewer bowlers who possessed the capability to impinge upon it. I wonder if Bradman ever found himself in the zone? I suspect he did. Watching England against New Zealand at Lord's in 1999, I saw that only Nasser Hussain was able to bat with this kind of equilibrium, watching the ball and allowing his natural instincts to predominate. I believe Michael Atherton and Steve Waugh play in that zone more than most. They have said that it was a surreal experience, but, on the contrary, it is very real. Psychologists identify it as the IPS (ideal performance state).

Just as technology is evolving and being put to beneficial use for the player, so it should be in terms of officialdom. Match referees are a relatively new inception and I am still not totally convinced that they are fulfilling the role expected of them, although some are far more diligent than others. The umpires on the square should have more control than they are allowed to have. Less experienced umpires can get conned quite easily by sharp practice on the field. I also feel it is necessary for match referees to report back on a whole host of matters outside matchplay. I was appalled, for instance, at the standard of net facilities, food and ablution facilities at Ahmedabad when we toured India in November and December 1996. The nets South Africa had to use at Derby in 1998 were also a disgrace to professional sport. There were holes in them and the ball was going through. If someone produced those facilities at a top baseball club in America, he would be out of a job. At Trent Bridge, too, there are no outdoor facilities separate from the main field. Test match grounds that cannot supply this facility should be fined or Test matches taken away.

Match referees should also assist the third umpire on decisions. In Pakistan in 1994, John Reid, the match referee, brought the third umpire down to our dressing room. We had just lost a limited-overs match to Australia at Rawalpindi by a very small margin. Dave Richardson had been given out run out when he was quite clearly in; in fact, he was so far in we were staggered when the red light beamed out to signal his dismissal. 'I am very sorry. I pressed the right button but the wrong light came on!' said the third umpire. It is my opinion that the standard of umpiring has deteriorated at international level despite the presence of neutral umpires. I believe that there should always be two neutral umpires who should be made to have a fitness examination which includes hearing and eyesight tests. Quite a lot of present-day umpires actually go for a run in the mornings and are a lot fitter as a consequence.

But to be a top umpire you have to have more than just good fitness levels, eyesight and hearing. I believe you have to have played some top-class cricket, to lend some weight to your judgements and lessen the possibility of losing the respect of a batsman, who might otherwise like to put one over you. Attitude is important too. I believe a good umpire has to be one who gets the crucial decisions correct, and is prepared to realise that he will make mistakes but works very hard to eradicate them. I am thinking in particular of the lbw law, which is probably the most questioned of them all, and certainly the most controversial. It cannot be long before science is applied in an effort to eliminate error. Surely if a missile can be pinpointed down a mineshaft, it is possible to tell, by use of a microchip, whether the ball is going to hit the stumps. I know the technology is there to be used and I am staggered by the debate over it, for the careers of many good players are on the line. I know also that the exams umpires have to take need to be practical as well as theoretical, and that no umpire is tested on his ability to give practical lbw decisions. You only have to watch a lowly league game where players have to umpire their own teams to see the damage this sort of approach can breed. I have heard some officials boast that they have never made a mistake in their lives and that they are never wrong. In fact, so contentious have some decisions been that batsmen have been known to go off the field, get into their cars and drive straight over the pitch at the offending umpire, taking out the stumps in the process. Why not introduce into the game a small machine that can tell when the ball's trajectory is going to take it into the stumps?

At times, TV cameras at the ground are not able to assist in making the correct decision, but again, I am sure this could be corrected. There is still a tremendous reluctance to use the technology available. To take one example: there is sometimes doubt as to whether or not the ball has carried to the catcher. The innovation of the camera square of the wicket was a good one, but the authorities need to train special cameras on the wicketkeeper and slip cordon from two angles. I was particularly impressed by Channel Four's innovations for their coverage of Test cricket in 1999, and this, I am sure, will lead to other companies coming up with a whole host of new ideas to assist the viewers in their understanding of the game. It is certainly well overdue, and will undoubtedly benefit the game.

As a result of hard work and focus, we were becoming a real force as a one-day side during the 1995/96 season. South Africa were blessed with a number of good all-rounders, although then they had not quite reached the level of maturity they have attained now. But certainly Hansie Cronje, Shaun Pollock and the young Jacques Kallis gave us a different dimension to the team, along with Brian McMillan, who at the time was the best all-round cricketer in the world. The side that eventually went to the Asian subcontinent for the World Cup was: Kirsten, Hudson, Cronje, Cullinan, Rhodes, McMillan, Kallis, Pollock, Palframan (who replaced Dave Richardson when he broke his finger), Donald, De Villiers, Symcox, Adams and Matthews, who was vice-captain.

It was a powerful party, whose morale was tested almost from the start. Attending the opening ceremony involved for us a thirteen-hour stop-start flight, during which we were garlanded at every airport we stopped at. Then there was a complete bog-up of an opening ceremony in which we were introduced as the United Arab Emirates, and the UAE were heralded as South Africa. That, plus the expensive lighting display that was blown about by a rogue wind and a thirteen-hour return trip. But the players handled it all with a smile on their faces, and made the episode a humorous rather than depressing one.

It was a good sign. While we were out there (we were based in Rawalpindi, which is a lovely place) I placed considerable emphasis on team building, involving the wives too as we were away from home so often. For instance, the World Cup party spent three days at the Fish River for some sun and interaction; the players also took in some golf and tennis, and we played touch rugby on the beach. We also talked about our goals in some depth, and how we would approach different matches. We re-examined our one-day disciplines as a team, paying attention to a lot of detail, relaxed in the knowledge that Cassiem Docrat, our team manager, had gone ahead to organise practice facilities and to make sure we had everything we needed.

When we got down to playing some cricket, we were virtually untested, despite our opponents being New Zealand, England and Pakistan. They were beaten by superb performances: New Zealand and Pakistan by five wickets, and England by 78 runs. Holland and the United Arab Emirates were cannon fodder for us. We had played five and won five, and were at the top of our group. Our confidence levels were high – with hindsight, too high. And there were two disturbing episodes for us during the week before our vital quarter-final against the West Indies: the first was the announcement that Brian McMillan was having discussions about the possibility of playing county cricket with Surrey; the second was that Jonty Rhodes wanted to play hockey for the South African side at Atlanta in the forthcoming Olympics. Dr Bacher was due to talk to both of them. I did not blame them at all for wanting to sort out their futures, but the timing was totally inappropriate. Any external distractions at that stage of a competition will affect the mental preparations of the individual and of the team. My gut instinct tells me this is so.

The night before the quarter-final we had a call from Nelson Mandela, and everyone decided that they wanted shirts and various pieces of memorabilia signed – 'just in case we don't get through'. Also that evening I bumped into three senior people in South African cricket and they said to me: 'Don't worry if we don't win tomorrow. We've already shown we're the best side at the World Cup.' I went to bed knowing that the atmosphere within the camp had changed, and that while we were in good shape there were too many external influences acting on the team. The West Indies, meanwhile, had scraped through into the quarter-finals, having lost to Kenya in a preliminary game; they knew they had to be properly focused for the game against us. The difference in attitude was small but telling. On the day of the match, 11 March in Karachi, I remember all too clearly walking on to the field for our warm-up and Brian Lara coming over to me and saying, 'Sorry Bobby, it's my day today.' He scored 111. In the first half an hour of the West Indies innings we dropped two catches and misfielded on two other occasions; they went on to bat exceptionally well as a team, posting a decent total of 264 for 8. Daryll Cullinan fought back with a 69, but we were dismissed for 245, twenty runs short of victory. But even as our World Cup ended, I realised the immense strides this team had made. We could now compete with the best, and on our day with the right focus would beat them.

One perception of the South African team at that time was that they could be a dour, expressionless bunch, lifted only by Jonty Rhodes' grin when he brought off a brilliant diving stop at cover, or by Pat Symcox's beery belligerence. Hansie Cronje was seen as the epitome of the unsmiling Afrikaaner. This image, though, camouflaged his brilliant after-dinner speaking and sense of humour. One of Hansie's victims during the World Cup was Paddy Upton, our fitness specialist. This particular jape, which took place the day before our match against the United Arab Emirates as we reckoned it would not be the hardest encounter of the tournament, involved sleeping pills.

Paddy was the fines master, and he had been put in charge of the social side of things. He introduced a lot of different exercises to help keep the team fit, and, as happens to anyone forcing people to exercise, he took some stick. Pat Symcox, for instance, often reminded him that Sebastian Coe could not bowl a decent off-break. Inevitably, when an opportunity arose to put one over on him it was exploited to the full. Numerous apple-pie beds, salt on the toothbrush and water buckets over doors led to a lively rough-and-tumble between the captain and Paddy. All good clean fun, until Paddy managed to lock Hansie out of his room by shutting the door and jumping across the balconies. This prompted the ultimate retribution. Hansie, being sharp of mind and wit, went to Professor Noakes, who had accompanied us on that trip to Pakistan, and asked if he could hand out the weekly malaria pills. These were almost identical in size and shape to some sleeping pills he had, and normally one would have been sufficient for a really good night's sleep. As we received two malaria pills every Thursday, Paddy received two sleeping pills.

The key to the success of the trick was that the pills took about twenty minutes to hit home – the approximate length of the bus trip to the ground. With the rest of the squad fully aware that Paddy was soon going to be struggling horribly, various people were prompted, each time he started to fall asleep, to ask him a question. By the time we arrived at the ground Paddy was in no fit state at all. He was only just about awake, but his legs were distinctly rubbery. Hansie asked him to keep the boys loosened up, saying that we should not be complacent just because we were playing against the United Arab Emirates. I am afraid to say that I gave Paddy a similar speech.

So off we went, jogging and stretching. It was incredible that the players were able to keep a straight face. I was asked to run a deep breathing and relaxation session as part of the plan. I included everyone, and we went through the programme, which took about five minutes. I then asked the first two batsmen to get ready, and the team rose and walked towards the net, only to be confronted by the sight of Paddy fast asleep on the grass. It was a wonderful scam. He somehow woke up and continued his duties in almost a comatose state, and only missed the team meeting that evening.

Moments like these make touring so much fun, especially in a country where the culture is so different from ours. Pakistan, of course, is a dry area (no alcohol), and the night life is very different, so our preparations had included taking videos and Playstation games for the younger members of the team. These helped to while away the spare hours. Cassiem Docrat, who had studied in Pakistan, was instrumental in obtaining invitations to people's houses, and we also made contact with the American and British clubs, which were frequented a lot by members of the side. When on any tour it is important to do two things: be part of the country you are in, and ensure that you have as many home comforts as possible. Bangers, beans and mash with a pint of beer are important home comforts for cricketers – not exactly what the nutritionist would prescribe, but an important part of the psychologist's fare.

But it was a credit to the set-up that high jinks could go hand in hand with serious thought on how to improve as a side. Following the 1996 World Cup, Noakes suggested we set up a cricket science meeting, which led to the formation of a working committee. I was then introduced to Tony Kirkbride from the CSIR, a scientific research organisation funded by the government. At these meetings we discussed a number of innovations, such as special innards for wicketkeeping gloves with state-of-the-art protection to prevent excessive bruising. We also wanted to produce lightweight pads so that running between the wickets would be easier, special gloves that would prevent broken fingers, and special vests to absorb sweat. The CSIR, based in Pretoria, had a number of scientists who were prepared to help in these endeavours, the point of which, of course, was to give us an edge over the opposition – something that was, for me, a never-ending quest.

During 1996, I kept a diary to remind myself of the myriad commitments and expectations that go with the job of national coach. The following extracts are taken from a week in September before a quadrangular tournament involving Kenya, Pakistan and Sri Lanka. The entries, with their immediacy, highlight the disparate happenings in a coach's existence better than I could ever record them in this book months or even years after the event. As you will see, it is seven-days-a-week work, morning, afternoon and evening. There is scant time for rest, for one's family, for escaping the all-pervasive cricket environment. I would not have wished to lead a nine-to-five office life, but I hope this account will give some indication of why I was reluctant to take on another international coaching job after standing down as head coach of South Africa. Not long after these entries finished, I had spent just 44 nights at home in a year and a half, and began to suffer from asthma as a result of so much touring.

We had just arrived in Johannesburg for training, only to find that the transport arranged to take us to our hotel had not materialised. A good start.

Monday, 23 September

Chatted with Hansie at breakfast – the top of his hand is still very sore and he is off to the specialist for bone scans and X-rays. Helped with the kit allocation. Had a brief team meeting to let everyone know what is going on. Lunch. Hansie returned and it seems he has a bad ligament strain/tear. He has had a cortisone injection and now has to wait two days for it to settle down. Contact made with the chairman of selectors and he said we should take the fourteen selected and that no stand-by should be prepared. The facilities at Pretoria University have always been great and they have prepared a middle wicket and four nets. There is also use of a bowling machine and four bowlers. Everyone looks in good nick and fairly fit. Had a two-hour practice which concluded with catches. Team meeting in the evening discussed a variety of matters; this followed a management meeting to discuss discipline, selection, etc. At the main meeting team objectives were discussed such as methods of playing, selected and achievable goals. Afterwards we went to a sports café and then for a pizza.

Tuesday, 24 September

Left at 8.15 for the university grounds. Each pair of batters had some excellent one-day practice. The bowlers struggled because they had not had much time in the middle due to the Cape's inclement spring. The practice consists of ten overs per pair and the bowlers bowl as in a match. Spare fielders are used. I have found that this is one of the best methods of making players aware of how to play in one-day cricket, although it is a long session and needs to be done at most three times a season. Hansie's hand is still sore, which is a worry. Jonty seems to be recovering well. Gazza [Gary Kirsten] had one of those nets that did not quite go right. All the players look fit and strong although the bleep test which preceded the practice took its toll due to some very strange atmospheric circumstances. For those who live at the coast it was probably the worst time to run because of the altitude change. Team dinner in the evening detailing the arrangements for the match tomorrow.

Wednesday, 25 September

Left at 8.15 again. Hansie had a function in Soweto at five a.m! He really is an amazing person. His hand seems to be a lot better, which I know has made him feel a lot more relieved. Both teams warmed up together: Cronje, Hudson, G. Kirsten, Boje, Gibbs, Rhodes, Crookes, Pothas, Donald,

Matthews, Adams versus P. Kirsten, Pienaar, Bacher, Cullinan, Kuiper, McMillan, Richardson, Symcox, Davis, De Villiers, Ntini. The heavens opened, but apart from losing three-quarters of an hour and having to reduce the game to 45 overs a side, it was an excellent work-out. Hansie came through with 24 not out and both Gazza and Jonty scored excellent half-centuries. We were able to get back to the hotel in good time for a shower and change for the Protea Assurance annual dinner, at which there was high praise for the UCB development programme. I had to go to see Dr Ferreria about my left foot, which is really playing up, and he took new X-rays and stuck two more cortisone injections into two very arthritic joints which he says will have to be operated on. I will have six weeks in plaster and six weeks' rehabilitation. Sounds great. He has to remove the cartilage from the foot and replace it with bone from my hip, but he says the chances are that I can start running again.

Thursday, 26 September

A seven a.m. meeting involving Ali and our backroom staff. Ali was quite hard on them, citing an unreasonable attitude towards wanting more money. The problem is that when South Africa came back into world cricket, the whole squad shared in the pool. In my view the players should earn the major share of prize money and the back-up staff should receive a bonus annually. Ali did give them assurances about clauses in their contracts. This was followed by a breakfast in aid of development in the townships, attended by the whole team, and a photo session at the hotel at which I took delivery of some very nice Adidas glasses. Left for the airport and mislaid my cell phone in the car. Nicky Boje retrieved it for me. No business-class seats on Kenyan airways – first and cattle class only. We are in cattle. Ushered through at Nairobi with the minimum of fuss, but the whole day has been very traumatic. Gill telephoned about some problems Dale is having at home. Team meeting that reaffirmed many of the one-day disciplines we have discussed previously. Had supper on Ali – bed lateish. I sleep very little.

Friday, 27 September

Practice facilities seem to be my biggest bugbear – especially when we are away from home. I expected that in Nairobi they would be inferior to those in South Africa, but why oh why can't there be two surfaces with nets available so that practice can be less tiring and lengthy? It is disappointing. It seems that the future of cricketers and their coaches lies in the hands of administrators who quite obviously have no idea of what the necessary requirements are to prepare a club side, let alone a national one. I always marvel how the West Indies manage on their facilities. We met with the ICC referee (my old captain, Mike Denness), the umpires Peter Robinson and Russell Tiffin (Zimbabwe) and K.S. Bansal (not sure where he's from). This was followed by a brief press conference at which we were asked how to pronounce 'Boje'. Then supper given by Standard Bank – the skewers included specialities such as crocodile, zebra and gemsbok. Telephoned Gill to discover if domestic difficulties have been sorted out. What a life cricket can be when so far away from home.

Saturday, 28 September

Played on a very different surface today that was similar to the old Newlands wicket. Although it was firm, it had a tennis-ball bounce and the batters had to adapt. The outfield was shocking. We spent time throwing at the stumps as we had not spent much time at this skill. We are playing against a Pakistan side that has changed much in composition through injury. Watched the Sri Lankans take on the Kenyans and it was, as expected, a very one-sided contest. That is not to say Kenya must be underestimated. At least the new season is upon us. The team meeting reflected a quiet calm and confident atmosphere. Had supper in the hotel carvery and, without wishing to moan, the food is very average in Kenya. I had a pizza which resembled a cheese omelette on a sponge pudding base. Worked with Hansie and found that his bottom hand grip had slipped a touch, reducing his hitting area, and this caused his top hand to start hurting again. We rectified it and he feels a lot happier. So to bed with expectations.

Sunday, 29 September

We were pushed to the limit by Pakistan, despite scoring 320 thanks to fine knocks by Daryll and Jonty. Craig Matthews suffered a recurrence of last year's injury (hamstring? We are not quite sure). Pat Symcox lost the plot a little and got some severe stick. Fielding was of a high standard although it was our first competitive game for five months. We would have had time to visit a game reserve tomorrow, but will still have to fit in a practice session, a selection meeting and a team meeting before the official banquet for the tournament. Prepared a piece for the team meeting and had to deal with Fanie, who thought I was laughing at him. I was merely amused by his English.

The following month we moved on to India for a Test series.

Wednesday, 16 October

What a day! Where can I start? Match referees meeting with John Reid, who really overplays his role, was followed by team meeting and then practice booked for four o'clock. From here on in, chaos ensued. India were also practising and the ground officials did not know they were coming. Then the crowd came on the field and we lost at least four balls. The nets were broken and the ball kept coming through – if it was not farcical it would be comical. The futures of both sets of players lie in the hands of the selectors and administrators, and for those responsible for these circumstances to go unpunished or without reprimand is unfair. Reid's piece of paper sounded like the Ten Commandments: thou shalt not swear at the umpire, thou shalt not show emotion, etc. Administrators must start getting their act together if they expect high-grade performances for poor financial returns.

Friday, 18 October

Left the hotel at six a.m. and travelled from Hyderabad to Indore via Mumbai. Had an optional practice. Security was poor and there were a lot of spectators on the field again. Worked with three players while Hansie lost his temper. It is a major problem keeping players in form with such putrid practice facilities. The boys look very determined, though. There is a good focus at the moment.

Wednesday, 23 October

At least I am getting a good night's sleep. I was in a bit of a relaxed state. This soon disappeared when I went to settle my account and was charged R35 [about £7] per page for a fax. I get really fed up when I have to communicate with home and pay a fortune. Warmed up a little casually and I felt the team was almost too relaxed for this particular game [against India at Jaipur]. Gazza played quite beautifully before not connecting with a sweep off Kumble – which later was very amusing as at the team meeting the day before he had stated quite categorically that we should be more circumspect against him and that the sweep was not really on. Daryll batted very well, especially as we had had a chat the night

Above On the offensive
for Kent against
Middlesex at Canterbury,
September 1979 (Photo:
Adrian Murrell/Allsport)

Right Running on to the
field for England at Trent
Bridge during the 1981
Ashes series (Photo:
Adrian Murrell/Allsport)

Brian Lara enjoys his world record score of 501 not out, scored for Warwickshire against Durham in June 1994 (Photo: Shaun Botterill/Allsport)

The Warwickshire team celebrate the victory that clinched the 1994 County Championship, Edgbaston, 2 September 1994 (Photo: Clive Mason/Allsport)

Above Dermot Reeve and Tim Munton proudly display the three trophies Warwickshire won during the unforgettable 1994 season (Photo: Clive Mason/Allsport)

Right If I can repeat the success of my first spell at Edgbaston during my second spell, I'll be a very happy man (Photo: Clive Mason/Allsport)

Right Turning my arm over during a practice session (Photo: Allsport)

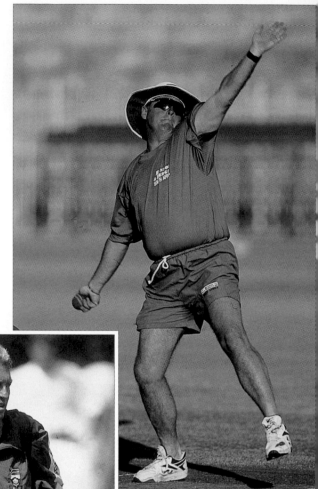

Left Lugging my 'coffin' around Lord's, May 1998 (Photo: Graham Chadwick/Allsport)

Above Meeting the
Queen at Rawalpindi,
Pakistan (Photo: Duif Du
Toit/Touchline)

Right Putting the
bowling machine to good
use while Hansie thinks
about his batting (Photo:
Duif Du Toit/Touchline)

Above Running through a technical point with Darryl Cullinan in Karachi, September 1997 (Photo: Duif Du Toit/Touchline)

Left Facing the press at Birmingham, June 1999 (Photo: Duif Du Toit/Touchline)

Right Dr Ali Bacher, chief executive of the United Cricket Board (Photo: Mike Hewitt/Allsport)

Doing what coaches do. Discussing the game with leg-spinner Paul Adams (Photo: Duif Du Toit/Touchline)

New technology has opened up a whole host of possibilities for the cricket coach. Much of my work is done hunched over my laptop in hotel bedrooms (Photo: Duif Du Toit/Touchline)

A genuine all-rounder should justify his place in the side as both a batsman and a bowler. Jacques Kallis unquestionably fits the bill (Photo: Laurence Griffiths/ Allsport)

Above and right The fifth
Test against England at
Leeds, August 1998. Allan
Donald ensnares Mike
Atherton and Shaun Pollock
dismisses Mark Ramprakash
(Photos: Stu Forster/
Allsport)

Left Powerful straight
hitting from Jonty Rhodes, a
fine batsman, a superb
fielder and one of the nicest
players I have ever worked
with (Photo: Laurence
Griffiths/Allsport)

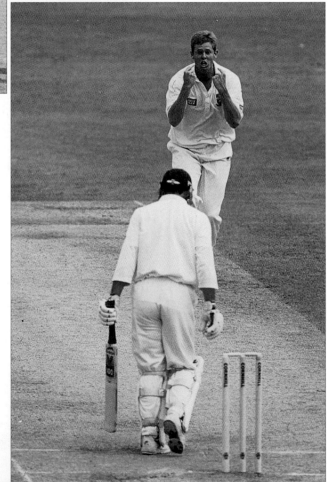

Left The deadliest pair of strike bowlers in world cricket. Donald and Pollock side by side during practice (Photo: Laurence Griffiths/ Allsport)

Below Jonty Rhodes pulls off a stunning catch to dismiss England's Robert Croft during an Emirates Tournament one-day international, Edgbaston, 18 August 1998 (Photo: Adrian Murrell/Allsport)

Right Jacques Kallis cuts during a World Cup warm-up game against Middlesex at Southgate (Photo: Stu Forster/Allsport)

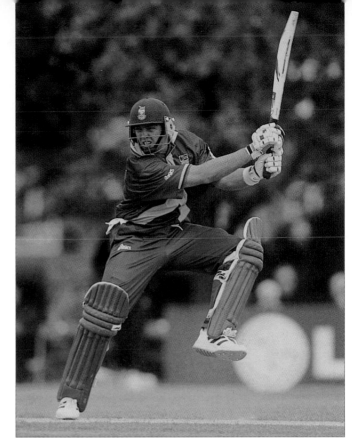

Below Lance Klusener had an awesome World Cup. On this occasion it's the Australian attack that's suffering, Headingley, 12 June (Photo: Adrian Murrell/ Allsport)

Mayhem at Edgbaston. Australia reach the 1999 World Cup final in the most dramatic circumstances as Allan Donald is run out. Note where Donald's bat is (Photo: Ross Kinnaird/Allsport)

Above David Lloyd getting down to business in the nets at Perth during the 1998/99 Ashes series (Photo: Graham Chadwick/Allsport)

Left What a contrast! Hansie Cronje and Steve Waugh come to terms with the events of a truly remarkable match (Photo: Ross Kinnaird/Allsport)

Right The man who replaced Lloyd was Duncan Fletcher, seen here facing the press for the first time at Lord's, 25 June 1999. Duncan is a talented coach who is capable of turning things around for England (Photo: Graham Chadwick/Allsport)

Left Darryl Cullinan attacks the English bowling during his fine century in the first Test at the Wanderers, Johannesburg, November 1999 (Photo: Stu Forster/Allsport)

Below The Warwickshire connection. Shaun Pollock, Brian McMillan and Allan Donald join me for a special photo opportunity. Great players, all three of them

before about his head and crouching. Interesting if he needs to be spoken to just before a big game? Hansie supported him very well and the singles they took ran the Indians into the ground. This itinerary is very hectic and the administrators will have to do something about it if they are not to create burn-out.

Thursday, 24 October

Up earlier than I would like for typically Indian interviews. Currently waiting for a man from the phone company. It seems that you need a separate 'sim card' [for cell phone operation] for each town and that the Internet only really works in Delhi and Bombay. It seems ridiculous that a bunch of people with families and loved ones at home cannot communicate without having to pay a fortune to do so. We spoke about too casual an attitude to the last game and the general consensus was that we needed to sharpen up our act. Had to have a change from curries – they are giving me indigestion.

Tuesday, 29 October

My health status is low. I washed out my sinuses last night only to get completely blocked up. I am concerned that the Indians are great copiers and to remain ahead of them we will need to combat their spinners. Received a fax from Nelson Mandela wishing us well. At the press conference we had quite an amusing question from one reporter. 'Mr Cronje, you have now won five on the trot just like you did in the World Cup. Are you worried you are going to lose the sixth game? After all, it is against Australia.' Which of course would mean that India would then have to beat the Aussies to get into the final.

Thursday, 14 November

Indo Petrochemicals Corp. ground [in Baroda] is a lovely setting and there are two reasonably good net surfaces. As usual the netting is arranged really badly – nothing is ever easy on the subcontinent. I had to have a long chat with Derek Crookes, as he felt I was not giving him the same treatment as the others. I tried to explain that life is not always fair and that I would make more of an effort in the future – but that there was only one of me and fourteen players. Final position went to Herschelle Gibbs instead of him and he was, of course, quite upset. He gives me the impression sometimes of being a petulant young man when he does not get his way. The main reason for Herschelle playing was to get him going.

Sunday, 17 November

Caught the bus to Ahmedabad. What a bus! It really is amazing that we have to travel on such rubbish. The driver smashed into a light and a hut on the way to the ground and then we travelled for the best part of three hours – without a police escort it would have taken four hours plus. Hotel really is low grade. Smog and pollution rife here and I suppose all the good work done on my sinuses could be undone. Will have to be very careful.

Monday, 18 November

Had a chat with the Christian group in the team (for want of a better phrase). Nice to talk about other things. Everyone seemed very committed and keen to prepare for the [first] Test. I had an interesting chat with Hansie about where we stand on the wheel of success and he is concerned that the team spirit is not what it might be. The crux of the matter would seem to be a push for places and fear of failure with the inevitable play-for-oneself syndrome.

Thursday, 21 November

Second day of the game and we finished off the Indians quickly for 223, but at 117 for 6 are in a lot of trouble. The most disturbing facet has been the poor umpiring. The comment of the day was from our chairman of selectors when he said it was no wonder India were difficult to beat at home. If I did not know better, I would say umpire Bansal was cheating, but I must give all umpires the benefit that they are doing their level best and trying to be impartial. However, it is blatantly obvious that Bansal is just not equipped to handle a Test match and should be banned from the panel sooner rather than later. If a player made a similar number of mistakes, he would be axed immediately. The heat, dirt, dust, continual horn blowing of cars in the street and the intense noise levels plus the language barrier, which is far worse than I experienced in 1976, mean one can understand the levels of intolerance among touring parties. It takes a special type of team to survive in these conditions for two months when the travelling and facilities are as abysmal as they are. The appearance of the wives therefore is vital for the party. The pressure is on those whose wives are not here and who have to continue.

Saturday, 23 November

Hansie slapped a piece of birthday cake into Gazza's face to wish him happy twenty-ninth birthday, and said, 'What a day to have it on.' We needed 170 to win. Well, disaster. Another shocking lbw decision got rid of Andrew Hudson (Bansal again) and the very next ball Daryll edged Srinath and we were 0 for 2. Jonty got another shocker from Bansal and we are staring down the end of the barrel. We cannot expect the tail to come good twice in a game and the end was swift, Srinath taking 6 for 21. Defeat is never easy to accept. It is harder when you feel events for two weeks have conspired against you. The important thing is to be realistic and get on with planning for the next game.

Monday, 25 November

Arrived in Calcutta a little late. I suspect they had a problem getting our luggage on the plane, plus one guy had got on thinking it was going to Bombay. Had a good hard practice as we need to harden the guys up if we are to get back into the [three-Test] series. Our team selection will be important. We are not yet convinced about Lance Klusener, yet Fanie de Villiers' performances are fairly variable and although he batted well, his bowling was fairly innocuous. Eventually decide Lance and Herschelle are to make their debuts. There is a cloud over Allan as he has a sore heel. It is vital to play him as he is our trump card but it is a risk as his recovery time has been short.

Wednesday, 27 November

Won the toss [for the second Test] on a wicket very different to that experienced in Ahmedabad. It is of greyish clay instead of red and much firmer. Hudders [Andrew Hudson], after a stern talking-to and after being given two lives, scored a great 145. It was quite a shock to learn from the selection panel about their reservations over him and I made the point that it would be hard to drop him without giving him a verbal warning of our intentions and one more chance. I am well aware of his limitations as an opener but to some extent this is compensated for by his fantastic ability to tear an attack apart. As one would expect, such a good day leads to a renewal of positive energy in the dressing room.

Friday, 29 November

Day three of the Test and wow! what a day. We were obviously hoping to get India to follow on, but Mohammed Azharuddin made sure that would never be the case. He played an unbelievable array of shots, in the process decimating Lance Klusener. I am sure Lance was nervous and he was asked to pepper Azhar and Kumble and followed orders and then lost it and in the process was slaughtered. We have dominated most of the Test series but for some reason when we lose a session we allow India right back into the game (so we lose it badly).

Saturday, 30 November

A superb partnership by Daryll and Gazza was broken by Gazza tripping over his own studs when attempting to give Daryll some runs to get his hundred. Unfortunately we mistimed the declaration because of the weird session times confused by the fact that tea is at 1.55. So instead of having twenty minutes to bowl at India we had early tea. With Azharuddin in positive frame we have a chance of getting him, although I am sure he will strike a few boundaries. I learnt from another source that the way he has played in this match was because he was threatened with being dropped. But really he has had nothing to lose as his colleagues have not played well at all.

Sunday, 1 December

Fifteen days to go on the tour. An aura of confidence was noticeable on the bus. We had a little huddle and reiterated where to bowl to Azhar and Dravid and stipulated a disciplined line. For the first twenty minutes Azhar tried to unsettle the ship but Lance and Mac [Brian McMillan] bowled well and we then stuck to the plan and started to pitch the ball up. Immediately Mac broke through and bowled

Dravid with a beauty. Azhar slammed two boundaries off Lance, desperately trying to knock him off his length, and then got his fifth Paaltjie [Afrikaans for 'wicket'] by having Azhar caught by Buckets McMillion (as he is called here). The game was all but over. Hirwani, who must be the worst number eleven in Test cricket, lasted two balls. What a great comeback to win at India's headquarters by 329 runs. This is tempered by the return of Allan and Jonty to South Africa. I have suggested to Jonty that he should consider alternative medicine for his hamstring injury because it is happening far too often.

Monday, 2 December

We leave for Nagpur via Bombay taking the wives and girlfriends back to Mumbai with us. We are charged 60,000 rupees for overweight baggage. Goolam [Rajah] persuaded the authorities to overlook the amount: 'They must see the broader picture.' Why are we travelling from Calcutta to Bombay if Nagpur is in the middle of the country? There is a serious rumour that a lot of backhanders and tips are being paid to a lot of officials and the more miles we travel the more money they make. The orange city, as Nagpur is known, is by Indian standards clean and neatly laid out.

Tuesday, 3 December

A good team meeting but unfortunately we harped on about wives and girlfriends on tour. It is obvious to me that the players want and need this 'extra', if that is what one can call it, and it is also obvious that both Peter Pollock and Robbie Muzzell [president of Border and tour manager] have serious doubts. It is debatable whether it is a moral or a financial decision. I do believe that the UCB should pay for wives and/or families and perhaps contribute to girlfriends. It is without question that on longer tours such as we are experiencing wives are a necessary factor. However, I do not support Tim Noakes' theory that it affected our performance at the World Cup. There is no doubt in my mind that the McMillan/Surrey affair and the Rhodes hockey affair plus a number of negative comments such as 'it doesn't matter if you win or lose as you have played so well already' and Mr Mandela's telephone call on the eve of the quarter-final as opposed to the final and then everyone getting the autographs done 'in case we lost' were as much contributory factors as the wives issue. It also worries me that the gulf between administrators and players is rather too large and some really hard talking between players and management needs to take place. Beware, however, the wrath of the selectors once an individual is tagged as a troublemaker. Nothing has changed from the pre-Packer era.

Thursday, 5 December

An amazing article in the Indian press with a headline about 'Woolmer curing Lance's no-ball problems'. I went round to check on why Lance was no-balling and I was concerned about his boots as he was wearing size twelves – the same as Brian McMillan – and he is only a size ten. The local press took it up as a sort of coaching phenomenon. Amazingly, as luck would have it Lance took two wickets in succession [against India A in Nagpur] and stopped bowling no-balls as well. Perhaps the bigger boots had kept him behind the line? It is of concern that he was unable to bring boots with him on the trip as Nike did not have any stock left before he left for India. This is definitely an area for us to improve. I think this must be part of a fast bowler's course I would like to hold next winter.

Friday, 6 December

Only half an hour's delay which meant I could finish *Pillars of the Earth* by Ken Follett as we flew to Kanpur. The wicket for the last Test reminds me of the one at Rajkot. It is a grey soil, similar to Calcutta, but not nearly as firm and rolled. Yes, we will miss Allan but Fanie will have to get off his backside and put in a real performance for us. I have a fantastic suite at the Landmark Hotel and have already been asked about my birthplace by numerous journalists. Darkness comes soon after 4.30.

Sunday, 8 December and Monday, 9 December

Unfortunately Hansie lost the toss. For the first time in the series we could not break through before lunch. The ball was not carrying to Dave [Richardson, the wicketkeeper]. Ganguly played some nice shots and his stand with Tendulkar lasted until tea. At close of play India were 205 for 6, which on that surface was a great effort. An abject collapse left us sixty behind on first innings and needing a complete reversal in batting performance to salvage this game. So much for the ninth day of the month. Still, I will always treat nine as a good number because I met Gill on 9 February, got engaged on 19 May and got married on 9 November. I am disappointed as I write and will have to remember to take every day as it comes otherwise I shall put myself under too much stress.

Tuesday, 10 December

It is always disappointing when you can feel a game inexorably escaping from your clutches. Today we followed up a poor batting display by bowling badly and Azharuddin, Tendulkar and then Dravid put on match-winning stands. Azhar in particular looked as though he was playing on a flat wicket. Paul [Adams] and Symmo [Pat Symcox] both bowled badly. At our team meeting I tried to present reality as opposed to complete optimism. I do not like to make comments such as 'we can knock them over tomorrow and then chase 360 in 180 overs'. Hansie was upset because he feels the batters are the ones who catch it in the neck when we have a bad day. The reality is that if you want to win games you have to make a big first-innings score. I suppose what is really galling is that despite all the hard work, all the modern techniques, we are coming second to an inferior outfit. Or are they? I suppose the conditions are far more suited to India. I really need to keep reactions to a minimum. Players are very sensitive to criticism.

Wednesday, 11 December

India declared at lunch with 400 on the board and we are chasing 461 in approximately 150 overs. Gazza was the first to go lbw. Herschelle looked nowhere and Daryll ran himself out. Hansie played really well until misjudging a drive at Joshi, and Hudders, having spent all but four hours at the crease, was undone at bat and pad off Kumble. In terms of the whole tour, we have played thirteen, won nine, drawn one and lost three. I suppose all in all a successful tour. On the other hand, I am seriously disappointed with our manager [Muzzell], especially as he has gone to Dr Bacher and said that he has had a disappointing tour and has not enjoyed it. This may be the case, but he has upset some of the players and has not in my opinion done enough for them. Our team has a special synergy and he has disrupted it on several occasions. As I write, we are resigned to a series defeat at 130 for 5. The inevitability about the result, though, helps me to handle the situation better.

6 The State of England

WHAT DOES IT FEEL LIKE to come home?

It was a question asked many times when I returned to England with South Africa. The general feeling among South African and Australian cricketers is that English cricket is not competitive enough, and that many of its players are arrogant know-it-alls. It is this perceived attitude that makes other countries try that much harder against England; they derive great pleasure from beating them. For many years England was the most revered cricketing nation in the world, the leaders in their field, and professional cricket there the ultimate finishing school. Overseas players today still enjoy the experience of county cricket, but now, because they are playing it daily, valuable knowledge is gleaned quickly.

So when the South African squad landed at Heathrow airport early in May 1998 there was a tangible determination to do well. The first two weeks of the tour were unbelievably warm, as if to make us feel at home; the entire team was able to train at Lord's in shorts (who would ever have imagined the MCC allowing that? Certainly not in my day). We were confident in ourselves, not least because we had just beaten Sri Lanka 2–0 at home, and the itinerary for England, in my opinion, was well structured. I had tried wherever possible to request that a three-day game be followed by a one-day fixture. This was partly because we would be playing the Texaco Trophy limited-overs internationals shortly after we landed, and partly because I did not want to overtax our bowling resources. I felt very strongly that as far as possible we should ensure our bowlers were still fit for the last part of the tour. Pleasingly, the schedule had accommodated my wishes.

The one fairly controversial selection had been the inclusion of Brian McMillan instead of Herschelle Gibbs or Hylton Ackerman; it was certainly the one a lot of critics would hang their hats on. At the time we were betwixt and between in terms of an opening partner for Gary Kirsten. Adam Bacher had been replaced by Gerry Liebenberg for the Tests against Sri Lanka in March and April, but Bacher still came on tour as the spare opener. Liebenberg continually did well against the counties, but failed in the Tests and one-dayers, and when Bacher finally made the team for the second Test at Lord's, he unluckily broke his collar bone. To compound the misfortune, the break went undiagnosed for over six weeks, and by the time we found out it was too late to send for a replacement. There was a lot of external pressure to push McMillan up the order to bat at number six, and for Kallis to open. There was also an element of the selection committee that had argued vehemently that Jonty Rhodes should not be selected. Fortunately he came, and he proved a revelation on the tour.

We made an excellent start. We played really well in the first two Texaco one-dayers to take the series, but had a poor final match at Headingley on 24 May on a pitch that did a lot for the first hour. Shaun Pollock's defiant 60 helped us to 205, but an opening partnership of 114 between Nick Knight and Alistair Brown sealed our fate. In hindsight, it would have been nice to have used the white ball in May to give us time to get used to how much it moved, and given that the World Cup was to be staged in England at the same time the following year. However, we were in pretty good nick by the time we got to Edgbaston for the first Test early in June, even though our seamers had not had particularly long bowls. I did not consider that too much of a bad thing as this was to be a long tour. Unfortunately Shaun Pollock started out not quite fully fit, and Lance Klusener ended his tour early with a foot injury. We would have to wait until the last Test at Headingley for Pollock and Donald to be at their most effective as an opening pair.

At Edgbaston I had billeted the team at the Forest of Arden Golf and Country Club because I thought it was a lovely place, and as it was out of the city it would keep the team together during the Test match. I misread the situation, though: the South African team preferred to stay in the hub of a town amid restaurants and other places to visit. It was an honest error of judgement on my part, but it was probably the start of a slight difference in thinking between coach and players. In conditions that were ideally suited to seam and swing bowling, we put England in and the ball went all over the place. If we beat the bat once we beat the bat fifty times, but Mike Atherton and Mark Butcher batted really well and we only managed to get the latter out when he swept Adams to deep square leg. England only lost one wicket on a day they should have been bowled out. Neither Pollock nor Donald could control the excessive movement. It was obviously disappointing for us that England managed to post a first-innings total of 462, but we also batted well and kept the deficit down to 119. We then bowled better in the second innings, reducing England to 170 for 8, leaving ourselves with an outside chance of winning on the final day, although I did not believe victory possible as scoring around 300 on the last day of a Test match is always difficult. As it turned out we never got the chance to have a go at the total as rain set in all day and the match was abandoned, but we felt we had done well to recover the ground lost on the first day and a half.

So we moved on to Lord's in good spirits, scoring plenty of runs between the Tests. Pollock and Adams were rested and given the opportunity to bowl in the middle at targets. My assistant coach, Corrie Van Zyl, had replaced Paddy Upton, our fitness specialist, because we had seventeen players in the party and needed another person to help the team. The South African work ethic is enormous, and to have another arm was absolutely essential for me. Corrie worked so hard it was mind-boggling. I also think it was a wonderful experience for him to have an insight into what was happening at international level. Of course, Corrie's selection for the tour caused a major fracas at home because already a lot of people were speculating about who my replacement after the World Cup would be. Duncan Fletcher, the man being earmarked for my role at the time, felt it gave him a negative message, and soon rumours were abounding about him signing for Glamorgan – which he did.

Little did Duncan know then that in little over a year he would be standing at the helm of the England ship. As England coach, he has swiftly found out that life is very tough at the top, while Graham Ford, the new South African coach, has had quite the opposite experience – although obviously the circumstances are completely different. Duncan has taken over a team whose confidence is at an all-time low. The media who cover England's demise are also very hard on them, and it will take time to reverse the downward spiral they are currently experiencing. South Africa, meanwhile, apart from their crushing defeat in the semi-final of the World Cup, are experiencing considerable success in Test cricket – and at the expense of England in South Africa as I write to boot. Duncan will obviously need time, patience and some positive results, and I say good luck to both him and Graham.

Lord's turned out to be a triumph for Jonty and Hansie. It was apparent, too, that Jacques Kallis was now a fine all-round cricketer whose real talents were only just beginning to emerge. At 46 for 4 in the first innings South Africa were in trouble, and it was a wonderful partnership by Jonty and Hansie that enabled us to turn the game round and put us in a position to win it. Donald was quick; Pollock was slightly injured and not quite himself, but he still bowled really well; and Jacques finished off England's first innings. They had to follow on, and in the end we won by ten wickets, which was almost a repeat of the great 1994 victory.

The third Test at Old Trafford was viewed by the England camp as the turning point of the series, because from South Africa's perspective it should have been a case of two up with two to play. Makhaya Ntini replaced Shaun Pollock, and Lance Klusener had to pull out during the game when his foot became so sore that it was unbearable – for a man like him to come off the field it would have to be a bad injury. So our attack was down to Allan, Makhaya, Jacques and Paul Adams, but, despite outplaying England from the very start, we could not quite finish them off. Robert Croft and Angus Fraser, the last-wicket pair in the second innings, managed to survive. The scenes in the England dressing room after the game put one in mind of a team that had won the World Cup; it was clear they had received a major psychological boost. Not having Pollock for that Test, and losing Lance in the middle of it, were key factors in our inability to win, but Allan Donald's bowling had been awesome. Called on time and again by Hansie, he made breakthrough after breakthrough and so nearly won us the game. In fact, we probably would have won but for one crucial moment. The New Zealand umpire, Doug Cowie, had made a dreadful blunder when he gave Fraser out lbw in the first innings to a ball quite clearly going down the leg side. Fraser was much closer in this next innings when Donald trapped him in front, but this vital decision when the scores were nearly level went in England's favour.

Despite this draw, I believed we were still in good spirits when we reached Trent Bridge for the fourth Test at the end of July. Our preparations had all gone according to plan. All the players had hit form somewhere along the line, and again we managed a small first-innings lead of 38. When we batted again, though, we stumbled. Jacques Kallis was given out when he did not hit the ball. Jacques never walks as he is a firm believer that good and bad decisions even themselves out, but the finger went up on this occasion and it was a key wicket for England. Jonty was also given out in dubious circumstances, caught off the foot down the leg side. In fact, it was an appalling decision, and having lost Gerry

Liebenberg early on we had too many wickets down. England were left with a very gettable target of 247.

Then, of course, came one of the most famous confrontations in Test cricket. Allan Donald steamed in to Mike Atherton, who has always been a key person in the England line-up, and at one stage during this ferocious spell the South Africans went up with an almighty shout. Atherton had fended off a fearsome bouncer which, had it not hit his left glove, would probably have decapitated him; the ball had carried into the middle of Mark Boucher's right-hand glove, and much jubilation ensued. The only problem was that umpire Steve Dunne, another New Zealander, remained unmoved. Atherton had got away with murder, and it led to what many pundits called the most intense Test cricket spectacle ever witnessed. Atherton and Donald engaged in some serious warfare out there, but this decision of Dunne's, in my view, changed the whole course of the series. If Graeme Hick had come to the crease early, we would have had that much better a chance of cleaning England up. Mark Boucher, who had so far caught every catch offered on tour, went on inexplicably to put down Nasser Hussain, and England ran out comfortable winners by eight wickets, Atherton finishing unbeaten on 98. We certainly felt that crucial decisions had gone against us, but we also knew that we had not batted well enough. During that tour we had decided on the bus that we needed to establish a batting culture, and everyone had been working hard to do so. We even had a two hundred club, and there were many century-makers during these three months. Yet suddenly, for one innings, we had lost our focus. Had we batted for a couple of sessions more, England would have been out of the series.

It is always amazing how the spirit can change. The selectors were criticised for not using McMillan enough, and I suppose if we had the tour again we might do that. But the reality was that we were just not mature enough as a side yet. Gerry Liebenberg, nicknamed 'the walking wicket', scored hundreds in between the Test matches and we were desperate for runs from him, but they were not forthcoming. Our starts were terrible throughout the series; even Gary Kirsten, who scored a fantastic double century at Old Trafford and made runs prolifically against the counties, under-achieved on that tour. As hard as Corrie and I worked on all our batsmen, when they walked over that boundary rope everything was up to them. I know how hard the players take failure and defeat. I know how hard they work to put it right. The push to give us greater resolve at Test level came when we held our batting camp in Bloemfontein later in the year, the immediate result of which was an historic whitewash of the West Indies.

So on to Headingley and the final Test. History records, very simply, that we went down by 23 runs. It was a great day for English cricket – their first series win for twelve years – but so disappointing for us. And there was a central figure in the middle during that Test match who I, personally, can never forgive: the umpire Javed Akhtar. As a coach I have no control over umpires, nor should I, but the difference between success and failure is a fine line. In this match Akhtar redefined that line totally. Of some eleven bad decisions he made during the course of the match, seven went against us, including five in our second innings. They were some of the worst mistakes I have ever seen. The South African dressing room was as miserable as it was at Edgbaston after the semi-final of the 1999 World Cup. The players knew they had not done themselves justice and we were all bitterly upset, but I still believe they were the victims of some ridiculous decisions. I will go to my grave thinking that, and nothing will change that viewpoint. Although England played very well in the last two Tests, it has to be said they were fortunate. So again I say the sooner umpires ask for full technological help the better. I know that if I had to stand at the highest level and there was the slightest element of doubt in my mind over a decision, I would be wanting as much technological assistance at my elbow as possible to make sure that I was not responsible for finishing some poor cricketer's career.

Unfortunately, losing a series gives everybody the chance to have a go at captain, coach, selectors and other individuals, but then adverse criticism comes with the territory and one has to be man enough to take it – and when the praise comes, take that as well! Pollock and Donald were superb, but our batting lacked the necessary maturity and confidence. On this tour, it just was not up to the required grade. The triangular one-day series against Sri Lanka and England that followed that defeat in August was not an ideal tonic. We had an off day against Sri Lanka but played near to our potential when we beat England at Edgbaston. But it was little consolation.

The defeat of South Africa was a real fillip for a demoralised England side, making them realise they were once again a force in world cricket, and alongside that came another realisation: luck is a vital part of being a good team. The reality was that England were for the most part outplayed on home soil, and this should be a lesson in itself. Winning is always easier at home, but when you are pushed to the nth degree in order to achieve it, you know there is a lot of room for improvement.

New Zealand the next year was a case in point. In Test cricket one can never go off the boil; the hallmark of a good team is consistency. The current Test match ratings show England firmly anchored at the bottom – which of course is rubbish, but what it does show up is the fact that there is too much complacency and lethargy and not enough urgency and dynamism in English cricket. Backwards-looking administrators have allowed football to blow cricket out of the water to such an extent that any young man with sporting talent will go to Manchester United's Old Trafford rather than Lancashire's Old Trafford. Still English cricket clings so desperately to the past; will they never learn that cricket is in constant competition with a number of other sports?

So whither English cricket? Having had the advantage of coaching abroad and listening to what visiting cricketers have said about the county system, I believe what they say is worth hearing. Many would say: Why bother to listen to them? Yet the England and Wales Cricket Board have copied the four-day game with covered pitches in Australia, cut down the overseas players to one per team, and introduced coloured clothing and night cricket as a supplement to help pay for the game. Although I do not believe in the wisdom of all these changes – the three-day game was not so taxing on players, with shorter batting times, shorter bowling times and less stress; to me, the four-day experiment is failing because, although it leads to a better game, less collusion for results and more results per games played, it puts a number of different stresses on the players – it is obvious that the England team is becoming more competitive. There is still a tangible desire to improve.

My personal belief is that the county game has become harder, but with less skill. The three-day game on uncovered pitches was very different. Facing Derek Underwood on a wet wicket was almost impossible, but I saw players like Rohan Kanhai, Mike Procter and especially Keith Fletcher display exceptional skill on such surfaces. In addition to their natural ability, it was their upbringing on beautiful wickets in their homelands that gave Rohan and Mike the confidence to play differently to English batsmen. I am not necessarily one who subscribes to uncovered pitches, or reverting to three-day Championship cricket. I believe the answer lies in a different field. My abiding early memories are of looking at the Kent team and thinking there were only two, maybe three places in dispute until the England players departed to play in the Tests. I had to be on top of my game to make the grade. I was taught early on by Alan Dixon that performance and not talking a good game was what made a county cricketer successful.

I had to laugh recently when Christopher Cowdrey wrote about me that I played more shots in the dressing room than in the middle. It is *de rigueur* on the county circuit that saying nice things about a fellow professional is not on. In fact, the Kent team of the 1970s, acknowledged as way ahead of its time and patently leaders in the one-day game, often having terrific tussles with Lancashire, could be vicious in the dressing room. The bandying around of cutting remarks was often the hallmark of a successful team during that era. A modern sports psychologist would have a cardiac arrest if he heard half the stories that used to permeate dressing rooms. I actually find it fascinating when today's cricketers look first to blame the support staff for their failures on the field. At the risk of being accused of saying 'in my day', we never had any real coaching (technically, that is) and we were reliant on the advice of our fellow players. Our second XI coach would batter the hell out of you if you thought you were any good, and the saying 'one swallow does not make a summer' was often heard in the dressing rooms.

Each era has changed progressively, and cricketers now are encouraged to 'be there for each other'. Shouts of encouragement have replaced sarcastic cries of 'What sort of f***ing shot was that?' But in an effort to introduce team ethics (which I believe is right) we may be losing some of the hardness necessary to become a Test cricketer. The one common denominator in any walk of life is that success demands hard work. Great players of any era will tell you the same story. There are exceptions to the rule, of course – the likes of Ian Botham, Gary Sobers and Graeme Pollock may have shied away from too much running, for instance – but the majority of superstars such as Alan Knott, the Chappell brothers and Barry Richards have all subscribed to the work ethic. My recent experience with the South Africans has shown that it is possible to create a magnificent team through a work ethic that is second to none.

Brian Lara once described Jonty Rhodes as someone 'who spends more time in the nets than in the middle'. Looking at their recent records, though, it would seem that Brian, whose West Indies team lurches from one disaster to another, could learn a little from Jonty's work ethic and his infectious enthusiasm. My late mother once (probably more than once) said to me that to get anywhere in life you need to use a lot of elbow grease. If the truth were known, I suspect even the Bothams and Sobers of this world worked pretty hard, albeit perhaps in different ways.

The game in England requires the skill levels of the players to be on a par with that of the opposition, but the desire must be greater than that of the opposition, the commitment to work greater, the flexibility of mind more pliable. The cricketer himself must want to get better every day. The administrators must have the same qualities. The clubs, and the players, need to understand that we really are in the entertainment business. Averages count, results count, we all count, and all of us must be held accountable. Four-day cricket on covered pitches is fine, and promotion and relegation will work. Clubs can market themselves more effectively, bring in more revenue and improve their practice facilities. In fact, one of the major keys to success is to bring practice facilities into line with, or even better than, those found abroad.

I detect that Lord MacLaurin has a similar vision and that English cricket is back on track, but it may still have a way to go. The counties are crucial to success, for they are the academies everyone talks about. Their common purpose must be to provide England with the most professional cricketers – to find athletic fast bowlers, to train brilliant fielders, to encourage youth. There is no doubt that, given the intensive international itineraries, youth has to be encouraged and brought through the system more quickly. England has to find those players, identify them early and work hard with them. Discipline is essential, and flair must be encouraged.

Promotion and relegation are now going to be part of English cricket in the new millennium, and a good thing it is too. It will be interesting to see how counties handle the pressures. Already, accusations of cheating and collusion are being made. Pitches will be scrutinised, and the points system for a draw will have to be changed. It will certainly be a fascinating time, and I am all for being even more radical. In addition to the eighteen counties playing in two divisions, I would like to see England divided into six regions, and the best players from each region fighting it out in five four-day games as part of a regional conference. The counties would, of course, have to forfeit their top players for these matches, as well as for Test matches, and those not selected would continue to try to perform for their counties in the hope of attaining regional, then national status. I believe such a system would sort the men from the boys, encourage the right type of competitiveness and provide a smaller base of elite players from which to choose the national squad.

I would also advocate an upgrading of club cricket to a three-day game, to be played in forty-over sessions lasting two-and-a-half hours each: two sessions on Friday afternoons between 1.30 p.m. and 7 p.m. (80 overs), and three each on Saturdays and Sundays, both between 10.30 a.m. and 7 p.m. (120 overs per day). A total of 320 overs a game would easily be enough for two innings per side and a positive result. Each league would consist of ten teams and they would play nine games, allowing the clubs to play traditional fixtures and a one-day competition as well. Cricket scheduled over the weekend would also enable more amateur cricketers to play (as well as more people to watch), and they could then come into the reckoning for county and regional representation. I am sure that businesses would allow any talented cricketers in their ranks half a day off work on Fridays. The regional competition, from which the England side is selected, would of course have no overseas players, but both the county competition and club cricket could have overseas players. County staffs could be trimmed, and would rely more on the playing strength of local clubs, to whom they would have to turn for their future players. This would, I hope, save club cricket and create strong teams with a vibrant work force. There would still be room for the traditional village game, of course – we must never forget that. The local community is important, and each county could look at ways of reintroducing the game at primary schools, and then secondary schools. Former players should be used in coaching and umpiring schemes, and gradually cricket will be looked upon as an attractive career route. Promotion and relegation will eventually see off the benefit system anyway, with transfer fees the next step.

The county system, as I have said, would remain in a four-day game format with one-day competitions, allowing Test matches and regional cricket to be fitted into a fixture list. Night cricket would become a compulsory feature. The regional games would be billed as a clash of the best that England has to offer, and should consequently attract the level of media attention a Test match gets. Whenever possible, Test players should play in these games.

I feel very much that county cricket is not so much dying as changing face, rather like a deciduous tree bearing fruit for the new season – although, of course, not changing as much as I have advocated above. The roots of cricket in England are as deep as those of any tree, however old, and the game will always flourish as long as the custodians of that tree are able to recognise what its needs are. If it needs pruning, for instance, so be it. I am a great believer that any system can work as long as the people in the system want to make it work. A Championship of eighteen counties is, at the moment, being severely criticised – it does not produce Test match cricketers, there are too many people just making a living out of it, etc. – yet it provides pleasure as well as employment. It is entertainment at its best – long, slow and interesting if it is allowed to be. Why have so many books been written about cricket? Why have so many people felt the need to wax lyrical about the game? Why do people go to such lengths to beat each other, praise each other, run each other down? It must have something! Cricket is a great sport.

Why have all the other national sides caught up and overtaken England? I think it is too glib just to say that our cricketers are raking the system and that they do not work hard enough, that they are too spoilt. There has to be more to it than that. The county game started to change in the 1950s and 1960s, when it became harder for top amateurs to get away from the City or other jobs to play county cricket. The game began to lose its appeal, and the three-day game was being played at a snail's pace. New sports started to become fashionable, and cricket countered the new threats slowly. Patience, after all, is its nature.

But in the 1960s the first limited-overs competition, the Gillette Cup, was initiated. Immediately Ted Dexter was criticised for defensive field placings, yet he reacted to the need for change more quickly than others, and, slowly, the other counties followed suit. But cricket fell back again to a certain extent during the 1970s and it needed Kerry Packer to give it fresh impetus. Even then, there were still those who wanted to hang on to the past. The lack of change in terms of remuneration gives one an indication of how reluctant English cricket was to move forward. England's players in 1968 received £180 a Test match, a lot of money when you consider that a capped county player earned £800 a year and another £200 in bonuses if he was lucky; by 1977, a full nine years later, an England player was earning £200 a Test. I know because I was one of them. Packer ensured that this ridiculous state of affairs changed, and with it the tempo of the game.

Aside from this rather hidebound mentality, I believe there are a number of factors that have led to the decline of English cricket:

- excessive one-day cricket;
- changing to the four-day Championship format from three days;
- reducing the number of overseas players per county to just the one (there should be a minimum of two, otherwise standards drop);
- the low standard of second XI cricket, the breeding ground of the game, which is not what it was;
- the vast reduction in the amount of schools cricket (what is the point of having schools if we cannot teach a proper sport there? It is sad that cricket is put aside because it takes up so much time);
- complacency within English cricket, and lack of recognition of the strides other countries are making.

Of course, I would never pretend that this is a closed list; there are other phenomena within the game that are partly responsible for the fall in standards. A considerable number of county cricketers, for instance, flounder when they experience the lifestyle offered by the game. It is all too easy to do just enough to obtain another contract for a year, and with eighteen counties to choose from the likelihood is that there will always be an employer for the underachievers. This tends to breed mediocrity, which is why I am in favour of a two-division structure and less cricket – say, sixteen three-day games, day/night cricket and Sunday league games combined, and a fifty-over NatWest Trophy – which will harden up and improve the health of the county set-up. Conversely, there are the ultra-motivated players who work like blazes and against the odds do eventually play for their country. In fact, county cricket throws up an extraordinary blend of professionals, and it is no wonder that players from overseas find it a fascinating place to play cricket. I was fortunate to play in an era when there was no restriction on overseas players; for English cricket to become strong again, competition for places has to be tough. It is no good an individual giving up and moving on just because someone else takes his place. Counties should resist contracting these types of players wherever possible. Central international contracts work as long as the salary structure ensures that the player chosen retains an identity with the club he belongs to and is prepared to perform for it when the time comes. Loyalty to one's team-mate and one's club is important, and when a player leaves it should be for one of two reasons: either he is too old or his desire to compete has deserted him.

The decline of English cricket can also be partly attributed to the increased, and therefore less attractive, workload being put on international players. Test matches are no longer special games because there are so many of them, and that is a shame. I have great admiration for the Australians because they retain tremendous pride in playing for their country. Their system tends to breed better players because talented youngsters take up cricket as it is still their national game. Their success is jealously guarded. I wonder how many of our really talented young men choose football, where they can earn in two weeks what a cricketer earns in six months? The national side – described by Tim Lamb, the chief executive of the England and Wales Cricket Board, as the shop window of the sport – is failing to produce the type of performances and results the country can take pride in, which in turn puts off the sponsors and results in less cash being made available to pay the talented sportsman. Football has become a religion in the UK, rightly or wrongly; cricket is a poor relation.

Of course some footballers earn ridiculous amounts of money. In fact, I cannot believe the sums of money some players earn these days – it is almost obscene. They are treated like demi-gods and heroes. I can survive very comfortably on a cricket salary, as can all the people involved in the game, but this should not stop me from striving for more by improving my performance. But the main problem here is that despite good earnings job security is virtually non-existent. Contracts cannot last longer than one year as there are going to be any number of players fighting to have their names on them. The pressure on the selectors will heighten as they will have to understand that continuity is fundamental to success. Players who need a rest will be upset if they do not play because they will miss out on large Test match fees. To avoid, for instance, players declaring they are match-fit when they are not, contracts will have to include rest pay. If smaller clubs struggle to cope in this respect then they should seek to amalgamate with other clubs in a similar position. It is of no use today saying to a cricketer that he might have a benefit if he hangs around for ten or fifteen seasons. The bottom line should always be how to improve standards and competitiveness. Rugby union also offers a short career, but is now offering the sort of money and benefits that will encourage people to take up the game.

Furthermore, how can the captain and the coach plan an effective strategy when the captain does not know how long he is in the job for? I am in no doubt whatsoever that there has to be a management committee appointed annually to identify players and work on them in order to turn them into an effective, and as far as possible long-term, unit. Australia, again, stand out in this regard. The side they choose week in and week out changes only because of injury and the occasional loss of form. The continuity practised by their selectors has been wonderful. Cast your mind back to 1976, too, and the start of the West Indies' domination of world cricket. What was their secret? Simple: they retained a settled hardcore unit and added to it only when players were injured or retired. Any business leader will tell you that he operates most effectively on the same principles. Warwickshire's and South Africa's success in the 1990s had a lot to do with those principles being followed as closely as possible too.

And, as I have advocated in other areas of this book, England must embrace new technology as a means of moving forward. I would like to see the day, for example, when every ground can show video replays of dismissals to the crowd, and there is full use of camera technology to help the umpires. I would like to see the day when we could cover a whole ground quickly, so that games always start or restart immediately the rain stops. I would also like to see the day when a perspex dome covers every ground in the country in the event of bad weather. Anything can be achieved if everybody desires it.

As for Warwickshire, they have always been a go-ahead county, and already the chief executive and the cricket committee are enabling them to make the most of new advances in technology and science. The big challenge for any coach in England is to use everything at his disposal to produce players and teams of genuine quality, players who are educated properly and treated with respect so that they can compete effectively in the modern cricketing world.

During the England tour of 1998 we learnt that, within two weeks of it finishing, we would be visiting Kuala Lumpur to participate in the Commonwealth Games. Given the choice – which I was not – I would have preferred a holiday. I was in the middle of a period of eighteen almost solid months of touring. In anyone's life that is unacceptable. I found that when we got back from England I could afford to grab just three days off, which I spent with Gill at the Ngala game reserve, part of the Conservation Corporation of South Africa. It certainly went some way towards refreshing me for the trip to the Commonwealth Games. During that trip Imtiaz Patel held a coach's conference without me. I found this strange. Eddie Barlow and Hansie were speakers and they publicly criticised my methods, in a way that Corrie Van Zyl thought was quite disgraceful.

We were to come across Mr Akhtar, our scourge during that final Test at Headingley, again at the Commonwealth Games. Reluctantly I joined the assembly at Johannesburg airport for our trip to Kuala Lumpur via Singapore. Immediately we were hauled up to a meeting room where Bacher had some stern words for a member of our team, Mark Boucher, who was accused of bringing the United Cricket Board into disrepute in front of a sponsor – the Standard Bank representative Bevan Barker. We had first come across him in Lahore and had become pretty friendly, but he was quick to take the bait when Daryll Cullinan started discussing finance and questioning his firm's performance. Playing games with such individuals is part of the fun all cricket teams have, and it is harmless. Mark had been playing in a golf day, had caught Barker in the pub afterwards and teased him along the same lines. Unfortunately, it appeared he had gone over the top, and he received a firm rap over the knuckles for his trouble.

After Ali left I sat everyone down and explained how we should approach the Games. While there were some who were upset they could not have a rest (myself included), I had decided that we had a job to do and that we may as well get stuck in. Apart from anything else we were part of Team South Africa. I reminded them that with anything we undertook we 'should go big or go home'. Shaun Pollock was adamant that he was going to win the medal that was the same colour as his hair, which I queried because there is no doubt in my mind that ginger is more closely identified with bronze than gold. By the end of the meeting we were in the right mood.

When we got to Malaysia we were immediately impressed by the cleanliness and order in the country. The tropical vegetation was very similar to that found in Durban, and we felt at home from the word go. As we drove into the Games village we were open-mouthed, for there, in the midst of several famous athletes, was the giant All Black Jonah Lomu. The main control centre was at the hub of the village and it was frequented most days by the team. Quite a number of our team had played hockey so we immediately struck up a friendship with the South African men's and ladies' hockey teams, although their curfews were much stricter than ours: we had to be in bed by half past ten, whereas they were kept to ten o'clock on the dot. They had also been off alcohol for four months. Which was the more professional outfit, I wondered?

Practice was difficult owing to bad weather, but we thoroughly enjoyed the fortnight. Northern Ireland had taken the place of England, who had decided that this competition was not important enough, and the upshot of a great thunderstorm during our match against them meant we were left having to chase 130 in 33 overs. At 45 for 5 we were in some difficulty too, but as with all South African teams, two players took responsibility. Shaun Pollock and Dale Benkenstein, two prime candidates for the future captaincy of their country, turned the game around, and we won by four wickets. I was unhappy with the performance, though, and told the team so. I reminded them of our responsibilities and why we had come. We went on to despatch Bangladesh easily enough, but again lost stupid wickets having bowled them out cheaply. Admittedly, though, the pitches were genuinely hard to bat on: they were damp at the start, which encouraged movement off the seam, and then broke up and turned square later on. Our third game, against Barbados, was our toughest encounter, not least because we came up against Philo Wallace, a big hitter of the ball. I was apprehensive as we were set a total to chase of more than 250, but we were assisted by half-centuries from Kallis and Gibbs and some terrible catching by the Bajans. This victory took us through to a semi-final against Sri Lanka. We bowled them out for just 130 and felt fairly confident in our innings until the spinners came on and the ball started to turn. Wickets fell regularly; before we knew it Alan Dawson, the last man in, was making his way to the middle to join Nicky Boje. South Africa still needed 36 to win. Dawson and Boje made them.

In the other group, a powerful Australian team was trouncing all and sundry, so there was no doubting who the favourites were for the final. Yet the game against Australia turned out to be a doddle for us. We had agreed at the team meeting that if we won the toss we would bat first, that we would not bowl on Mark Waugh's legs, and that we would keep the ball up to Adam Gilchrist and Ricky Ponting because they enjoy pulling. We also played three spinners and left out Steve Elworthy, because we thought the pitch would turn square. The other contentious issue was the choice of umpires for the game. During the semi-final we had been on the receiving end of another dreadful error by Javed Akhtar. As the third umpire, he had given Elworthy out stumped when quite clearly the cameras had not been able to give him a clear picture, and when the producer of the TV unit responsible for the sideways-on shots clearly told him that was all that was available. 'How can I give a decision with these pictures?' Akhtar had asked. To which Richard Parker, the producer, had said: 'It's not for me to give you advice, but you know who you should give the benefit of the doubt to.' Akhtar had said he was going to give Elworthy out, and pressed the red light. Naturally I was shocked when I heard the whole story, and I went straight to Cammie Smith, the match referee, and told him that in my capacity as coach of South Africa I was making an official request that Javed Akhtar should never umpire another game in which we were involved. I turned and walked off without waiting for a response.

Akhtar did not umpire the final, which was played in a good spirit. We had Mark Waugh caught down the leg side, Pollock bounced out Ponting and Gilchrist, and the Australians managed just 183, nearly half of them made by Steve Waugh. We made the total with four wickets to spare. Standing on the podium with a medal round your neck must be a fantastic feeling. I sat opposite the players with Derek Crookes' camera. When the national anthem started to play, there were tears in my eyes. We partied until late that night and came home a very happy team.

Our victory in this tournament had proved that practice is not always necessary, especially in the one-day game. I remember talking to Shane Warne just after we were defeated in another limited-overs series, and he said the Aussies too had taken that tournament fairly easily and had just had one or two practices. That is not to disparage the work ethic, of course; I firmly believe in practising well wherever and whenever you can, but not just for the sake of it. Sometimes we forget the value of rest, and for a modern-day cricketer, rest is truly a luxury.

But it was an important tournament for us, not least because it began the run-in to the World Cup the following May, and I remember it for another reason too. While we were in Kuala Lumpur, Imtiaz Patel, the UCB's director of professional cricket, had organised the aforementioned conference at which all the coaches in South Africa were to meet and discuss coaching. My ears must have been burning in Kuala Lumpur as apparently my name was mud at that conference – or at least certain people came away with that impression. It is human nature in any walk of life to be critical, but the reports that filtered back to me concerned me. I had no choice but to soldier on until June 1999. Our triumph at the Games was a nice riposte to my critics, but it did not change the fact that Eddie Barlow was back in favour.

The reports of cholera, disease and floods made us all apprehensive several weeks later when the time came for a visit to Bangladesh for the mini World Cup. It is, however, a lovely place to visit by subcontinental standards. The enthusiasm and support for the game there is unmatched anywhere in the world. The stadiums, mostly just concrete bowls, have large dressing rooms and are generally very comfortable. The Bangladeshis do have a habit of preparing food in their dressing rooms, though, and this cannot be hygienic. It also means you have a procession of people walking in and out, which can easily distract you. To be able to handle such conditions you have to be patient, always in good humour and have, as Daryll Cullinan once said in Hyderabad, 'a return air ticket'.

Although the host country was not included in the tournament, every fixture was a sell-out. Our first game was against England on a magnificent surface. They played well to reach 260, and I remember Peter Deeley of the *Daily Telegraph* saying to me: 'Is that enough?' I replied that I thought it was thirty or forty runs short, and he grimaced in disagreement. We won with four overs to spare and only four wickets down. Our next game was against Sri Lanka, for which we devised a complete reversal of tactics. The team meeting had centred on how to handle Muttiah Muralitharan. After much discussion, we agreed our aim should be to allow him to bowl all ten overs for no wicket and between 35 and 42 runs conceded. We did not want to take a risk against him, and opted to collect singles rather than try to hit boundaries. Jacques Kallis then proceeded to rip into Muralitharan's first over, scoring 22 runs including two enormous sixes. He bowled only eight overs, for 70 runs, and went off with a sore shoulder.

We finally met the West Indies in the final, and despite Philo Wallace scoring a good hundred, Jacques Kallis took 5 for 30 and Hansie steered us home with an unbeaten 61. Having been defeated in England in August, here we were a couple of months later with gold medals galore and an international trophy – and in a totally different frame of mind to face the West Indies again, this time in a five-Test series at home.

7 Whitewash

THE 1998/99 WEST INDIES series proved to be one of the most bizarre I have ever taken part in. Given all the pre-tour shenanigans, it was not long before the cynics began to write off the West Indies team. Then the inevitable stories started, of disharmony, lack of spirit, a beaten camp. Brian Lara, the captain, Clive Lloyd, the manager, and Malcolm Marshall, the coach, three of the most respected names in world cricket, had to be given the sack, and anyone who moved within the West Indies party was being castigated from all quarters. One newspaper reporter actually wanted his money back on a bet because the team had not so much lost fair and square as, he thought, not competed at all.

I am always amazed how certain people, mostly through complete ignorance, can make such comments after a series in which one side has slowly, methodically and brilliantly beaten the opposition. Nothing has changed from the days when I played, which is a great pity. It sometimes seems that we all want to rubbish our game instead of building it up. New Zealand's achievement in beating England in 1999 was not given due recognition as it was generally agreed they had been up against an abject England team. Bill Shankly, the legendary Liverpool football manager, once said: 'You only play as well as you're allowed to!' It seemed to us in the South African camp that the consistency of our performances against the West Indies in this series was overlooked, all our efforts somewhat undermined. Comments that the West Indies were past it, over the hill, were all over the news pages, yet the reality was very different.

The West Indies players were, of course, in the eyes of the selectors, the best available. Newspaper reports and statements that emanated from the Caribbean suggested they were confident of beating South Africa away from home. Inevitably, the media and the public overreacted when their troubles started. There were many quotes before the series started suggesting that it would be an even series which South Africa would win 2–1, or perhaps 3–2; all these were quickly forgotten. The West Indies were apparently in disarray, stories were rife about a split between senior and junior ranks, and I guess that as in any dressing room in times of adversity, communication was poor. In 1999, when South Africa were knocked out of the World Cup, we were on the receiving end of similar stories of dressing-room rifts, of a fractured team, and I can tell you it hurts, for I know all about the effort and time it takes to build team spirit, work on technique, throw balls to batsmen, plan schedules and accommodation, run fielding practices, and so forth. Criticism is fine, as long as it is deserved and it is constructive.

The West Indies team has an icon as its leader in Brian Lara, of course, a fact which tends to attract perhaps more than its fair share of media attention. Lara is certainly almost constantly engulfed in controversy – a lot of which, it has to be said, has been self-inflicted. I once overheard a journalist describing his arrangements to have an interview with Lara at a practice session. According to him, when Lara had failed to turn up, he asked the coach where Brian was, and the reply was just 'F*** knows!' Stories that Lara had played every golf course in South Africa got worse, and were probably exaggerated. His laxity in time-keeping had become almost legendary, and his high profile as one of the great players of the modern era was in serious jeopardy. But I know that Brian's pride was affected by this, and his acknowledgement to Hansie Cronje during the series – 'I need to learn from you how to get the team to play together' – was evidence enough that he wanted to bring about an improvement.

The West Indies' preparations for the tour were certainly less than perfect. Following our one-day final against each other in Bangladesh, both teams were due to land in South Africa simultaneously. And we did, at Jan Smuts airport at 0600 hours on 4 November 1998. Well, actually, not quite. There were noticeable absentees and some troubled faces among the administrators; I remember thinking at the time that the reaction to our triumph in Bangladesh was a bit subdued. I thought we would get a terrific welcome, but, on arrival, Dr Bacher and his colleagues were very quiet.

It was later when I learnt that the reason for our less-than-ecstatic reception was the news that Brian Lara, Carl Hooper, Curtly Ambrose and Courtney Walsh had flown straight to a hotel on the outskirts of London and had presented the West Indies Board with an ultimatum. All four players seemed to be incensed by their treatment. There was a lot of speculation about tour fees and meal allowances, but in fact their gripes were centred on all manner of conditions as well as money. Eventually, eleven distinct points surfaced that the West Indies Board had to deal with. For years the West Indies had relied on a tremendous team spirit, fashioned by Clive Lloyd after their 5–1 thrashing in 1975 by Australia; ironically, now Lloyd was the West Indies manager, this sense of comradeship had dissipated. By the time Lara had been sacked and then reinstated as captain, the party was clearly not mentally or physically fit for Test cricket.

A letter from Nelson Mandela was brought by Ali Bacher to London as an urgent peace offering. For the UCB, the ramifications of a cancelled tour were too horrendous to contemplate. With the ICC tour schedule already drawn up for years to come, it would take some while for another tour to be arranged – the quartet had chosen their moment well. The previous year Ali had had to put up with the first Test against Pakistan being delayed by a day owing to those bizarre claims that two of their players had been mugged.

Now, a year later, here he was in the midst of an even greater crisis. I remember how mentally tired and exhausted he was after fighting for his country's cricketing financial survival. Ali, in his own words, had been a workmanlike cricketer, but he possessed excellent motivational skills and an astute cricket brain. He had had to battle his way into the side and then fight like crazy to stay in it. Rightly or wrongly, he nursed South African cricket, his baby, jealously and zealously; he was not especially keen on allowing his cohorts to run their own ship, and had to know what was going on at every turn. He worked night and day – I really mean that. So with this latest crisis I was surprised that his health, which was not in great shape, was not even more badly affected.

While all this was going on, the South African team was safely ensconced at a batting camp in Bloemfontein, an idea that had been mooted in England. We had, in fact, batted well throughout the tour of England, making big totals at Edgbaston, Lord's and Old Trafford. Our batsmen had scored heavily throughout the county matches too, so there was no great scope for panic there. The natural disappointment engendered by defeat was the catalyst for action. Initially, Hansie Cronje felt the players needed a rest, especially after their defeat at Headingley; later, he had telephoned me to ask if I could arrange the camp and whether we could get Eddie Barlow involved as he had given Hansie some thoughts on how to beat the West Indies.

So Hansie and I invited the most controversial of all South African characters to join us. Friends of mine thought I was mad, that he would undermine my role and was trying to muscle in on what was my squad. My view on the matter was straightforward: I knew we needed other, fresh voices. Hansie and I often discussed this, for we felt the team was only half listening to us as they had heard our advice so often. I had always adopted the policy of gaining outside help, and had also asked Graeme Pollock, Pat Trimborn, Jimmy Cook and Kepler Wessels to talk to the players at some point or other during my tenure as coach. I believed not that they would necessarily say anything new, but that they would put across their thoughts in a different way, and that this might appeal to certain people.

But Eddie Barlow was nonetheless a slightly different proposition. He had written some pretty mucky articles full of unanswered questions and had always found little good in what we were doing. He had also castigated the administration each week through his Bunter's Bouncers column in the *Cape Times*. In fact, his relationship with the hierarchy in South African cricket was dreadful. He had also fallen out with Griqualand West, whom he had started coaching only that season, and had returned to his wine farm in Robertson under a cloud of controversy. I never asked what went wrong there, and still wanted him to become involved with the team, especially as he was one of the few outstanding players from the 1970s who had remained in coaching. I had played for and against Eddie many times and had always been an admirer of his all-round skills. Yet his articles, which were fairly nasty at times, had certainly affected my relationship with him, even though, knowing him as I did, I managed not to let his words get too deep under my skin.

Hansie saw Eddie in a completely different light. As a young cricketer in the Free State he had seen him in his own inimitable fashion transform a bunch of talented low achievers into a winning combination. Eddie had lasted just one season, but in that time he had disciplined and bullied (nicely) these young Afrikaaner cricketers virtually into believing that they could fly off Table Mountain. He made them strive for results. His main method was to show them that they had to put runs on the board quickly – three or more an over in those days – and that they had to bowl with the utmost discipline. There was nothing wrong in that. The Free State youngsters lapped it up and responded magnificently, so Hansie's regard for Eddie was undiminished.

It made sense for me as coach to have Eddie involved if the captain admired him so much, and his visit did indeed turn out to be a success. Eddie was emphatic that we could beat the West Indies. He reckoned we needed to score at 2.8 runs per over (he had moved his initial target down slightly after looking at the Test match record of the great South African side of the 1960s and 1970s, who had scored at that pace). The Australians had used such statistics successfully against the West Indies, both home and away. If we were sufficiently aggressive, we would, he said, be good enough to win. Eddie was also hard on our batsmen, saying that they had to achieve more. He was a stirring influence, and his talks constantly reiterated the harsh responsibilities of Test cricket. However, the question now was: How were we going to score at 2.8 runs per over against Ambrose, Walsh and co.?

For two days at Bloemfontein Eddie and I drilled the batsmen into scoring off short-pitched bowling. The Free State prepared ideal pitches for us and we had a bowling machine thundering balls into ribs and throats as we prepared to take the West Indies on at their own game. Eddie stood behind the net, and as each person went in he would tell him to get into line and play straight. His stern, almost gruff bark instilled discipline into each individual, and the faster the bowling machine propelled the ball the more the players appeared to thrive on it. Except one. Herschelle Gibbs hated that bowling machine. This was too much for Eddie, who was very disappointed in him. Instead, Corrie Van Zyl, my assistant coach in England and the coach of the Free State side, threw balls to Gibbs and tried that way to simulate the problems he would face against the West Indies – if he was selected.

I sensed quickly that Hansie was happy with Eddie's contribution. Eddie, in turn, was keen to continue with the team, so I then had to persuade Ali that we should keep him involved. That in itself did not particularly concern me, for I have never been one to stand in the way of progress. 'He can stay for a while and then he must go,' was Ali's decision. Changing Bacher's mind was always difficult, and it was evident that Eddie's fall-out with the Griqualand West chairman, Mike Doherty, was more disputatious than we had thought. So Eddie finished his work for us after the second Test in Port Elizabeth, but the significance of that camp was that we were properly prepared. Hansie certainly credited our success to the batting-camp preparation. The West Indies were stuck at Heathrow and the South Africans were beating themselves into excellent shape in Bloemfontein. There is no doubt in my mind that this was a hugely significant factor in the weeks to come.

We had managed to persuade Ali that Eddie could come to the first Test, yet as soon as he started to appear on TV there were inevitably those who inferred that he was trying to take over and was undermining me. I certainly was unconcerned about the fact that there were a few in the dressing room who related to him; on the contrary, as I have said, it was good to have a new voice around. By the second Test Eddie was only there for the preparation. After that he was given the chance to attend the pre-match practice, but he wanted to stay for the whole five days, so his input, as I said, ended there and then. He was later quoted in a Cape Town paper as saying that he had been sacked. It is such a shame. Eddie brought to the camp a desire to improve individual performance and to lift up averages into the forties, the accepted benchmark for a good Test player. He was also adamant that players should have standards of performance. I was happy that he talked in such a way to them. The South African side went from strength to strength against the West Indies, and continued where they left off against New Zealand when we toured there later in the season.

Barlow, as I have said, was not the only South African cricketer from the last great Test side to be invited to help out the current squad. One of South Africa's main problems upon returning to Test cricket after the dismantling of apartheid was the lack of peer influence. One symptom of this was that the batting might well be brilliant one day and abject another – not through lack of application or commitment to practice, I might add, but simply through lack of knowledge of the way players are expected to bat in a Test match. They had been brought up on one-day cricket, which had affected both their technique and the quality of their mental application. Occasionally Gary Kirsten or Daryll Cullinan would play an exceptional innings, followed by a gem from Jonty Rhodes or a powerful and graceful innings from Hansie Cronje which would give the bowlers the chance to win Tests, but the consistency needed at Test level was lacking and it was difficult for me, as a coach, to emphasise this continually. Hence players like Graeme Pollock and Barry Richards were brought in to assist. These guys were legends to the younger players, who sometimes could not believe what was being said to them.

Yet in a sense their message was simple: hit the bad ball for four, and often, and do not get out. I am simplifying what was said, obviously, during the course of many involved debates. Once, when Barry remarked that Brian Lara would have been an average player in the 1970s, I am afraid Gary Kirsten was left wondering to himself, 'If he thinks that, then what in hell does he think of me?' At the time our batsmen were also having to contend with television commentators castigating them at every turn, although it was glaringly obvious to me that they were excellent players. They were experiencing technical difficulties, but they made up for them through guts, determination and hard work. Still some commentators boxed them in and refused to change their minds. It was very important, then, to ensure that new players were not exposed to this type of negativity. In one-day cricket we had already achieved the right way of thinking for that format, and this had, I believe, clouded our approach to the longer game, so the type of batting of which all these players were capable was strictly nursed in terms of the needs of the Test arena. A great deal of the squad's improvement in this sense was down to Eddie's involvement.

Lara and company apparently got what they wanted because all four were present and correct for the first Test at the Wanderers, which was a fluctuating affair. Both sides were in a position to win at various times, but it took a couple of crucial innings by Cullinan and Cronje when we batted a second time to take the game away from the West Indies. There were two defining moments in the match, the first of them when the West Indies were 177 for 4, Williams and

Chanderpaul at the crease and batting well. In team meetings Pat Symcox would make an oft-repeated contribution: 'We have to identify crucial periods of the game and change them.' In this respect, Hansie excels. He initiated a ploy in which David Terbrugge, a fine bowler who is quicker than you think, as well as tall and very accurate, took the first of what should be many Test wickets when he had Williams out pulling at a ball too wide for the shot. This was a tactical triumph over a player who was too reliant on this method of scoring runs. Hansie, who hardly ever drops a catch, pouched the chance easily at mid-on. Immediately Donald returned, and Chanderpaul was beaten by a superb in-swinger. The second such instance came on the second morning when the West Indies were 249 for 7. McLean is a dangerous hitter of the ball, and Lewis, his partner, an obdurate defensive batsman. We needed a breakthrough. Hansie turned to his opening pair of Donald and Pollock, who had taken three early wickets. The end came in seven overs, with only a further twelve runs conceded. Two–nil to South Africa in terms of the tactical battle, and eventually 1–0 up in the series too.

We had been unable to find a steady opening partner for Gary Kirsten for some time. Adam Bacher and Gerry Liebenberg had been vying for the place during the England tour, and the former was selected for this first Test, albeit under extreme pressure to maintain his position in the team. In England he had played nicely at Lord's before breaking his collar bone diving in the field. For that Test match he had replaced Liebenberg, who had promised much but had been affected by his tendency to plant his front leg on middle and off stump regardless of the line of the ball – hence he was bowled or lbw far too often for a Test-class player. As a coach it is often easy to identify a fault and to assist a player in getting it right; unfortunately, the only person who can actually ensure a fault is eradicated is the player himself. Gerry was a prolific batsman at school level who has underachieved at the higher levels simply because of this basic failing. I am still convinced that by eradicating this he will become a fine Test cricketer.

Adam had also employed various methods against the new ball, some of which were more successful than others. While I am a firm believer that any batsman should establish his own technique and preliminary movements, I reckon also that he should make sure he understands them. During my own career Geoffrey Boycott queried my preliminary foot movements and for months afterwards I was in a state of flux trying to come to terms with what he said. At the time I was upset, but in retrospect his remarks were very pertinent. I was taught to move back and across the stumps with my back foot by Colin Cowdrey, a method which had been very effective when playing quick bowling. The timing of the foot movements was vital, though, but initially I had no idea what that timing was, and in fact I never worried about it as I had been very successful opening for Kent. However, when things go wrong at Test level doubts can crowd in and one poor innings can trigger off a chain reaction. Form can disappear. Consider my own experience of scoring 79, 120, 136 and 0 not out against Australia, and following that with a poor game for Kent at Tunbridge Wells and a first-ball duck at Trent Bridge. Suddenly I started to experience doubts about my ability.

I therefore empathised with Adam Bacher and other players who had experienced similar reactions. Geoffrey had posed to me the simple question 'What do you do with your front foot?', but a better question might have been 'When do you move your front foot?' So I asked Adam whether he was happy with his movements and he replied that he was intending to stick with them. Unfortunately he had a tough match at the Wanderers, receiving a superb ball from Courtney Walsh in the first innings. Walsh is not only a great performer, he is a particularly awkward bowler as he gives the batsman the impression he is going to move the ball in at them and then achieves late away movement. His height makes judging the length of the ball difficult, so the batsman's feet generally do not move as he would like. On this occasion Walsh dragged Adam's feet together and opened him up, and the ball tickled the outside edge. My heart went out to Adam as I had hoped he would just play and miss at a couple of those so that he could settle in. It was a classic case of wanting desperately to help an individual when you know the individual has to make the play himself. I reprimanded myself for not being firmer with him. I felt I had failed someone who was a wonderful team member, who played the game for all the right reasons, who had a wonderful attitude and a real passion for South Africa.

His second innings was of vital importance, and he decided to make sure he got forward without his feet together. It was almost as easy to see what was going to happen. Walsh, with his extra bounce, made one come back and Adam got an inside edge on to his pad and was caught at short leg. The difference between success and failure really is the proverbial coat of paint when it comes to cricket. After an Under-24 tour on which Adam had done so well and had been an avid listener, he had decided that he must stick to one game plan. He is not the first and will not be the last person who has decided that there is only one way to play cricket.

I often listen to coaches saying exactly the right things to the player concerned but never explaining the differences between the many great batsmen who have graced the stage. No two players are alike, but it is important to find out what is right for one individual on any given day, against different bowlers. Preliminary movements are the key to success with the bat, and the basic principles of the game have not changed for a hundred years. Sir Donald Bradman must have understood what was needed as he was quite simply the best exponent at not getting out. Through coaching and studying I believe what is required is simply this: a batsman must be still at the crease when the ball is delivered, in order that he can judge length, make the correct foot movements and get his body into the correct place to hit or leave the ball. There are a few more factors that come into play, such as swinging the bat in a straight line, but this sequence is not affected by them. Great players who follow this precept perform consistently well. The balance at the crease allows them every chance to do well, and consequently they are more consistent and average more runs per innings. It is an understanding of these principles that, in my opinion, makes them great players. It is probably unfair to single out Adam Bacher here, as many other players have suffered from the same problem, but he is certainly a good example of the importance of this basic coaching principle. It does not matter where or how you make your preliminary move-ments, it is when.

We chose Herschelle Gibbs ahead of Adam for the second Test at Port Elizabeth. It was perhaps just as well Adam did not play because this was a low-scoring affair on a well-grassed pitch. Ambrose and Walsh took fifteen of South Africa's twenty wickets, but our quick bowling was even more impressive: Donald, Pollock and Terbrugge dismissed the West Indies for 121 and 141, and the game was over before tea on the third day. Lara dropped himself two places down the order from number three in the second innings, which hardly helped their cause. Unwisely, Ambrose had struck Donald on the side of his head with a short-pitched ball, which only served to fire him up. He finished off proceedings with a vengeful bouncer at Ambrose, which the tall West Indian could only fend off in the direction of the slips.

The West Indies made five changes for the third Test at Durban over the Christmas period, but to little effect. Put in to bat, they mustered only 198. Franklyn Rose, one of their relatively unknown fast bowlers, took 7 for 84, but we still managed to gain a lead of 114. Jonty Rhodes struck 87, and even though Lara was at last his recognisable self during a stand of 160 with Shivnarine Chanderpaul, the West Indies' second-innings total of 259 was still insufficient. On our way to winning by nine wickets, Courtney Walsh was carried off the field after tearing his left hamstring – a sad symbol of their decline.

By the time of the fourth Test in Cape Town in the New Year, much of their cricket was shambolic. We made a good start: Daryll hit a superb 168 and Jacques 110 in a first innings total of 406 for 8 declared which, considering the

West Indians' mental state, was a mountain to climb. It was inevitable that a player of Carl Hooper's ability would come good at some stage, but even when he did his dismissal encapsulated much of what was wrong with their game. He had accumulated 86 immaculate runs before being run out by an unbelievable throw from Hansie at the boundary edge, so unbelievable that Carl was jogging the third as opposed to running because Hansie's pick-up and turn had been so quick. After that we were able to bowl the West Indies out for a modest 212. Donald had created mayhem early on – indeed throughout those Test matches he generally had the better of the West Indian batsmen, Brian Lara included – but after six overs and figures of 3 for 20 he had to come off the field. This was the beginning of Allan's infamous left ankle injury, and he needed a cortisone jab as soon as he came off. Such injuries have greatly affected our bowling attack. More recently, David Terbrugge's future was in jeopardy and it looked as though he would have to have an operation. Shaun Pollock had also had to come home with an ankle injury during his season with Warwickshire, and Lance Klusener, of course, had had to return early from the England tour. It was a problem our physio, Craig Smith, was struggling to come to terms with.

The West Indies had just managed to save the follow-on, although enforcing it in modern cricket does not occur as frequently as it did in the 1970s, as there is no longer a rest day on which to give the bowlers some well-earned respite. The number of overs in which the opposition have been dismissed, the state of the weather and the general conditions will now determine a captain's decision in this respect. With plenty of time left and very little likelihood of rain or bad light in Cape Town at this time of the year, we batted again. Ambrose had joined Walsh on the injury list, so it was the youngsters, McLean and Dillon, and the seasoned pro, Otis Gibson, who had to hold the attack together. Hooper bowled a long and excellent spell to keep one end going, and we struggled to reach the figure we felt we needed in order to declare – around 225 – but overall batted very sensibly on a pitch that was getting tougher to bat on. Ridley Jacobs, the wicketkeeper/batsman who had been the find of the tour, held us up on our way to victory, as did the West Indies tail. Without Donald, and with Terbrugge not himself, we did not have sufficient pace in our attack. Jacques Kallis, who had scored 88 in the second innings to add to his century in the first, was entrusted with the new ball, and it was during this match that I declared he was on the way to becoming one of the finest cricketers in South Africa's history, because at times he bowled every bit as fast as Donald and he and Shaun Pollock decimated the upper order. Kallis just bowled and bowled and bowled. If ever there was a time when he needed more petrol for his radiator, this was it! Eventually he knocked over Dillon's stumps and the game was over. Four–nil in the series to us.

The final Test in this series, at Centurion Park, gave South Africa the chance to make history. Hansie said in his pre-match address at the team meeting that if we won this Test it would be recognised as one of the great achievements ever by a South African team, and that each of the players held the team's destiny in his hands. The West Indies won the toss and there was plenty in the pitch; in fact, I had never seen so much grass on a track. Most of it was dry, but it was very thick and this caused major indentation marks. There was some sideways movement, but the major problem was steep bounce. If you present those conditions to a man of Courtney Walsh's ability (for he was back in the side for this Test) it makes life tough for any batsman. Sure enough, he was responsible for removing both our openers, Kirsten and Gibbs, for five runs and creating an opening for his back-up bowlers. Unfortunately for the West Indies Ambrose was still injured, so there was not quite the same oomph in their attack.

Nevertheless, the West Indies kept eating into any attempt of ours at recovery. It took a remarkable performance by Mark Boucher, who scored his maiden Test hundred, to enable us to reach 313. Mark was under severe pressure virtually throughout this innings, so it was a great knock. I know from talking to, and playing with, Alan Knott that a wicketkeeper's opportunities to score runs are few and far between, especially low down in the order where the tail tends to collapse around you. In South Africa's case this is not so, and while Mark plugged away so admirably at one end, Lance Klusener, Allan Donald and finally Paul Adams ably supported him. This total of 313 was a good one, well over par for this type of track, and a defeated and demoralised West Indian batting line-up was always going to struggle. Unfortunately for them, they also managed to catch Donald at his best. He took half of their first-innings wickets as they collapsed to 144 all out, and centuries by Kirsten and Rhodes enabled us to declare and set them no fewer than 569 to win. Unsurprisingly, they never came close to it, and to my delight Paul Adams collected four wickets.

Who would have guessed that the West Indies would ever lose a series 5–0? I did not find it hard to feel for them as I watched their gradual but total humiliation, even though I had been on the receiving end of some of their strings of victories. I shall always remember my days playing for England when I just could not see a way in which they could be beaten. Now here were two of my antagonists, Clive Lloyd and Malcolm Marshall, who so sadly died later that year, facing the kind of drubbing they had inflicted on opponents for years. It is amazing what changes in fortune can occur if you become at all complacent, or reliant on certain individuals to win games for you, and West Indies cricket is still beset by problems, some of which are prevalent in all countries, especially by the threat of the increasing popularity of basketball. But at the same time I was very proud of the South African team, and of the excellent cricket they had played. We had done what would have been considered impossible fewer than five years before.

But I have to say that the West Indies, unfortunately for them, encountered Allan Donald at his best and most ferocious. In fact, the needle between Allan and Brian Lara resembled at times the intensity of the Donald–Atherton confrontation at Trent Bridge in 1998. Allan had targeted

Brian from the word go on the tour, and in his autobiography he made his feelings quite clear as to what he thought of the little West Indian. His main gripe was the terrible year Warwickshire had had under Brian's leadership. Allan, considered an honorary Brummie by the Warwickshire supporters, did not like to hear of unrest at the club. Brian Lara therefore became a prime target – and I, for one, certainly would not relish being a prime target in Allan's sights.

Every time Brian came in to bat in this series, Allan wanted the ball. In one encounter at Centurion Park he bowled short and Brian immediately cut him for a blistering four. Allan responded by bowling even quicker. At lunch, Brian was not out and on top. At that stage Allan had bowled over the wicket in an attempt to get him out by angling the ball across him. I suggested that no batsman enjoyed having it coming in at the head and that it was easier to cover the leg side for the hook than the off side for the slash over point. Also, if Allan bowled again straight after lunch, Brian would have to get his eye back in as he had had a break and might not sight the ball so easily. Conrad Hunte, the former West Indies opener who had had much to do with the development of cricket in the townships, had even suggested during this series that Brian needed to have his eyes tested.

Three balls after lunch, Brian was back in the pavilion after fending off a vicious bouncer that was seriously threatening to rearrange his face. It was fearsome and awesome stuff. I cannot think of a worse scenario for a batsman than to have to view that sort of thing from the balcony, or watch it from the non-striker's end. It would not be easy to stay focused or relaxed after watching bowling like that. Allan finished the innings with 5 for 49 (his seventeenth five-wicket haul) and the West Indies suffered a fifth consecutive defeat.

But if I was asked for a defining moment for the series, I would pick the third Test match in Durban when Herschelle Gibbs held two terrific catches – moreover, two of four he pouched in that second innings alone. In fact, not only was it a defining moment for the team, but for Gibbs himself. The

West Indies at the time were 114 runs behind in the first innings and were 201 for 2 in their second, with Lara and Chanderpaul batting easily. The game was fast slipping away from us. Immediately after tea, David Terbrugge bowled a short delivery, a loosener in effect, which Lara, on 79, pulled firmly and square of the wicket. Gibbs took off like a goalkeeper and at full stretch held a stunning one-handed catch. It is amazing how often the remaining batsman of a partnership quickly follows his colleague's lonely path to the dressing room, and, sure enough, Shaun Pollock brought off a brilliant catch off his own bowling to get rid of Chanderpaul. The second of Gibbs's splendid catches came when Darren Ganga tried to hook Pollock and mishit the ball off the splice. Gibbs turned, sprinted, dived and again hung on to the ball one-handed. From 201 for 2, the West Indies collapsed to 259 all out. We all knew then that this was going to be our day. With only 147 needed to win and the pitch becoming easier as the game progressed, an opening partnership of 97 paved the way to a nine-wicket win.

It was during this Test that Gary Kirsten scored his 3,000th Test run in his 48th consecutive match, becoming only the third South African batsman to pass this milestone. Gary is probably the most liked man in cricket. He is admired for the way he plays all the fast bowling he has to face. If he has a weakness, it is early on in an innings against a spinner; if he remains patient, there is only one winner. For many seasons Gary has held the South African batting together, and I was so proud of him when he made the first of his centuries against England in 1995 in Johannesburg. He has become a prolific batsman in both forms of the game, and is having another splendid series against England as I write. I was delighted when Gill and I were invited to his wedding to Debbie Cassidy in September 1999, and to witness how adored he is by so many Capetonians. They care about him too: I have received a number of letters from concerned members of the public about the best way to go about rectifying his tendency to drag the ball from outside off stump on to the wicket. He knows full well that when he is playing a forcing shot his backward defensive shape alters, and if his timing is not right the ball makes contact with the inside edge, although he always reminds me that on occasion the Chinese cut, as it is known, has been a very profitable one. During the series against the West Indies he was also given out caught down the leg side off a glove and unfortunately off the thigh pad as well. The lot of an opening batsman suggests that this kind of dismissal will occur fairly often, but if you average 40, which Gary does, you can truly say that you have fulfilled your role.

Daryll Cullinan also played quite superbly in this series. In many ways he reminded me of Colin Cowdrey: stylish, with time to play, obviously an excellent judge of length. He is his own worst critic though, too often finding fault with his technique, just like Colin. Colin's peers thought he was getting himself into a technical morass, and for weeks he would underperform as a consequence. Daryll also has this trait. If only he could relax and let his instincts take over I am convinced he would be even more prolific. It is clear that the newspaper reporter who wrote that he would be the next Graeme Pollock after he scored his maiden first-class hundred at the age of sixteen did him a disservice. Mind you, anyone lucky enough, as I was, to see him score that sumptuous 275 against New Zealand in the first Test at Auckland in 1999, breaking Graeme's South African record, would reckon that judgement was not far wrong. But I can just imagine what Daryll had to go through when playing against seasoned pros in his late teens after a comment like that. He is, and always will be, very sensitive to that type of remark, and in many ways it has been his Achilles' heel.

Recently, however, and happily, Daryll has recognised this and has worked very hard to overcome it. I can say quite categorically that he will. Like a lot of other players, he always wants to know where he stands in terms of selection, coaching and administration, and events of late have sadly conspired against the stability he craves. For example, he learnt of his non-selection for a limited-overs tournament in Kenya only through the media. His province, Gauteng (formerly Transvaal), has also gone through a complete change of coaching and administration. Internal ructions are normally, if not always, reflected in performance on the field, and South African cricket as a whole is currently going through huge changes. Inevitably, and sadly, some of these will be painful and will take some time to come right, especially when ambitious people believe they can run a club better than those already entrusted with the task.

8 The Spectre of a New System

THERE WAS A TWIST TO THIS HISTORIC series win over the West Indies. For the first time for some while we had left out Paul Adams, the 'frog in the blender' bowler, due to a complete lack of form. In his place for that first Test at the Wanderers we picked Pat Symcox. As the Test unfolded, it became abundantly clear that we were going to face criticism for picking an all-white side.

For years, as I have mentioned, the United Cricket Board had been championing a development programme that had encouraged young blacks (Africans) and coloureds (essentially of Indian, Pakistan and Malay extract, albeit third-generation).

The seeds of this programme had been sown largely by Dr Ali Bacher in the early 1980s when he took over the role of managing director of the South African Cricket Union and was involved in organising the rebel tours. I took part in the first one in 1982, led by Graham Gooch and set up by Geoff Boycott. It was the first of a number that Ali organised in order to keep South African cricket alive. This, of course, enabled him to bring players from other countries to the Republic as well, top players like Alvin Kallicharran and Sylvester Clarke. Joe Pamensky – life vice-president of the

UCB and a prominent lawyer during the apartheid years – and Ali were, I am sure, responsible for a change of heart over apartheid in sport within the ruling National Party. I remember in 1973 sitting with Dr Piet Koornhof, then Minister of Sport, while he explained to me how they would gradually be relaxing legislation to allow black players into the fold. By 1982 there had been some changes as far as integration of players of colour was concerned, and certainly Ali had much to do with this.

But in the end Ali organised one breakaway tour too many. The 1989/90 tour of an England team under the leadership of Mike Gatting was cancelled owing to the vehemence of the opposition to it. The changes that followed that episode were extraordinary. Mini-cricket was born, thanks to a blueprint drawn up by Alvin Kallicharran and put into operation by Ali Bacher. He had decided that now was the time South African cricket had to show a completely different face, and the township programme – which, of course, had actually started in 1986 – was to be the catalyst for a new South Africa on the cricket field.

The main source of players of colour has always been the western Cape. The Western Province Board side was traditionally strong. The main source of 'African' players of colour has always been the Transkei and the Ciskei, not least during the John Passmore cricket week. Other pockets obviously existed and there were a number of promising black cricketers, but the volume was always very small. The development programme with its mini-cricket, known as kwik cricket in England and kanga cricket in Australia, was unearthing great numbers of cricket-loving children, but from the age of eleven onwards the infrastructure could not handle so many.

For five seasons, it will be remembered, I had been involved with Passmore in his aim to bring the best ten black teams together for a week, at the end of which we would pick the best twelve players and take them to participate in the Nuffield week, the elite white cricket tournament where these boys would be exposed to a standard they would never have experienced before. The upshot of this was that talented black boys would be brought into the provinces system. A number of them made the grade: Morgan Mfobo and Freeman Simelela from Langa, Nigel Roberts and Darryl Williams from Avendale, and Lulama Mazikazana and Kenneth Mahua from Eastern Province were among those who progressed through the ranks. Of the black players to show genuine Test match potential, Makhaya Ntini was probably the pick, but without the Passmore week none of them would even have carried on playing. John Passmore was almost single-handedly responsible for keeping things going, and it was no wonder that Ali turned to him for advice. He was quick to appreciate that a special type of person was needed to foster the game, and he soon identified several role models, including Arthur Turner from the Free State, Greg Hayes from East London and Imtiaz Patel from Transvaal, who were to take the game to the townships. It was a huge undertaking which is still very much a part of the development programme to this day. Enthusiasm for the project is greater today than it was twenty or thirty years ago, and this fact remains the major problem facing South African cricket. It is being addressed at pace, but will it ever be quick enough to satisfy the new South Africa?

For his part, Ali worked extremely hard to sign up sponsors – Plascon, Standard Bank, Nedbank, Pick 'n' Pay and, more recently, the cell phone network MTN – who gave millions of rand to the cause. I was swept along, as were many others. I was fortunate to have had five years' experience in the townships, so I was able to help out from the beginning. Ali involved me and was always very supportive. The only sponsors initially were Bakers mini biscuits, and I still have a promotional film in which the young white boy, my son Dale, was filmed getting out of bed and preparing for a mini-cricket festival. His life was compared to that of a young black boy from Langa going to the same event. They were early days, but already Ali was acutely aware of the need to publicise sponsorship deals. As a result, when unity was officially announced in 1992, the development programme's roots were already firmly embedded and it was carried on by other willing individuals. The speed of change was very fast in some areas and more sedate in others, but there was no doubt that the whole process needed an exceptional man to oversee what was happening. Ali was that man, and he did the job quite brilliantly.

And the programme always had widespread support in cricketing circles. Indeed, it had been at the instigation of Hansie – with my full support – that Adams, and later Ntini, played in the side, with absolutely no interference from the UCB. Adams had emerged suddenly as a good prospect, and Ntini had been given an opportunity on the most seamer-friendly pitch in the world, at Perth, in 1997/98. But the advent of unity in 1992 and South Africa's return to international cricket had posed numerous questions as to how the national team would go about properly reflecting the demographics of the country. Unfortunately, the politics of the country demanded a quick rate of change. The development programme, started in 1986, had been heralded as a new dawn – and rightly so. But when would it really start to take effect?

It can easily be argued that the integration of white, coloured and black cricketers is already working – Adams, Gibbs and Ntini, among others, bear testimony to that – and that there will be a natural progression of players into the system. Recently, however, there has been a much bigger push. Early in 1999 I was involved in assessing a practical for the Level IV coaching course; of the team that one individual, Deon Muller, chose to coach, ten were black or coloured and only one was white. In Western Province there was likewise a greater number of coloured players to coach than whites. The change is quite marked, and it is also reflected in administration, where black and coloured administrators exceed in number those who are white. The eastern Cape also reflects a major change, although the northern provinces do not. Free State, Easterns, Gauteng and Northern Transvaal are producing the new black and coloured cricketers.

Why is this? Simple. Cricket in the black and coloured areas on the coastal regions has been played through the generations and therefore these have a greater base of players. For the sake of explanation, there are two distinct areas of black cricket: the first is distinctly Asian, the other ethnic African. The problem in simplifying this is that the Asian content is now third-generation South African and therefore the reality is that these people are simply South Africans. It would be a lot simpler if selection was based on that premise alone, but, owing obviously to the injustices of the past, the reality is that it will be a long time before there is enough talent at the top level to break through, although junior provincial teams are beginning to show the fruits of the vast and comprehensive development programme. The push, however, continues for the best representative South African side, but racism in South African cricket is dead and it is time the politicians allowed the United Cricket Board to concentrate on making cricket the number one sport in the country. The players of colour in South Africa certainly have talent, though. We will see a lot more of them coming to the fore year by year, and already there are signs that Justin Ontong of Boland and Robyn Peterson of Eastern Province, to name but two, have something special. It is up to them to prove that they are special. The infrastructure is there, the coaches are there, the will is there.

If we go north, in particular to Soweto where in excess of one million people live, there is only one club. The base is still very small and is clearly reflected in the Gauteng team. The recently introduced quota system has put tremendous strain on the northern provinces owing to the small base of black cricketers; the southern sides have greater numbers and therefore it is easier to pick a team on merit. The quota system will be a thing of the past very soon: in three seasons' time the number of black players in the game will be more than enough. What is imperative, though, is that these players are good enough to hold their places. What must not happen is that players are selected for the wrong reasons. South Africa must be represented by its best players; the national team has to win Test matches.

We can see how English cricket is being affected by bad results at Test level and how the drift towards football gets greater by the day. Already there are rumblings among white cricketers who cannot see a future for themselves in South African cricket, and those with English passports may well look to go abroad. Should the authorities be stopping top players from playing at the highest level? Why can you not play for the country that is your domicile? I am sure Zimbabwe, who have exported so many talented cricketers, would be especially happy to have all their players back. Graeme Hick, Steve Elworthy, Dale Benkenstein and Trevor Penney would make a huge difference to their international squad, but they cannot play for Zimbabwe because the current regulations are too stiff. Hick, for example, has been out of favour with England but would certainly be able to hold down a place in the Zimbabwe team. There is no regulation to stop a coach from changing countries, and recently we have seen the improvement in Wales' and Scotland's rugby union fortunes since the influx of New Zealand-bred players. It has certainly improved the overall standard of the sport. Tiaan Strauss, playing for Australia, is another case in point.

A quota system should never be applied to an international team. This might fly in the face of current South African policy, but I do believe that international caps should not be given away. They have to be earned. Of the coloured and black South Africans playing cricket today, Herschelle Gibbs is chosen for the national squad totally on merit. So is Paul Adams, although his form on occasion has been wayward. The wonderful aspect of his cricket has been his ability to take wickets despite having to deal with many derisive comments about his action and accuracy. Paul will do very well as he grows older, and as long as his body can take the contortions it goes through when bowling. There are many who think he is not up to coping with the strains, but every year Paul surprises us.

Paul's action has obviously been the focal point of most commentary. When he was young and tried to bowl, it was obvious his coordination was slightly awry and he could not find a position for his head as his arm came over. So like a lot of kids, he ducked his head down and bowled with this peculiar action. I suspect over the years many boys have slowly had this coached out of them, but Paul, who may not have had any good coaching at an early age, would have just got stuck into it. I suspect, too, that he was ribbed by a number of his team-mates. Such was his determination that when he eventually got to Plumstead High School he was good enough to make the first team as a quick bowler! He had also found a way to take wickets by spinning the ball (which indicates a high sporting intelligence): he found he was able to bowl the googly with a very different grip to what is normal, holding the seam of the ball with thumb and first finger and spinning the ball off the tip of the first finger (a reason why he does not get as much spin as an orthodox leg-spinner coming off the third finger). By the time he was up for selection for the Western Province sides he was obviously a wicket-taker.

A great friend of mine, Keith Richardson, was convenor of selectors and Paul was selected for the Western Province B team because of his unusual action. I suspect that Keith was highly sceptical of this action, as I would think 99 per cent of coaches would be, so Paul never made it to Western Province A, but this was probably a good thing in that Paul worked even harder subsequently. His destiny was to meet Eddie Barlow, who saw his potential at the Western Province Academy and encouraged him as only Eddie can do to work even harder. The South African squad was practising before a Test in 1995 and this young person came up to bowl to us. His rise to fame since has been nothing but meteoric. The UCB also recognised his talent, and he was helped by Ashley Mallett, the former Australian off-spinner, and Terry Jenner, the leg-spinner turned coach (who also did a lot of work with Shane Warne). Terry is an excellent wrist-spin coach and has travelled the world to help teach the art. It was Terry who said that he could not understand why South African coaches and players could not fully recognise the jewel they had in Adams.

Paul was drafted into the team to play the West Indies in the fourth Test at Cape Town instead of Pat Symcox. He proceeded to bowl really badly, sending down 39 overs for 141 runs and just three wickets. He got rid of Lara with a low full toss in the second innings but had bowled a number of long hops and full tosses, so before the next Test at Centurion Park we had some work to do with him. We talked mainly about how we could improve two areas: accuracy – although we dared not touch his bizarre action – and how to obtain greater revolutions on the ball, as too many deliveries were going straight on. Paul was able to play for Western Province before the fifth Test, and did indeed bowl a lot better against Eastern Province. Spin bowling, as I have mentioned before, is an art and is all about hard work.

Paul's strike rate actually rivals that of Shane Warne, who without doubt is the spinning icon of this era – Shane averages a wicket every 64 balls, while Paul's is a wicket every 68 balls – and at the tender age of 22 Paul has taken 81 wickets (as a spin bowler he should only start to mature at the age of 27, so this would suggest that Paul will be in his pomp between the ages of 27 and 34, say), yet the two are chalk and cheese in terms of control of line and length and in the amount of spin imparted. Paul has the advantage of an awkward action and some incredible deliveries that come from nowhere, but although at times he has bowled brilliantly, at others he has looked a real novice. I am on record as saying that he has a great future, although after working with him extensively for some time I feel I have to qualify that.

Paul has a problem bowling a chinaman (the left-armer's leg-break) as his action is so unorthodox (Craig Matthews once joked that Paul's head is positioned in such a way at the point of delivery because he used to steal hubcaps off moving cars when he was a kid). The arm position is inevitably too high and therefore what is delivered is an improvised leg-spinner that is not as effective as the googly. Furthermore, in order to obtain enough revolutions on the ball, he has to bowl it quickly. Once a batsman is used to these variations, it is easier to read him. On a good day he gains loop, or 'dip' as some call it. In Cape Town, with the south-easter – a wind of high velocity – blowing, he is able to get that dip; up country, in the thinner air, his dip seems to go and he is easier to handle.

One of Shane's fortes is that he is particularly good at bowling to a field. His secret is that he obtains what is known as in-drift just before the ball lands. It swings into and down to the right-hander and this upsets the foot position – witness Mike Gatting and, more recently, Herschelle Gibbs. For years Warne took wickets with his fabled flipper, but this is easier to spot as there is a distinctive change in grip and action. If any spinner is allowed to settle, he can spin the mystery web around your mind, affecting your feet movement, so spinners have to be taken on.

I wish we knew all the variations that Shane bowls and could read them, as that would make life easier for our batsmen. They are not easy to describe on paper, but I will give it a bash. Analysing his two main varieties of leg-break will be easier if you can visualise the face of a clock. From the batsman's point of view, the leg-spinner which bounces and turns at a steep angle will probably come from a fairly high arm position – say five to twelve – with the wrist rotating from half past to quarter past the hour in a clockwise direction. The second leg-break, which turns across the face of the batsman at a greater angle and can bowl batsmen around their legs, will start with the arm at ten to twelve and the wrist will rotate from quarter to twelve to quarter past, again in a clockwise direction. These deliveries will be bowled at subtly different paces and will need careful watching. The batsman must also be wary of the top-spinner, which dips late and often deceives the batsman into driving when the ball is not quite there.

Then there is his flipper, which drifts in towards the batsman before hitting the pitch and hurrying on. The flipper is actually quite simple to understand, but it takes years of practice to achieve real control over it. The technique is similar to that of clicking your thumb and first finger to call a waiter (as one does). You just have to do it using a forward motion of the wrist and at the same time bowl the ball – easy, eh? What sets Shane apart from other spinners is the incredibly young age at which he achieved all these varieties. Owing to his sore shoulder, he does not now bowl the googly as well as he did. The arm height for this is at twelve o'clock or a few minutes past, and the ball comes out of the back of the hand and turns in the opposite direction.

Shane remains the ideal model for a young leg-spinner. What is so remarkable about him is that he is not as erratic as most of his ilk. A contorting wrist and exaggerated shoulder movements usually make it very difficult for such bowlers to keep their heads still. It is important for them to use the front arm and turn sideways, which helps to direct the ball to the right place. Shane keeps his head still and level and parallel to the ground as he runs in to bowl. As he moves into the actual delivery stride, his front arm takes him towards the target and his bowling arm works across the body as his wrist and fingers spin the ball. I was fortunate as South Africa's coach in that our encounters with him were markedly few, as they were often telling – witness his domination of Daryll Cullinan (among others) and his bowling in our great World Cup semi-final of 1999. Even his great compatriot Richie Benaud concedes that Shane was the better bowler.

Comparing Paul Adams to a great bowler such as Shane Warne is perhaps a little unfair, for Paul is undoubtedly Test material, but I cannot say the same for Makhaya Ntini. I do not believe he has the necessary level of skill to play regular top-grade cricket, although he certainly worked hard when he was selected at the age of twenty. The son of a servant in the eastern Cape, he was the first player to come through the development programme and be chosen for Test cricket. He had little scope to excel on our 1997/98 tour to Australia, but took two wickets in each of his Tests against Sri Lanka in 1998. Again, his selection was hastened by criticism of the selectors for choosing an all-white team for the final Test of the preceding series against Pakistan, when Ali Bacher was quoted as saying that this was no longer acceptable – although, as I have said, it was to occur again. I am not saying that Ntini will never be included at Test level again, but he has to develop greater variety and be able to make the ball move laterally both in the air and off the seam. Victor Mpitsang, who has also been taken on tours for experience, is also short of the required standard, but could yet improve. Including him at the highest level now would be too soon. Inexperience is too easily found out both on and off the field of play.

Over the many years I have been involved in the development of non-white cricketers – since 1981, in fact, and my first acquaintance with Avendale – the biggest dilemma has been how to strengthen the minds of the players, and build up their self-esteem. For years they were considered to be second-class citizens, and to persuade some of them to express their ability was difficult. Adams, Gibbs, Ntini and Mpitsang belong to a new breed of mentally tough cricketers of colour, and there are more and more following this example. The young wicketkeeper–batsman Thami Tsolekile from the western Cape is another, but for every one with this toughness I could name twenty who have not got what it takes and will not come through. The trick, then, in my opinion, is to deploy sports psychologists to identify the ones who will make the grade.

I am very much in favour of giving the disadvantaged the chance to prove their worth, but not at the expense of good cricketers and good administrators, whatever the colour of their skin. Love of the game and fostering it for all the right reasons will eventually lead to just rewards. I am in no doubt that cricket in South Africa will eventually reflect the demographic make-up of its people, but the process must be left to take its natural course. The South African international team must comprise at all times the best available players, otherwise we will be permanently at a disadvantage as all other countries field their best possible teams.

Pat Symcox managed to remain focused on his performances throughout 1999, but the increasing tide of criticism from some politicians might have adversely affected his performance, for he was effectively taking Paul Adams's place. One remark in particular by Steve Tshwete was particularly damaging: he said he could no longer support the South African team if it was not properly reflective of the make-up of South African society. Initially, Tshwete had been an inspiration to South African cricket. In the early 1990s his influence was instrumental in helping South Africa to take part in the World Cup in Australia, and, along with India, he was also instrumental in South Africa's rapid return to Test cricket. On a personal level, I had long discussions with him and Jannie Momberg, once president of Boland and now an ANC member of parliament, about the expansion of the Castle Cup and why Boland should be part of that expansion. I suspect Steve was also influential during talks about getting a higher representation of players of colour into the first-class game – and that he reckoned the transformation in cricket at the highest level was going too slowly. As Minister of Sport, his influence was less appreciated by the team when he criticised the selection of Pat Symcox on account of his age and, especially, the fact that he was keeping Adams out of the team. I do not have any proof, but I suspect the order to implement the quota system came from his office.

Certainly the pressure Hansie and I felt during the West Indies series was as a direct result of the decisions made in the Minister of Sport's office. Hansie and I were pretty upset about this as we were instrumental in the actual selection of both Adams and Ntini in the beginning. The pressure on the political parties is, of course, huge; unfortunately, cricketers are the pawns in the game. Politics regards sport as a great weapon, especially during the apartheid struggle, and today it is still being wielded liberally, causing unrest in South African cricketing circles.

If anything, Pat Symcox became even more determined to succeed in the face of affirmative action, as the policy of selecting coloured players under a quota system is called, because he is a strong character. But everybody wants to feel needed and important, and it is crucial that at all times players feel they are being treated fairly, even though this is an almost impossible task because no one has ever quantified what is fair for an international player. Leaving Allan Donald out of a World Cup quarter-final in Karachi – was that fair? Dropping Pat Symcox after he scored a hundred against Pakistan at the Wanderers in 1998 – was that fair? There are many more examples, but that crucial statement always remains: South Africa must at all times pick its best team from the available pool of players, whoever they are.

Affirmative action came to a head again early in 1999. The selection of the one-day squad for a forthcoming triangular tournament coincided with the final day's play in the Test series whitewash over the West Indies in January. The selectors and I met in the morning. Hansie Cronje and I had hoped for fourteen names plus one affirmative action player – that is, a product of the development programme in the townships. We wanted this team to reflect the make-up of the World Cup squad, which was just four months away, and then we could have plenty of time to work on strategy and one-day techniques. The selectors in the end picked seventeen players. Hansie was not happy about this, so I had to ask Peter Pollock to come round and talk him through what had happened. Hansie thought I had not fought hard enough for our original plan, but when I tried to do so Peter had simply and firmly informed me that we had no other choice. The government had made its decision on the matter: of the seventeen players, a minimum of three had to be of colour, and during each of the triangular games we had to play at least one and preferably two of them.

Suddenly, we were being told what to do. Even the selectors were taken aback. The bearer of the news, Peter Pollock, is a man I have tremendous respect for. He made it quite clear that this had to happen, and that he was sure we could manage the team within those parameters. The squad named was: Kirsten, Gibbs (player of colour one), Kallis, Cullinan, Cronje, Rhodes, Pollock, Klusener, Boucher, Symcox, Boje, Elworthy, Benkenstein, Williams (player of colour two) Hall, Rindel and Mpitsang (player of colour three). Seventeen players for a seven-match series! When I gave the list of names to Goolam Rajah, his face was a picture. He had to organise all the clothing, plane tickets and hotel rooms, and when I told him what the policy was he just shook his head.

A wonderful man, Goolam. He was unfortunately caught inextricably in the middle of this delicate situation. He was a third-generation South African whose great grandfather had come to South Africa as a migrant worker and had exercised his right after five years to stay on. Goolam, Hansie and I had worked together for four years and each of us knew almost instinctively what the other would do. We had become an extremely powerful triumvirate, and the results were beginning to show on and off the field.

Hansie came to accept the idea of a squad of seventeen. I then naively, but honestly, told him that we would have to play one player of colour as a minimum requirement. He was less than enamoured about this aspect, and told me so. In fact I had been categorically told that the selection was a way of resolving the colour issue and that when the World Cup party was finally selected, we would be able to select whoever we wanted providing we acquiesced to these demands. Hansie, however, with his strong beliefs was not as pliable as me. I hasten to add here that he would have had the total support of the team as well as that of all the management and staff.

Given that we had just beaten the West Indies 5–0, the victory ceremony should have been a marvellous occasion, but as we waited for the TV production crew to get the presentation areas ready, I saw Hansie in deep and heated conversation with Dr Bacher. Hansie's face is like a book: when he is cross he has very frightening facial features. He smoulders. For years I had been a buffer to his moods, tantrums and troubled states of mind. When upset, he used to roar in torrents – and today he was upset. A very large and partisan South African crowd had turned up that day to watch their heroes create history. The roar was deafening. In the dressing room the atmosphere was almost one of disbelief that we had completed such a rout. I turned to Peter Pollock and hugged him, and there were high fives all around. The management had been told in no uncertain terms that we had to focus on beating the West Indies and winning the World Cup as this would unite the country and help cricket to grow and prosper in the new South Africa. The players could rightly be proud of what they had achieved thus far as they had shown an inordinate amount of discipline, courage, commitment and dedication, but what should have been a day of joy and celebration nearly turned into a disaster.

It has to be said that some success had come from affirmative action, if Herschelle Gibbs, a coloured batsman who had won a sports scholarship to the most prominent school in the country, Bishop's in Cape Town, can be thought to have come from an underprivileged background. He was a choice forced upon us by the government which was to have fantastic results. We all knew he was a good player, but we did not know whether he had the mental strength to make it at the top level. He had played before, but had not shown he was equipped for Test cricket, having got himself out rather naively on a few occasions. The situation has now changed dramatically, and I believe he is going to be one of the great players in the history of South African cricket. I have known and enjoyed Herschelle's company since I met him when he was eleven years old at Avendale. He has always had a rare talent, allied to a wonderful sporting intelligence. People talk of Tendulkar and Lara and Waugh as great players, and Gibbs, as well as his contemporary, Jacques Kallis, has an excellent chance of being mentioned in the same company. Only one thing will stop him, and that is not being able to handle fame and its accompanying riches. Technically he needs to work on how he is going to dominate the short ball in one-day cricket, but apart from that he has everything. (I will, one day, forgive him for his arrogant habit of tossing the ball up after catching it. Remember that dropped catch – and dropped World Cup?)

It is interesting, though, that the majority of affirmative action players have come through good cricket schools, a state of affairs that will not change for some time to come. They have had the best facilities, the best education and the best coaches. Makhaya Ntini is from Dale College in East London, and Victor Mpitsang from Grey College in Bloemfontein, which has also spawned such fine cricketers as Kepler Wessels, Hansie Cronje, Corrie Van Zyl and, for a while, Allan Donald.

Take Grey College and Wynberg Boys High School in Cape Town, both of which have cricket-loving headmasters who are excellent coaches. Johaan Volsteedt and Keith Richardson have done wonders for the game in South Africa. Then there are the many schools in Natal, East London and Port Elizabeth. They are, and will always be, the base of South African cricket. New areas of development are still in their infancy, except, perhaps, for Langa and Soweto townships, the club sides that have vast junior sections. Other areas of expansion for blacks include East London and Port Elizabeth; most of the development for Indians is in Natal. The western Cape looks after many such club schemes, including Avendale, which has been close to my heart for many years. Since unity, there are two or three more clubs in the disadvantaged areas in the Cape that have created vibrant junior sections, and there is evidence already of talent coming through. My first involvement with the fast-tracking of players of colour has led me to believe that the ability is there, even if the experience is not. Unfortunately, all the nets in the world cannot teach you what is necessary to succeed out in the middle.

The reality for all potential cricketers, regardless of colour, is that they must perform. My view is that if good young black players do not get selected for their home province, it might well be worth grouping them in a separate team and pitting them against the provincial sides in the domestic Supersport series, under a good captain and coach. This would hurry the process up. It is a radical plan which could be perceived as a racial one, but my common sense tells me that each year a promising player would flourish and perform because he has the opportunity to do so, and then he would be snapped up by a provincial union. We must broaden the base still further and help those who are not able to force their way into a team.

No other country has had to develop from a system that was totally abhorrent to mankind, and Dr Bacher and the UCB are committed to the transformation of the new South Africa. Peter Pollock and the new chairman of selectors, Rushdie Majiet, will continue to try to carry this out in terms of selection, but Hansie, as captain, is under different pressures. He must win series – just look at the reaction of the public if he fails! The coach and captain now feel strongly that affirmative action can only be carried out at a lower level, simply because no other country is going to weaken their best team to include players of colour. The players I coached are proud of their performances and proud to play for South Africa. They are worried in case players of lesser ability take their places. They all understand that perform-ance is a prerequisite to being selected and therefore they are keen to do well.

A meeting on these burning issues took place the day after the final Test match against the West Indies in January 1999. It was heated, and such sentiments were expressed time and again. Ali was in a corner and urged the players to see the bigger picture. Alas, if anything, feelings were only hardened. Hansie left the room with his face wearing its stormy look. It has been reported that he took Ali by the lapels and held him against the wall, but that is completely untrue. But he did come up to me to shake my hand, thanking me for everything, telling me that it had been a pleasure working with me, and adding that he would not be playing any more cricket for South Africa. Hansie, a man entrusted with the job of guiding South Africa towards high-level goals, was now being told how to do it, and, in his own words, he felt like a chess player with someone else moving the pieces, and that his position as a result was untenable. He was being compromised at every turn. Nothing anyone could say prevented him from packing his bags that morning and leaving for the airport.

I felt desperate. It took a while for what he had said to sink in, and then I rushed to his room to try to calm him down and talk him out of it. He was absolutely adamant he was not being racist; his job was to take South Africa to the heights of the game and he felt his position was being compromised. It was hard to disagree with him; his arguments were, in fact, highly rational. I had managed to calm him down, but the only effect that had was to make him even more clear in his mind about what he needed to do. I knew he was deadly serious so I alerted Ali and Goolam. Then Hansie went to the airport to go home and did not turn up for a round of golf with his great friend, Gavin Zeitsman. Gavin then did some work behind the scenes, telephoning friends whose opinions Hansie respected. In the end, Hansie relented, which meant that we had him back in the fold just in time for the first one-day international of the triangular tournament.

The frightening thing about that episode was that if Hansie had stuck with his decision and not played we would have been down to very few men – of that I am certain. The support he had from his team-mates was solid. I knew that, which is why I was so distraught at the thought of his leaving South African cricket, for here we were about to start our build-up campaign for the World Cup. I would like to think I would have resigned had Hansie stayed out and others had gone with him, but I cannot say that for sure. Thank goodness I was not pushed into making that choice. Goolam Rajah was absolutely wonderful during that period, and I can imagine the turmoil that went through his mind. Our World Cup preparations were off to a seriously rocky start.

Our first game in this triangular tournament was rain-affected but was won by some late hitting by Lance Klusener (who else?). We lost the second at East London, and then went on to win the next five. The series was significant in that different tactics were needed to contend with the Duke ball. There was significantly more movement at the start of an innings and it remained harder at the death, which meant more runs could be scored in the last ten overs. Hansie and I discussed a change to the pinch-hitter role and concluded that Klusener would be more effective going in after 35 overs than at number three in the order. We also asked our management to look into further use of the Duke ball in New Zealand on our forthcoming tour, although this request was to be turned down.

Another idea, that Daryll Cullinan should open, was shelved. I had asked him if he minded experimenting, as he is, to my mind, clearly the best technical player in South Africa and his ability to perform as Mark Waugh does for Australia was uppermost in my mind. He had been successful in Bangladesh earlier in the year and had expressed a desire to be moved up the order. However, owing to the concerns over affirmative action, players did not feel secure within the team at that time and inevitably this led to a degree of selfishness. It is annoying when selectors do not recognise the sacrifices players have made for the team. What eventually occurs is that for fear of failure players do not want to be part of a flexible batting order, which, I believe, is one of the secrets to success in one-day cricket. It has always been my maxim never to apportion blame for failure in limited-overs cricket. Success depends upon teamwork, and on any occasion certain people are going to succeed when others do not – but that is not to say they are not trying their hardest.

On top of all this anguish over the policy of affirmative action, as we came to the end of this limited-overs series I received a phone call from Gill saying that my father had fallen ill with pneumonia and that our doctor felt he only had a few days to live. He had slowly lost his will to survive. He had been suffering from Alzheimer's for twenty years and on recent visits he had only just been able to recognise me. I returned home immediately and went to his bedside.

It was a very sad time for me, as I imagine it is for anyone to see a parent in such poor shape. My mind went back to the time when he took me into the garden in Kanpur and then Calcutta, and threw a ball to me in the nets at Tollygunge Cricket Club in Calcutta. On one occasion he took me to a field next to the flats where we lived in Alipore estate, and he became so incensed with some local boys playing football and interfering with our game that eventually he took their ball and hit it with my cricket bat. To a six-year-old it seemed he had hit it into space, as if he were Superman! So keen was he for me to play sport, especially cricket, that when I was born he put a bat and a shiny new cricket ball in my cot and reportedly said, 'Son, I hope and pray that this will be your life!' For that statement I can never ever thank my father enough. The gift I received from God has given me the utmost pleasure and satisfaction. If I think of the sacrifices my family has made for me in helping me pursue a career in sport, I cannot ask for better parents and I hope that I can learn from them. It would be remiss of me here not to mention my mother as well, without whose guidance and energy I would not be where I am today.

I shall never forget my father – who never gave praise readily – saying to me, after I had scored 149 against Australia at the Oval in 1975, 'Son, I am still the top scorer in the family!' He had made 150 against Crowborough second XI at the age of 51. I knew deep down he was very proud of me and would have bought a drink for his work colleagues, but he would never let me get too big-headed. Mum used to get cross with him, but it never really worried me. Perhaps the proudest moment in my cricketing career was batting with him against Tonbridge Onward, a village side, for Tonbridge Town second XI at the age of thirteen. We were chasing around 180, and when I came in we were 80 for 9 and in deep trouble. Dad had made sixty and there must have been over an hour to go. The exact details escape me, but by the close of play I was on nine, Dad had reached 120, and the match was drawn. I will always remember him hitting the ball into the Medway, the river that ran next to the Tonbridge sports ground.

It was with a doubly heavy heart that, after his funeral, I boarded the plane to travel to New Zealand, for I knew this was to be my last tour. We had taken Graham Ford, who would eventually replace me, because Corrie Van Zyl had made himself unavailable for family reasons. One often forgets the tremendous pressures the families of cricketers are put under, and Gill, my wife of a quarter of a century, is a real saint. My sons, Dale and Russell, have been wonderful as well, despite not having seen their father that much – they have supported their mother very well. Being the coach of a national side is an eighteen-hour-a-day job owing to the huge desire to gain an edge over the opposition. To remain one step ahead demands research, diligence and attention to detail. International burn-out is always going to happen, and I have not spent as much time as I would like at home, but as my life becomes less pressurised I will enjoy it even more.

For our tour to New Zealand, a nineteen year-old black 'Sotho' African born in Kimberley was asked to accompany the team. He had a very promising action, played for Free State, and was a graduate, as I have mentioned, of Grey College: Victor Mpitsang. Victor joined the tour as an affirmative action selection so that he could be encouraged and taught the ropes. There is no doubt in my mind that he will become a formidable bowler. He is strong, accurate, eager to learn and is playing in the right environment. The rest of the touring party comprised the prospective World Cup squad players.

New Zealand had just beaten India at home and had a formidable one-day team and record against South Africa on their own grounds. In fact, South Africa had not beaten New Zealand in New Zealand. They were our last opponents before the World Cup and we knew that the Test series would be a tough one (as it was, the first Test was played on a glued pitch in Auckland and the second at Christchurch on one of the best batting wickets one could wish for). I arrived in Dunedin, having attended my father's funeral, as the first limited-overs international was starting, and was extremely touched to see the team wearing black armbands. I know he would have been very proud and deeply honoured. It was an emotional moment for me, too, and brought back some happy memories. Kallis hit a century as we notched up 211, having batted our way into and out of a hole, and then we bowled magnificently, almost to victory, but the New Zealanders took the match in the end. We were then confronted by a turning pitch in Christchurch and decided to change the team. One must remember that we were experimenting for the World Cup, so we decided to play two spinners in Pat Symcox and Nicky Boje. This meant leaving out one of our top-order batsmen, and Herschelle Gibbs, who really was still learning his trade, was asked to sit out. Despite leaving him out for this match, we felt certain he would figure in our one-day plans in England.

Both in Christchurch and in Auckland in the third one-dayer we played an all-white team purely on cricketing grounds, winning by seven wickets in Christchurch but losing by the same margin in Auckland. It could be argued that it would have been more politic to leave out someone else, but we felt that the team we selected was right for the surface we played on. Having gone 2–1 down in the series thanks to a fine century in Auckland by Nathan Astle, we were on our way to Hamilton for the first of our three-day games when we received a call from the president, Ray White, saying that we were out of order to play an all-white team. Yet again Hansie and I were being accused of racism and being told that we had to pick at least one 'player of colour'. The telephone call came on the evening of the first day, which had been notable for splendid hundreds by Gibbs and Cullinan. We had bowled the opposition out cheaply, and Hansie and I were discussing our *modus operandi*. We felt this intrusion was out of order. We were being captained from 13,000 miles away. Both of us felt very disillusioned by this new development, as the main goal was preparation for the World Cup.

In fact, it was almost the last straw. Hansie and I decided to say that we were prepared to continue on tour but we would no longer be on the tour selection committee. Eventually the players, led by Goolam, persuaded us to continue, and reluctantly we did so. But we were right to be angry: our goals were clearly set, and it would have been stupid to upset them at such a relatively late stage when the prize was so big. It was not the first time pressure had been applied by the politicians, and now, in the build-up to the World Cup, it was beginning to wear us down.

Pressure is a funny word. In cricket there are many occasions on which it can be averted by simple discussion and reasoning. I believe that the UCB are ahead of the pack when it comes to opportunity and development, yet there is little trust apparent between them and the players. The petty bickering over selection being racially motivated must come to an end. The reality is that there will still have to be a lot more work put into the fostering of the game in South Africa before the critics will be satisfied. If they are not satisfied soon, there could well be a drain of players from the country. This would be a great pity, because in the end the same selection criteria should apply to all sportsmen regardless of colour. And the sooner this happens the better it will be for all the cricketers in the country.

9 The 1999 World Cup

WHEN MY DEPARTURE FROM THE POSITION of coach to South Africa grew closer, there were a number of offers I had to deal with. One of the rumours was that I would be returning to Warwickshire, which must have led to much local speculation, and consequently Phil Neale soon found himself in an untenable position. He wanted to know what his future was as coach with the club. He probably knew they had been in contact with me because when I left in 1994 I had been told that when I finished with South Africa they would like first refusal.

It was an intolerable time for me as well. The major tournament in world cricket was about to start. After the ups and downs of five years with the national side, this would be the culmination of all my efforts. Everything that went before it would pale by comparison. We had beaten the West Indies 5–0 and New Zealand away from home, and this was be the grand finale. It took all my English restraint not to become too excited. Yet the press was hounding me after the resignation of David Lloyd, trying to discover whether I would take on the England job. In New Zealand, Chris Doig had come up to me and had asked me where my future lay. Northamptonshire had also asked me what my plans were, and later Sri Lanka and Pakistan would get in contact. I wanted desperately to concentrate on my final task with

South Africa. Obviously it was nice to be in demand, but I felt I was being constantly sidetracked from the task ahead.

I was also being ribbed by the players on a daily basis. It was amazing how the same sayings came back to haunt me. In 1975 when I played for England, opponents and team-mates would thrust 'Bob England' down my throat, and the comment was bandied around again now by my own players. People would pass on comments that Neale was upset about what was happening with Warwickshire, and that I was definitely going back to the club. If I was going to return to Edgbaston, I was told that I had to make a decision immediately after the World Cup so that they could offer Neale something else within the club set-up. All the time I was still on the shortlist for the England job, and I had been told to make a decision about that *before* the World Cup as they wanted to appoint the new coach immediately afterwards. Everyone was under pressure, and the timing of it all was awful.

I was aware that changing countries so immediately would be problematical. From hero to traitor in one bound. When I took the South African job in 1994 I got a Christmas card from the UK saying that I should rot in hell for betraying my country. There were a number of people who really felt that I should take on the England position, and I suppose subsequently there were a number who believed I had chickened out. When the pressure to make up my mind was at its height we had already launched our World Cup campaign, and it was all too clear to me that I was emotionally far too close to the South African side, and that I would need a break after the tournament. Gill and I had never been on holiday for longer than three days and our relationship effectively had been put on hold because of the amount of time I had spent away from home. There had to be an easier way of working. Three days before the semi-final against Australia I pulled out of the race and said that any decision I would make would have to come after the World Cup was over.

South Africa had been posted as pre-tournament favourites, mainly on the strength of our one-day success over the previous year. We were Commonwealth champions, had won the mini World Cup and, after going down 2–1 at Auckland in our most recent one-day series, with New Zealand, had come back at Napier and Auckland again with convincing victories to take the rubber 3–2. Our first match, against India at Hove on 15 May, was overshadowed by the controversy over our decision to equip Hansie Cronje with an earpiece so that I might communicate tactical advice to him from the dressing room.

It was difficult to understand the complete disdain with which certain people treated the innovation. The International Cricket Council has now decided to ban this sort of technology. But there is no legislation to say that earpieces cannot be used, and if they are deemed unnecessary, or it is thought that their use brings the game into disrepute, then the ICC must say so. As technology has developed through the deployment of a third umpire and radios are now being used for decisions over run-outs, I see no reason why what is effectively a walkie-talkie should not be brought into play. The next step for cricket will be two-way communication between the field and the dressing room, if only to avoid wasting so much time in terms of bringing out drinks, gloves and messages. I suppose there will be the odd occasion when the battery runs flat or the earpiece gets knocked out or falls out of an ear, but its use will have many benefits, and if every team is allowed to use such technology then the playing field is level. If youngsters are thus equipped it will be infinitely easier to explain fielding positions, or why they should walk in as the bowler is bowling, watch the captain and so on. In fact, under certain conditions, such as in the great Calcutta stadium in front of a very noisy crowd, the captain could move his fielders wherever he wants without recourse to shouting or crossing to the other side of the pitch. The advantages, to my mind, are clear.

Anyway, we gained a relatively straightforward five-wicket victory over India, Jacques Kallis making 96 and Lance Klusener providing a foretaste of what was to come by hitting his first three balls to the boundary. There were fourteen balls to spare at the moment of our triumph, and it was a good win. We moved on to Northampton, where four days after the victory over India we overcame Sri Lanka by 89 runs in spite of two controversial umpiring decisions by the third umpire, Ken Palmer. Daryll Cullinan struck 49 and Klusener, relying on a wonderful eye and sense of timing, smashed 22 off the last over of the innings.

On to the Oval, and the most overwhelming of victories against England, who only just avoided making their lowest-ever total in the World Cup. They were all out for 103, Donald taking 4 for 17 coming on at second change. When limited-overs cricket began, there was no question over whether or not a bowler such as Allan Donald should open the bowling, but this particular little change worked very well for us. There were important runs from Klusener again – this time an unbeaten 48 from 40 balls. A resounding victory, but sometimes this can make you feel a touch unsettled. There was a feeling that perhaps we were peaking too soon. When we took part in the first international contest to be staged in Holland, in Amsterdam, we beat Kenya with nine overs remaining. Lance Klusener emphasised, in taking 5 for 21, that he could still bowl a bit too.

Thus we reached the qualifying stages of the tournament with scant difficulty. If we needed a reminder that we were not invincible – and we probably did – it came in our next match in Essex on 29 May. Subconsciously, perhaps, we relaxed. Zimbabwe not only beat us, but brought about the elimination of England from the competition in the process. Neil Johnson, who had once played for South Africa A, made 76 in Zimbabwe's total of 233 for 6. This was not an insurmountable target, for the straight boundaries at Chelmsford are not long ones, yet we collapsed to 40 for 6, Johnson taking three of these wickets. We still finished top of Group A by two points, but the manner of the defeat at the hands of our continental neighbours was a concern.

In the meantime, Australia were running ominously into form, beating India at the Oval and dismissing Sachin Tendulkar for a duck. At Trent Bridge on 5 June, we had the first of our three memorable matches, beating Pakistan by three wickets at the Super Six stage after Shoaib Akhtar, who registered 95 mph on the speedometer that monitored fast bowlers, had removed Gibbs and Cronje all too swiftly. Once again we needed to make only a relatively low total, 221, but we were greatly dependent on the brilliance of Jacques Kallis, who I felt was looking increasingly as if he would become a truly great all-rounder, and, once more, on Klusener. He came to the wicket at the stage of the innings, give or take a couple of overs, we had had in mind when deciding he should go in lower down the order. His striking of the ball at a time when 41 runs were required from 26 balls was stupendous. He was dropped off a skier, which was the little bit of luck that is so necessary in such situations, and we won with an over to spare.

The deciding feature of a convincing victory over New Zealand in our next game five days later was an opening partnership of 176 by Kirsten and Gibbs. We did promote Klusener now, for he had made more than 400 runs in the tournament without being dismissed. For once he failed, but it scarcely mattered. Kallis won the Man of the Match award for an unbeaten half-century and two early wickets.

So to the first of our great struggles with Australia. The Australians, our great antagonists, are an excellent team with some outstanding players and characters. They are a collection of hard people who hate losing. I thought we had managed to overcome them, psychologically, at the Commonwealth Games in 1998. During that tournament they had decimated the opposition with what was tantamount to their first XI (with the exception of Warne, who would have made a huge difference on those Kuala Lumpur wickets). In the final, though, which we had just scraped into, they did not perform at all. I have always had a suspicion that an eleven that walks into a final without having overcome tough competition does not win it. When I think back to games I have watched, I know the team that squeaks through the semi-finals usually triumphs in the final. South Africa in the 1995 rugby union World Cup, South Africa at the Commonwealth Games, Australia in the 1999 World Cup semi-final at Edgbaston – there is a pattern. Australia had really made life difficult for themselves during the World Cup, yet gradually improved and were ominously near to their best by the time of the final.

In that first match with Australia on 13 June at Headingley, our total of 271 for 7, which included a century by Gibbs and a half-century by Cullinan, was a substantial one in fifty-over cricket, yet we had one notable absentee: the injured Kallis. It was to tell. At one stage we had Australia 48 for 3, yet still they won. The inestimable Steve Waugh is not a man to give a life, but we were more generous: when he was on 58 he clipped a straightforward catch to Gibbs at mid-wicket, who, in looking to hurl the ball up in celebration, lamely dropped it. Herschelle had a habit of catching and flicking the ball in the air somewhat flamboyantly, and in this instance accidentally hit his knee in the process. The ball dropped down, and there was immediate doubt over whether or not he had had the ball under his control. Srinivas Venkataraghavan, the square leg umpire, thought he had, and said he would have given Waugh out, but Peter Willey, the umpire at the bowler's end, said it was not out and the Australian batsmen ran a single. The Australians, fairly or unfairly, have a reputation for being the worst sledgers in the game. Certainly when I spent eight and a quarter hours at the crease in 1975 I really copped it. Upon the umpire's decision that the catch was invalid, Steve Waugh, who was upset at nearly getting out, turned to Gibbs and said, 'What does it feel like to drop the World Cup, Herschelle?' The words were a bit over the top at the time, but they would come back to haunt us.

I know the ICC are very concerned about the behaviour of players on the field and will soon, I am pretty sure, give umpires more power to prevent unnecessary sledging. I actually believe sledging is more fun now than when I was playing against the Australians in 1975. I remember Les Ames saying long ago that in his day they used to congratulate the batsman if he performed well. However, with the extra money that has come into the game, and the consequent pressures to win, this outlook has changed a little. In fact, the match referees still fail to interpret sledging in a consistent way. Some are much more lenient than others.

But as I said, some comments on the field have been amusing in the heat of the moment. Take another instance involving Waugh, this time at Centurion Park in 1997. We were 2–0 down in the series and really motivated to record a victory, especially as we had thrown away the previous Test at Port Elizabeth. Allan Donald had ripped out Mark Waugh's off stump to leave them 40 for 3. Pat Symcox, fielding at mid-on, ran deliberately across the path of Steve Waugh and shouted, 'Come on lads, another wicket and they'll be forty for four,' giving Steve the eagle eye on the way. Steve replied, 'Hell, Symmo, you really have got the hang of this game!'

Waugh's superb innings in that last Super Six match had given Australia an edge over us, and he was to excel again in our semi-final at Edgbaston four days later. It was an epic contest, one that he was to describe as 'the best game of cricket I ever played'. It was a great game, and one we should have won. We had Kallis back for the match, and some fine bowling from Donald and Pollock, who took nine wickets between them, restricted Australia to a total of 213. Waugh made 56 and Michael Bevan, one of the best strikers of a ball in the limited-overs game, 65. Shane Warne then found a tremendous amount of turn, taking four wickets in his ten overs. But in spite of Warne's expertise, we made sufficient runs. Kallis contributed 53, Jonty Rhodes 43, and we had the match in the bag. Or so I thought.

Although we lost wickets as we came closer and closer to reaching the target, Klusener's astounding hitting meant that a place in the final was within our compass. He hit the first two balls of the last over, bowled by Damien Fleming, for four, which left us needing only one more run to win. He was unable to score off the third ball, from which Allan Donald was almost run out at the non-striker's end as he backed up too far. When Lance failed to time the next ball properly, hitting it off the bottom of his bat between bowler and mid-off, in the heat of the moment he unwisely set off for the required single. Allan, unaware of what was going on, had turned round and scuttled back into his crease. Reacting far too late to Klusener's sprint as a result, and dropping his bat as he desperately tried to make the elusive run, he was unable to beat Fleming's throw to the other end. It was desperately cruel.

The scene in South Africa's dressing room at Edgbaston resembled that of a refuge in the midst of a natural disaster. The team sat in their chairs completely stunned. Of course, this disaster did not suffer any human tragedy, but by cricketing standards it measured 10.6 on the Richter scale. Towels covered the faces of Donald, Kallis, Cronje and probably others, but I cannot and do not particularly want to remember who they were. I know there were tears shed under those towels, though. I felt sick to my stomach. I could not cry, which might have helped; I was just sort of resigned to it all. There was nothing I could do or say that was going to help, and I remember going round to each player to commiserate and to thank them for everything. It was my last official day with them and it hurt more than anyone could believe. It hurt not because I wanted to win the World Cup more than anything else, but because we were comfortably the best-equipped team in the competition. Our tactics and our build-up had been as good as anyone could have wished for, and there were millions of people who thought we would go all the way.

I do not know what my face looked like, but I distinctly remember the Australian coach Geoff Marsh's expression when we shook hands. There was a look of total disbelief and total relief, and I even felt that the Australians were sorry for us. I suppose it was such a great game that no one deserved to win. I remember reading when I returned home that our top order did not fire and that when it came to the crunch we choked. I suppose there are things we would do differently if we had the opportunity, not just in terms of that semi-final, but the whole tournament. Perhaps we would ask the ICC for permission to wear the earpieces, for instance, although I doubt that would have changed anything. But I still think our preparation as a squad and our attitude to the games was as good as that of any other country.

Allan Donald was run out at 6.10 p.m., and an hour and fifty minutes later I signed for Warwickshire. I then got on the bus to go back to the Crown Plaza Hotel in Birmingham. I was devastated and numb after the defeat. All that hard work, all that planning down the drain for .02 of a run. Against Australia as well – it was unbearable. We crowded into the lift with not a word said. There was an American couple in it, and as we all pressed the button for the ninth floor where the majority of the team were billeted, the man said, 'Jesus, we missed our floor,' to which Corrie Van Zyl responded, 'Sorry, it doesn't go that far!' Humour of the highest order at the toughest time. After showering and changing I knocked on Hansie's door, but his wife was with him. I wanted to take him out for dinner and just chat. I went down to the bar instead and met some very good friends, including Michael Cohen, who had come up for the game, and I sat down and shared a bottle of champagne with them. It was another of those surreal moments that one encounters in cricket. Clearly the best side in the competition had failed at the final hurdle. The disappointment was almost too much to bear.

Five years was about the right length of time for me to spend with South Africa. I would have liked to continue, but that issue had already been resolved eighteen months earlier. It was a very sad time. I had derived terrific enjoyment from being with the team – who would not, watching Lance Klusener, Jacques Kallis, Shaun Pollock, Allan Donald, Jonty Rhodes, Daryll Cullinan and Hansie himself out in the middle? All of them were great. I often laughed when the media said that we had no superstars.

I needed a break, and I also needed to come to terms with our defeat, so I went on Sky Television's World Cup programme and spoke about the desperation of that last ball. But I could never blame Lance or Allan, only empathise with them for something that will live in their minds for ever. They will be stronger for it and they will learn from it; more importantly, they will pass on what they have learnt. As for the World Cup final, it was a disaster again for me. I put my money on Pakistan at the Sky studios. I knew Australia would triumph, but somehow I just wanted them to lose.

In a strange way, all great sides cause resentment, and Australia have always been the side to beat. What people forget is that it took them ten years to reach their current position, for they, too, went through some tough periods. That is why I say South Africa will be stronger for their semi-final defeat. The Australians have become a great side because they are able to cope with the basics of the game better than other teams – in other words, their skill levels are very high. They are not a convincing team on the subcontinent, but then who is? They have produced consistently good batsmen and two great bowlers, Shane Warne and Glenn McGrath, backed up by other very skilful bowlers like Paul Reiffel, Craig McDermott, Damien Fleming and Stuart McGill. In Border, Taylor and now Steve Waugh they have had three of the toughest men on a cricket field you could wish for. No excuses, just guts, determination and high skill. South African cricketers in general still have to reach these levels. They are not far away from achieving them though, and in recent months have shown many signs that this will occur. They are certainly ahead of all the other countries.

On South Africa's development in the seven years since 1992, the *Cape Times* had this to say:

When South Africa returned from isolation in 1992, they found the perfect combination to head the team in the form of Kepler Wessels and Mike Procter. The latter did not have much experience as a coach, but what South Africa needed at that stage was not a coach but a figurehead. Two years later the honeymoon had effect-ively ended. The players needed a technical coach rather than a figurehead. They effectively told the United Cricket

Board to get rid of Procter. Their choice of successor could hardly have been better qualified. Woolmer had already made his mark both at Warwickshire and in the Boland, where he had handled both the rich and the poor in terms of cricket resources and ability with equal skill.

From a South African point of view, the big advantage that he brought to the national team was the fact that he was a Test cricketer of considerable experience. That was what the South African team needed. The selectors had prematurely put Peter Kirsten out to pasture in the belief that Wessels would still be available to bat on under Cronje's captaincy. Wessels, however, was not interested, and the Woolmer–Cronje partnership suddenly found themselves handling a Test team that had very little experience. It was in such a crisis that Brian McMillan was promoted to bat at number three.

Had Woolmer been coaching England – his record at that stage was seven defeats in six one-dayers and a solitary Test match – he would no doubt have been given his marching orders by the tabloids without further ado. But the UCB fortunately knew what it was doing. Cronje needed a father figure as much as he needed a coach, and the entire side, with the possible exception of Allan Donald and McMillan, still had to learn how to play Test cricket. Teaching them how to play it was probably the greatest contribution Woolmer made to South Africa.

After five years of virtually living with those players, it was certainly a strange feeling going to a cricket ground and seeing them all running around the field and practising without me. I actually did not miss being with them, though, and I knew then that I had made the right decision. I had been particularly keen to coach an international side and had enjoyed it tremendously, but clearly it had been the toughest period of my career. The expectations of the public, expressed in the media, at times were hard to bear; the expectations of the captain and the team were sometimes unrealistic too, and at other times not sufficient. The delicate handling of people, the negotiations over assistance and equipment, the frustration of being told 'you have to make the most of it' – these aspects of the job were just too much. I could have handled the role for a little longer, but the relief and absence of stress after I had finished was so considerable that I actually wondered if it had all been worthwhile.

The South African team, as the *Cape Times* implied, has gone from being hesitant newcomers to being one of the best sides in the world, and quite a few other cricketing pundits would be in agreement with that statement. In my new role as a roving coach for the UCB, I have been lucky enough to visit a number of provinces to see various players earmarked for success by the selectors, and to watch a number of promising players of colour. There is without a doubt boundless talent coming through the ranks. Whether these players make it to the top will ultimately be in their hands, but the support system now in place will surely create even more fine players for the Republic. The future still looks bright.

10 The Coaching Game

MY PRIORITY WHEN I COACH anyone, or any team, is to try to be enthusiastic. It is advice well learnt from the very first full-time international coach, Bobby Simpson, who was so successful with Australia. His words have stuck with me always, but the priority is to ensure that all those whom you tutor have a love for the game and a desire to understand it. If this were my only goal, I reckon I have done very well, but as with all sports, whatever the age group and whether the coaching be at school, club, county, provincial or international level, a coach has to know what he needs to achieve. It is the easiest thing in the world to stand behind a net – or, indeed, in front of one – and simply shout out the odds. Those coaches are two a penny, and quite frankly almost always a complete waste of time.

A coach must have a plan and must work out that plan. For example, a schoolboy coach should follow a set curriculum throughout the term, educating the youngster in the various disciplines of the game. The reason for this is that cricket has basic principles and necessities that must be taught before the array of shots can be understood properly. The fact that the bat shape is unique, for instance, is a factor too often disregarded. Paying attention to detail is a prerequisite of this game, so long as by doing so you do not discourage flair.

Moreover, as you move through the ranks as a coach you must retain and expand on this philosophy. I was fortunate to be involved in some excellent coaching courses run by the South African Men's Hockey Association, and also to be involved in the Plascon training camps (before unity) when areas of the game such as nutrition and psychology were touched on by some very interesting speakers. On top of this I had my own playing experience at the highest level to call on, as well as my English coaching courses under Harry Crabtree and knowledge garnered from Colin Page when I played for Kent. It is amazing how my coaching style has changed, developed and adapted according to the boys/men I coached. It was those courses and experiences which gave me a new insight into the extent to which technology could advance coaching and playing.

For example, some twelve years ago, Mel Siff from Pretoria Technikon introduced me to the philosophy of the 'six sesses': the six sesses for success are skill, speed, strength, stamina, suppleness and spirit. This philosophy made it easy for me to have goals not only for myself but also for each individual in the team. For example, if speed is one of the sesses and Jonty Rhodes is your benchmark in terms of speed off the mark, then attempt to ensure each individual narrows the gap on Rhodes. If skill is another, work the player up through technical appreciation towards Don Bradman's standard. The six sesses have both physical and mental interpretations and can be used at any time during the season. Another great coach was Pat Riley, who introduced me through Hansie Cronje to what was called the team cycle of success. This, too, was cleverly thought out and put on to paper what goes wrong when teams go through a bad patch and how they put things right. I have used both these coaching aids many times and have had a lot of success with them.

The other factor which many coaches fail to get to grips with is that the player's self-determination is a key element to his success. Once he walks over the boundary rope it is he who has to do the business. He can blame the coach for not preparing him well enough or he can take responsibility for his failures by saying that he has prepared properly but has not made the grade on a given occasion. The coach who takes all the praise and avoids responsibility when disaster strikes is also wrong. Both parties should always look in the mirror and ask themselves if what they are doing is right or whether it is enough. If there is too much reliance or too much blame apportioned then the parties concerned are wrong. The balance is a fine one, though, and can easily be upset by temperamental people.

The real reason for coaching, obviously, is to get the best out of your players. I also firmly believe that by making the players contribute to meetings, they will learn more quickly and feel more a part of the team. This all-team philosophy flies in the face of the overbearing senior player syndrome, which has permeated cricket for years: 'How many Tests have you played, youngster?' followed by a forbidding 'And how many more do you think you're going to play?' By involving players I believe you make them part of the team. At the same time, of course, the youngster should respect the elder statesman in the side and also be prepared to learn from him. It is this very peer influence that has made the Australians such a great outfit – and it has been almost wholly absent within the England team of recent years.

I remember only too well my one England tour, of India, Sri Lanka and Australia for the Centenary Test in 1976/77. Devoid of preparation due to an ankle injury, I missed the first two weeks allotted to practice; when I was ready to play, we were already on our travels around India. My practice sessions were few and far between and usually not controlled. As a new boy, I just made the most of it. We did not have a coach, so had to rely on our fellow professionals for help and advice. Unfortunately, this was like looking for blood out of a stone. Everyone wanted to play, and if there was a chance that a regular in the team was perceived to be in trouble, he was abandoned like the young runt in a litter, the one that cannot keep up. This experience made me determined it should not be repeated when I became a coach.

By setting up a mentor system, I made two players in the team work together and help each other, setting each other little goals and targets.

I wish I had had a set-up like that when I played, being given the freedom to set myself attainable goals, especially when batting – a minimum number of runs per game, for instance. Something like forty an innings as a minimum goal would, I am sure, have driven me to a greater number of better scores. I think the reason that I did not do this was that I started batting at number nine for Kent, and in those days I bowled more. Taking responsibility for winning a game or putting runs on the board was not in my repertoire. There were plenty of individuals, I am sure, who did set themselves targets, for such things can motivate certain people. Personally, I found I became more determined to go on to a good score if I got hit early on in an innings. What motivated Geoff Boycott and David Gower, two completely different animals, to score runs? What spurred on Graeme Pollock and Eddie Barlow? What were the deciding factors that kept them at the crease? Was it the challenge? Was it their average? What was the deciding force?

Bradman is always the ideal example: what kept him going every time he walked out to bat? I am sure he relished the challenge of the game. Reading his book, *The Art of Cricket*, forces you to realise the amount of thought he put into the game of cricket. I suspect his peers did not follow his example and were therefore shown up, although of course this may be an unfair statement, because the great players of the time would have recognised the necessity of out-thinking Bradman. Douglas Jardine, for instance, took an England side to Australia with the express intention of getting rid of Bradman and winning the Ashes with bodyline bowling, and he was successful.

I believe (and I am not alone) that, technically, Bradman was far ahead of his time, as was C.B. Fry, who wrote a wonderful book on the art of batting, *Batsmanship* published in 1912, and which should be compulsory reading for every coach. I am indebted to Sir Paul Getty for my copy, and I have had genuine pleasure translating into modern English some of the basics of the game. Fry was the first person to talk about the importance of understanding timing, so much so that I believe these words to be quite fantastic: 'In actual play a perfect stroke is the combined result of perfect mechanism and perfect timing; and this combination must be preceded by perfect selection.' In that sentence Fry has settled the issues that cause coaches to pontificate over how to play a shot. In today's English: 'You must pick length perfectly, then get your body in the perfect position and then time the ball to perfection before you can be satisfied.' One hoick, however successful, does not make an innings.

There is so much wonderful coaching literature available, and digesting some of it has been a godsend to me. It has taught me one of the most valuable facts any coach can learn, that there is no one source of knowledge in this game. So many have thought it through and so many have had theories and so many have lived for the game. I am just one of those humble servants. The pleasure lies in assisting a person to find some success on the cricket field. Nothing can give me greater pleasure than to watch a player score a hundred soon after the unlocking of a problem. A player may make the same mistake many times, but it is the one who makes the least mistakes who will go on to be the most successful. The coach acts as this player's catalyst for success by providing the bowling machine, the video, the chances he himself never had. To this day I will never forget members of the Kent team ridiculing me for bringing down my own camera to identify faults in my batting so that I could correct myself. Well, let us see who is laughing now! If you can help people to love and understand the game, then you will have achieved a lot.

One of the many reasons why we all play cricket is what might be termed the 'adrenalin factor'. Implicit in that phrase is an acknowledgement of the fear of failure, which has to be overcome at both a young age and then again when the player in question is past his best, when there are good young cricketers coming through to Test level from the A team and he is looking over his shoulder at their performances and thereby putting more pressure on himself. But cricket, like golf, is one of the great levellers, and it is quite normal to fail. Success is a bonus. Moreover, standards for success and failure differ; people set their sights in different ways. Some players think they are doing all right if they average 29 with the bat – dare I say in county cricket – and others aim for much more. What is important for all of them is that they eliminate as many fundamental errors from their game as possible, and the key to that is to focus on your own game. To understand his game better, a cricketer should ask himself these questions:

- What is the level of my own skills?
- How fit am I?
- Why am I in the team and not the guys in the second XI?
- Why am I playing the game?
- Am I concerned about the team's performance?
- How can I help others who feel as I do?

Most importantly, though, ask yourself how much you love the game and then make a promise always to try your hardest, to give one hundred per cent, and understand that no one can ever ask for more. Even if you get dropped from the team, you should always keep these values. Never worry about how other people's performances affect your position; cricket is a team game and the team's success is the most important thing. If it is you who makes the runs, so be it. You will take the plaudits. But learn to be pleased by the success of others as well.

I am often asked at what age boys and girls should be introduced to the game. This question has been made easier to answer by the many innovations cricket has thrown up over the past few years, principally kwik cricket in England, kanga cricket in Australia and mini-cricket in South Africa, where lightweight plastic bats and stumps allow youngsters of only six or seven years of age to enjoy a form of the game. I was introduced to cricket by my father when I was three –

not that I remember anything about it. I know my father was fairly impatient to get me involved. But the real question is not when to introduce a child, but when he or she should discover the finer points and be coached with a hard ball and pads.

The ideal time for this, of course, varies from child to child, with factors such as coordination, natural ability and strength to take into consideration, but my experience is that a child around the age of ten is more likely to make meaningful progress than anyone of a younger age. It is important to ensure that the bat the child uses is not too heavy as this can cause untold damage in the early stages of learning technique. I would also like to see a change in the way junior cricket is played. Instead of schools wanting to win at all costs, I would like to see all the players getting a chance to bat and bowl and enjoy the game fully. Nothing is more of a turn-off to the budding cricketer than turning up to play and neither batting nor bowling, just running from fine leg to fine leg at the end of each over. I remember a county match between Kent and Essex at Folkestone when the young Keith Pont, an all-rounder who was something of a practical joker, showed that the best way to deal with such a situation was to borrow a bicycle and ride it to the other end of the ground. It caused hysterics, not least among his own players.

Young cricketers are great fun to coach, not least because, generally speaking, they are an inquisitive, eager bunch. Since I began coaching I have often been asked by schoolboys and schoolgirls to explain aspects of coaching and technique – and by adults too. I have been contacted on occasion via *Wisden Cricket Monthly*, on whose editorial board I sit, by cricket enthusiasts who enjoy watching the game but say that their hand–eye coordination is too limited to gain much enjoyment from playing sport. Is there anything that can be done to improve your eye for a ball, or is this just something you are born with? There is no doubt in my mind that improvement is possible, assuming there is nothing wrong with the person's eyesight. Numerous gadgets that can help are on the market. In the Varsity Tavern on the Pershore

Road, just outside Edgbaston, there used to be a machine that asked you to press a button when a red light came on, and then recorded your reaction time. Dermot Reeve and I used to compete over that. In South Africa, Stellenbosch University and the Sports Science Institute have a series of tests and games that will help speed up those reactions. The South African team and English counties have benefited from this.

Nobody, to my mind, epitomises near-perfect hand–eye coordination more than Jonty Rhodes – yet nobody I have coached has benefited from technical assistance as much as he has. Sorting out his technique was one of the toughest jobs I have ever had, although it was made easier because Jonty is one of the nicest players I have ever met. When I became coach of South Africa, I decided to call all the contracted players together to introduce myself and find out what they required. So, armed with home telephone numbers supplied by the United Cricket Board, I rang around. By now Jonty was a legend, the jack-in-the-box boy who had run out Inzamam-ul-Haq so spectacularly in the 1992 World Cup (mind you, who hasn't run out Inzamam?). At the time, it was the making of the competition. When I rang him, Kate, his wife, had no idea who I was. We have had a laugh about it ever since.

I will try and put Jonty's status into perspective. He was a tremendous marketing tool for South African cricket, particularly in those days for Bakers Biscuits, who had introduced mini-cricket to the country. He had saved South Africa's cause in two Tests, one in Sri Lanka and one in Sydney, and was averaging in the thirties with the bat. Yet when we started to work together, his star was fading despite his continuing brilliance in the field. Other cricketers saw themselves as better and more consistent players. I remember Dr Bacher saying to me that there were two individuals South Africa needed in their team and that I had to do everything I could to keep them in it. Jonty was on that shortlist. Almost immediately I, too, had sensed the positive effect Jonty has on any team, but he had to bat better.

I got to know him in Pakistan, where he and Gary Kirsten worked together every practice session. I still have film of Jonty from that 1994 trip, and the difference between the way he was batting then and the way he bats now is quite phenomenal. My first effort at improving his game was to explain that he should try and drive under his eyes – in other words, get his head over the ball – and that a slight alteration to his grip was necessary. This was going to take time, of which I had little. His two weaknesses were associated with the very basics of the game. In fact, to say that I was making technical changes is rather overstating the case. I knew from past experience that trying to change Jonty overnight was not going to be possible, even if he was to accept that change was necessary. I would have needed to work with Jonty every day for months, but I was lucky to have an ally in Graham Ford who recognised that what I had initially told Jonty was correct. Imagine the tension if Graham, Jonty and I had disagreed.

Jonty was in and out of the team during this period. He was certainly in it for the one-day internationals, but for Test matches we started to look elsewhere. Kirsten, Hudson, Commins, Cullinan, Cronje and McMillan became the top six in the order and they batted fairly well, but the life had drained out of the fielding performances. It is a credit to Jonty that he worked so hard to regain his place. He received sound advice from Kate and Kepler Wessels, and he had a terrific rapport with Ford.

Before long, he began to score heavily in the Supersport series, and the time was soon judged right for a return to the Test team. Fortune smiled on him: Brian McMillan's fitness problems, the immaturity of Herschelle Gibbs and other matters enabled him to regain his place fairly easily. How can he bat at number six in a Test match? the selectors asked. He has just scored four hundreds for Natal in the four-day game, was my response. But he hasn't done that at Test level, they came back. He has the temperament and now he is batting better, I insisted. Eventually he regained his place and has since proved that he can be consistent and dynamic down the order. Leave him out at your peril now!

Jonty's brilliance in the field is something all cricketers can work towards, and in terms of throwing the ball much can be learnt from the techniques of baseball players. Sport has instigated much research into throwing methods and the rehabilitation of shoulder injuries. The main difference in the throw itself is the position of the throwing arm on the backswing. In baseball this is much higher than in cricket's traditional round-arm method. The more round-arm the thrower, though, the more strain he puts on the biceps, which is how a lot of cricketers' injuries start. In baseball, the thrower follows the line of the bicep tendon and is therefore less likely to cause an injury. The amazing speed and accuracy of the baseball thrower would certainly be an advantage for a cricketer, especially with the advent of the video replay which has reduced the margins of error in run-outs. A number of Australian and South African cricketers have played both sports and have benefited accordingly. This is not to say, of course, that there are not situations in cricket in which round-arm or underarm throws can be invaluable, but the best advice for all cricketers who want to improve their throwing is to try to track down a baseball coach as well as a cricket coach, and also to go to a local gym where they can be advised on how injuries can be prevented through strengthening the shoulder.

A fielder should always be able to improve the length of his throw. If he feels his basic technique is satisfactory, then he needs to strengthen his shoulder muscles, especially those used for throwing. Then throwing shorter distances should be practised, and a net can be used for this. The fielder should start at ten metres' distance and throw twenty balls, gradually increasing the pace and distance until he is throwing as hard as he can at a target just above his own height.

Excellence in the field is becoming ever more important given the developments in the game. The most notable change in one-day cricket has been the increased pressure on the fielding side because of restrictions on field placings. The first fifteen overs of an innings have become more significant. In Test cricket there is little need for batsmen to take unnecessary risks and hence there should be few run-outs, but if the ball is hit square of the wicket in the limited-overs game and the batsmen do not run, the whole team groans in the pavilion. Pressure also increases on the fielders if batsmen run on a misfield. There is no doubt that years ago I would never have advised them to do so, but developments in the game have radically changed my mind. 'Never run to a ball square of the wicket as it causes confusion in calling' was the sage advice in my youth. Not so now.

I can remember running out Mark Benson, my opening partner at Kent, while playing against Sussex. I hit the ball square and to the left of Paul Parker, a terrific fielder, but right-handed. I was convinced there was a single there. Mark responded straight away – and Parker threw down the stumps. He had to hit the stumps from sideways on, and did, but that is the risk batsmen have to take sometimes. Most of the time the fielder in question will not be as good as that.

One of my other tasks when working with Jonty, as indeed with all cricketers, was to emphasise how necessary it is to select the right equipment. I tell young people not to use a bat that is too heavy, and that applies to some Test players, too. I had a horrendous experience once when I experimented with one weighing in excess of 3lb. The first time I used it I scored well, benefiting from the pace of the ball for deflections, and I had reached twenty-odd when a leg-spinner came on. I went down the wicket and started to drive, realised I was struggling, and nearly fell over as the momentum of the bat carried me forward. Needless to say I was stumped by an embarrassingly large margin.

If you have a nice bat which you would like to use but which is too heavy, then go to the gym and start pushing weights. Many great players of today have used a heavy bat and have been very successful. I believe this is a major cause of the ball going out of shape so quickly these days. If there is a key to choosing a bat, it must be the pick-up. I have often used bats of 2lb 10oz which have picked up lighter once I have put extra grips on the handle. I ended up with three as I enjoyed that feel, but I know a lot of very fine players who prefer just the one grip. There is no easy recommendation – only by trial and error will the right combination be found. I started with a 2lb 2oz bat in my early days and graduated to about 2lb 8oz, and sometimes 2lb 10oz. As this is a cricketer's most important possession, it is worth spending time getting the bat right.

Should a batsman wear a helmet? What I would say is that if someone is prepared to protect his legs and thighs, then it makes far more sense to wear a helmet as this can prevent fatalities. I recall Graeme Pollock, towards the end of his career, being asked why he wore one – after all, it had not been a part of his game until he was almost in his forties. 'If the protection is there,' he said, 'then why not make use of it?' Viv Richards was another great batsman who never wore one, although he was rumoured to carry one in his 'coffin' and, of course, he had to face the West Indian fast bowlers only on occasion. Gary Sobers says he would never have worn one – and one has to take him at his word. Likewise, I cannot imagine Tom Graveney, Colin Cowdrey or Brian Close decked out in that way. Who could ever forget the famous photograph of Brian catching Sobers at short leg off John Snow at the Oval in 1966, the ball having come off the top edge after a mistimed hook? Anybody else would have been diving for cover.

Had these famous names grown up in what might be termed the 'helmet generation', it might, of course, have been a different matter. I recall vividly the amount of publicity I created when I was the only England batsman not to wear one upon my return to the Test team to play the West Indies in 1980. They had, at the time, any number of genuinely quick and extremely good fast bowlers – a fearsome roll-call that comprised Michael Holding, Malcolm Marshall, Andy Roberts, Colin Croft and Joel Garner – but I was not used to the helmet. I was fortunate in that I played the hook shot well and could pick up the length of the ball quickly. I only got hit on the head once in seventeen years of first-class cricket when not protected: Malcolm Marshall struck me on the right cheekbone on a quick pitch at Maidstone, and I was out of action for six weeks. When I returned I scored a half-century, but I was genuinely scared for the first time in my career. It took me about eighteen months to shake off that feeling, and to this day the sinuses on the right side of my face play up when I have a cold. This particularly affects me on aeroplanes, and was a factor in my deciding to cut down on the amount of travelling I would do when I stood down as South Africa's coach. Had I taken the England job, I would have been even more affected than I am already.

So why tempt fate and not wear a helmet? A batsman will get used to a helmet by wearing it in the nets and in the middle, and by doing some neck-strengthening exercises. If he still feels uncomfortable, as he might well do, or less mobile, or thinks his vision might be impaired by the grill that is commonplace nowadays, he has to ask himself these questions:

- Am I good enough technically to deal with extra pace?
- Are the pitches I play on good enough that I am not worried about the steeply rising ball off the dandelion stem on a good length?
- Am I always fully in control of the hook or sweep shots on these surfaces?
- How long might it take me to get used to the helmet – can I strengthen my neck and work on my balance?
- If I could not bat because of an injury, would that affect the team's performances, and would I keep my place in the team when I came back from injury?

Now that Richards has retired, I cannot think of one Test cricketer who does not wear a helmet, unless the spinners are on. This does not make the game aesthetically pleasing, granted: I myself do not always recognise a batsman if his name has not been announced over the Tannoy. Players often seem identical in terms of appearance and clothing. There is another drawback, too, in that many cricketers have lost the knack of swaying out of the line of the ball; they do not always watch it properly, and that in itself can lead to them becoming injured. The advent of helmets came about partly through World Series cricket, when Kerry Packer encouraged, if not ordered, his players to put them on as the matches were marketed and played in a confrontational way. They gained popularity also because fast bowlers grew stronger and became fitter – and, indeed, better. Who would have wanted to face Malcolm Marshall or Colin Croft without a helmet? I took to one eventually.

I mentioned earlier that heavier bats was one reason why cricket balls go out of shape so quickly these days. I remember one correspondent writing to me to ask why there is so much fuss made by the fielders when the ball goes out of shape. I am often asked why this should matter, as, from a bowler's point of view, a deformed ball should deviate more in the air or off the pitch. I recall a conversation I had once with the great Les Ames when he was Kent's manager. We were bowled out cheaply during a Sunday League game when the ball had swung prodigiously, but when our turn came to field it would not move at all through the air. It felt and looked out of shape and just drifted into the bat – shades of reverse swing. We lost by nine wickets and were naturally upset. The obvious reason was that we had not scored enough runs, but we also believed that had our ball swung like the opposition's we might have been able to defend our total. Les queried that by saying, 'Surely if the ball is out of shape then it makes it just as hard for the batsman to know what the ball is doing?'

That seemed a fair point. As a long-suffering bowler, I found that the reality was that unless the ball had reacted conventionally, there was no deception when it did change. Reverse swing is not so effective unless the ball has swung conventionally in the first place. Also, some balls reacted differently to others and some bowlers could make one ball do all sorts of tricks, which led to onfield arguments about whether the ball should be changed or not. The main lesson here is that there is a need to experiment and to discuss with your fellow bowlers how the ball can be polished, wetted or legally manipulated to create lateral movement. If all else fails, then a concerted effort to change the ball is made. Different umpires have different views on the matter; some might just throw the ball back to you and say, 'Bowl a few more and the batter will soon knock it back into shape for you.'

Reverse swing is regarded as a recent phenomenon, although evidently it occurred in the past without bowlers being aware of what was happening. It is most apparent on rough or worn pitches, because it happens naturally when the unpolished side of the ball begins to scuff up. Throwing the ball in from the outfield one bounce on to the rough side scuffs the ball up, as does a rough outfield, which is far more common on the subcontinent. And there are some means of achieving this that are not subtle and are against the rules and spirit of the game, such as scratching it. In both Tests and one-day internationals nowadays, it is central to many teams' strategies. With the ball being shone normally on one side and with a slight change in action (more round-arm) the bowler can defy the normal scientific principles of the shiny side going through the air quicker than the dull side. The change of action also creates a different shape for the ball. In the final few feet of its path it not only swings but dips as well. This is a difficult delivery for an observant batsman to cope with, and is even harder for a tailender, especially against bowlers of the pace of Donald, McGrath, Wasim Akram and Shoaib Akhtar. (One could argue that a batsman of Test class should be able to play the swinging ball – as usual, it is a question of quality of foot movement when considering how to combat this.) I remember as a youngster being taught very early on, particularly by the Kent vice-captain Alan Dixon, to 'work on the ball'. I did not realise just how hard that was until I had the experience of bowling with John Shepherd for Kent and John Snow for England, both of whom were adamant that the ball had to be looked after immaculately.

The first task of a captain whose team is defending a low total such as Kent's that day in the Sunday League is to keep the runs down and his fielders alert, and to find out where his players want to field. An alert batsman could target the fielders at mid-off or mid-on for quick singles. The slower fielders should have cover – in other words, they should have the support of quicker individuals in positions near them. If they cost their team an extra twenty runs then someone is going to have to score them. The more you try to hide someone, the more the ball will come to that fielder, and of course the better batsmen have the ability to pick out the weak links. The captain will have no shortage of problems, and this will only add to them. A quarter of a century ago, most counties had one or two individuals who were not particularly mobile. Colin Milburn, wonderful striker of the ball that he was, would not be given a place in a 45-overs-a-side game today. Colin Cowdrey will not mind me reminding him that, once there was no need for a slip, we would position him just behind the square leg umpire and reckoned on him doing no more than stopping the shot that came straight at him. He played one-day cricket when he was over forty; very few will do that in the future.

The main reason, of course, why players are not continuing after forty is the sheer amount of cricket they are having to play. Modern players spend hours in the gym building up their strength, or are out running shuttles or jogging five miles. They have to survive a constant year-round onslaught on their bodies. I advise sedentary people who ask me how to gain strength for a season to start gently, walking the dog, and building up to a five-mile walk. Then visit a gym and do a few runs on the treadmill. Pick up a bat and shadow-play all the shots in front of a long mirror. Next, spend a couple of evenings at the local disco to get the feet moving (Bradman and Fry often mentioned the wonders of ballroom dancing in this respect, which taught one balance, poise and silky foot movement). Anyone who works in an office can – their boss permitting – roll up a piece of wastepaper into a ball and bowl it down the corridor. At least this will help bodies to become reaccustomed to cricketing movements.

Once outside, do not be deceived by the crisp spring air. Long-johns are a must in the spring – thermal, of course, with a thermal vest. Warm up by stretching. Arm circles are essential. Then jog gently up and down on the ground before moving on to five or six twenty-yard shuttle runs. Anybody should then be ready for hamstring, groin and side stretches. The dedicated cricketer in England will have started his season in February, and the chances are that having played a winter sport of some sort he will be reasonably fit. To achieve cricket fitness, an aerobic and an anaerobic base are required. The first, which builds up stamina, is achieved by running long distances; the second, required to sharpen running between the wickets, running in to bowl and chasing the ball to the boundary, is gained through 300- or 400-metre sprints, flat out, followed by recovery and repetition – a minimum of six times but no more than twelve.

Stretching, by the way, is not just something that should be done before the start of play, but at the end of a bowling spell too – and even during it – and straight after an innings has finished. Most muscle injuries occur when the muscle is tired. There is no substitute for actually playing the game, for the more overs you bowl the better you will feel; the more time spent in the middle, the more comfortable you will be; the more fielding you do, the easier it becomes.

Net practices should be concentrated and efficient, for nothing is worse than having a disorganised net. Over the years, a lot of players who shall be nameless have used nets to have a slog rather than practise properly. With the advent of bowling machines, things have changed – a little. Ideally, six people should go into one net for an hour, which means ten minutes' batting each, and each batsman faces a minimum of four bowlers to test his skills in a variety of ways. If you stay too long in a net, you will be at risk from shin splints, an injury caused by hard surfaces. Bowlers also run the risk of back problems. They must wear extremely good training shoes with plenty of padding.

Whether in the nets or in the middle, the batsman has to sort out his guard. This is necessary as he has to know where he is relative to the stumps, primarily the off stump. Shot selection is based on positioning and adjusting to the surface.

I tried most guards when I played, but found that batting with my feet outside leg stump enabled me to have more room to hit the ball, and that anything directed down the leg side became a free hit. This made the bowlers bowl straighter, which I found a great help as I could then play straighter myself, not flashing at wide half-volleys, which I often used to edge to wicketkeeper or slip. One of the batsmen I found hardest to bowl against was Mike Smedley of Nottinghamshire, who also stood outside leg stump and made it difficult for me to put my out-swinger in the right place. I remember Tony Greig standing outside off stump to Derek Underwood on a vicious wet pitch at Hove in an attempt to nullify his tremendous turn and bounce. I also remember batting against John Emburey on a wet turner in South Africa and deciding that, as the ball was turning so much, I would station myself outside leg stump so I could play down the line. It worked for me on the day.

There is no such thing as a right or wrong guard to take; there have been many variations of the stance, some more successful than others. The usual coaching method is to ask a player to stand with the feet four to six inches apart, with knees bent ready to move forward or back. This policy is favoured by the vast majority of modern batsmen. As the standard of the opposition – of fast bowling in particular – improves, one has to learn more about getting into position. One way of dealing with extra pace is to move the back foot back and across the pitch, lining up with off stump. If the ball is pitched up, then the batsman just has to move forward, thereby limiting the amount of movement involved in countering a very quick delivery. I first came across this technique as early as 1970, while talking to Colin Cowdrey. It certainly helped me against pace bowling early in my career.

Alec Stewart's approach is particularly interesting. He stands with his feet wide apart and still moves back and across, and ends up playing only inches from the stumps. He was very successful with this method in the West Indies. When I bowled against the great Graeme Pollock for Natal, he scored 196 with his feet wide apart. He always looked as if he was in the correct position without doing anything more than rocking back or forth, or moving his front foot into line if the ball was slightly wide. Pollock found the stance advantageous; others might not. It should be remembered, too, that Bradman rested the bat between his feet, so his stance must have been further apart than most. I can only tell you that the stiller your head is (or the less or later you move) the better your chance of reading length and line and so making fewer mistakes. If you move around the crease but get the timing wrong you are in trouble. It always comes down to what suits the individual on the day, but the principles of batting are clear: stand still when the ball is delivered, pick the length as quickly as possible, move into position smoothly and play the appropriate shot.

Just as the stance can differ from that recommended in the textbook, so, of course, can the shots. Coaches would emphasise in the past that batsmen should not play across the line, yet the developments in limited-overs cricket are such that this has become an accepted part of the game. Peter May, a truly great batsman, intensely disliked the reverse sweep, which was becoming more and more prevalent when he was chairman of the England selectors in the 1980s, and there is no doubt that playing across the line is sometimes a dangerous thing to do. But a spin bowler on a turning pitch can make life very difficult if the batsman is trying to play straight. I have often seen players who, when tied down in this way, will try to get themselves out of a rut and are dismissed through spooning up an easy catch. Sweeping the ball is an alternative, and acceptable, method of scoring off a spin bowler. The reverse sweep, which was utilised more by the Warwickshire players I coached than the South Africans, is played mainly against the spin of an off-spin bowler. By rolling the wrists and turning the face of the bat so that it faces the off side, the ball can be directed towards fine third man. It is especially useful when there are six fielders on the leg side and only three on the off, all of whom will almost certainly be in front of the bat, thus leaving plenty of space for runs. Like any shot, it takes time to perfect. We found that time in my years with Warwickshire, and it was played to great effect, particularly by Dermot Reeve.

Field settings and the type of pitch will, to a large extent, dictate how much the sweep is deployed, but it has distinct advantages. It helps to keep the scoreboard ticking over and thus reduces the pressure on the batsmen, and it can also force a captain to move fielders from other positions to counter the sweep, which in turn allows the batsmen to score off the spinner in a more orthodox manner through the now vacant positions. There are actually five sweep shots, if one includes the slog and the reverse sweep.

One shot that has gone out of fashion, perhaps because few can play it effectively, is the paddle. This smothers the ball in a paddling motion, guiding it very fine just past the wicketkeeper at an acute angle to the pitch. Colin Cowdrey and Basil D'Oliveira were great exponents of it, and given the restrictive field settings in the one-day game today it would be of considerable benefit nowadays. The paddle is a felicitous shot of a kind which is not best played with a heavy bat. Perhaps years of relentless pace in Test cricket dulled enthusiasm for it, just as batsmen became unaccustomed to coping with different kinds of spin bowling.

I am often also asked how a batsman should play the yorker. Graeme Hick has had a somewhat topsy-turvy Test career (although he is more highly rated abroad than he is in England) and is identified by some bowlers as a batsman who does not have the capability of countering this delivery, partly because he is such a tall man. I well remember Tony Greig, my first England captain and another tall man (six foot seven inches), becoming entangled when he could not bring his bat down quickly enough against the likes of Michael Holding. Many of the bowlers who have used this weapon in recent times – the likes of Waqar Younis, Curtly Ambrose and Joel Garner – are experts whose arm would release the ball from such a height that it was actually coming down from above the sightscreen.

If the bowler is obtaining late inswing or reverse swing at high speed, then getting into line, the normal method of countering pace, becomes dangerous. If the batsman is hit on the foot he is liable to be lbw; if he moves his feet out of the way he will probably be bowled. Batsmen, though, can practise against bowling machines that can be set to deliver yorkers. Somebody who bowls them really well will deliver them perfectly more often than not, but we are talking about only a handful of top bowlers. Most will overpitch and deliver juicy full tosses, which in county or Test cricket are put away to the boundary. I advise my batsmen to stand inside the crease but outside leg stump, to reduce the backlift and play with a straight bat towards mid-off. They would then have more room to hit the ball swinging in towards the stumps, while anything going down the leg side becomes a free hit. What is vital is that they must take advantage of it. Many are the batsmen who have failed to take advantage of loose deliveries through toppling over as the ball passes, taking their eye off the ball and misdirecting their backlift over gully, and hence drawing the hands away from the body, causing weight transference to the off side and moving across the stumps as the ball is bowled.

Jacques Kallis is one of the younger fast bowlers who is working on perfecting the yorker. Given that he is capable of bowling as quickly as Allan Donald, it should be quite a delivery if he gets it right. Until a knee injury sidelined him from bowling quickly for a short period in 1999, he was rapidly becoming the best all-round cricketer in the world. It could be argued that he is already. I was introduced to him when he was just sixteen and invited him to join Warwickshire during a pre-season training trip. It was obvious then that he was a boy of incredible talent. Even at that age he did not look out of place among seasoned English pros. Educated at Wynberg Boys High School in Cape Town, he is from a humble family background and one of the nicest young men that you could wish to meet. His technique stands scrutiny against the best bowling and he is a hard worker. He has unfairly been accused of being less than bright – Clive Rice, a national selector, caused some fuss when he wrote this in a newspaper column – which is far from the truth.

This perception has now been exaggerated by comments made in fun while touring. At the start of his Test career Jacques was a quiet and shy person, but he has matured into someone with an impish humour and a more worldly outlook.

I see in him already an all-rounder of greater stature than Eddie Barlow, who opened the batting. Jacques has a marvellous technique. He has a determination not to get out, too. He loves batting and it is this desire that has enabled him to raise his average from 26 to 40 in under eighteen months. If he has one failing, then it is his occasional inability to move the scoreboard along. He does tend sometimes to get bogged down and score at one pace, yet at his young age I do not see that as a major problem.

I hope he looks after his suspect knee, as it is vital for South Africa and the balance of the team that he continues to bowl. He is now genuinely quick and can swing the ball large distances in and out. His action is not classic, and when his head falls away he can lose his line, but I shall watch his future with considerable interest as I have been with him since an early age and have taken a lot of responsibility for his future. An abiding memory for me is of the time in 1994 when I asked him to come and bowl in the Edgbaston nets to Brian Lara, and Jacques knocked his middle stump into the back of the net first ball. I knew then that here was a special talent.

The same can be said of Saqlain Mushtaq, the Pakistani off-spinner who has mastered the 'arm ball', which in his case is more of a top-spinner. Ray Illingworth, the one-time England captain and manager, was a very fine off-spinner. He once told me that no bowler of his type would go far in the game unless he could beat the bat 'on both sides'. I trust that statement is self-explanatory. The off-spinner will naturally go past the right-hander's inside edge, but to be able to beat the outside edge as well makes him that much better a bowler. The method of beating the batsman on the outside of the bat is the arm ball. Other terms are the floater, the top-spinner and the drifter, which are really all different names for a similar skill. The game's greatest exponent of bowling a mystery ball from an off-spinner's action was not Saqlain Mushtaq, but John Gleeson, who played for Australia in the 1960s and who actually produced a leg-break. Few players could read him, but he had a relatively short Test career. He is best remembered now from an after-dinner anecdote that is told about Geoff Boycott, who during the 1968 series between England and Australia was batting against Gleeson with Basil D'Oliveira at the other end. At the conclusion of one of his overs, Basil came down the pitch and told Geoff that he had managed to work him out. 'Yes, I have too,' Boycott allegedly replied. 'But don't tell the others how to do it!'

How is the arm ball, which drifts on after pitching, bowled? Saqlain Mushtaq does it by holding the ball as if he were going to spin it from off to leg, but adjusts his wrist position until the seam is going away from the bat. A bowler with enough flexibility in his wrist can practise this variation, but it is extremely hard to master, and patience and perseverance are required. The real secret is to hold the ball as normal. As your arm circles to bowl, allow it to slip in your fingers. Probably the best way to practise this is to stand in front of a mirror holding a ball with the shiny side on the leg side in an off-spin grip. I think that John Emburey used to bowl his off one finger. The key is to ensure that as the ball comes out of the hand, it is held in an upright position and allowed to swing away. It is also important to vary one's pace. Sometimes, inevitably, it will slip out.

The principles of delivery have not changed down the years. The momentum created by a smooth run-up must be strong enough to propel the body through the action. At the start of this, the body must be wound up correctly: the front elbow must be above shoulder height and, as the bowler is about to bowl, the front arm must lead the head and finally the delivery arm on to the target. The head should travel parallel to the ground before and after release to ensure fuller length (Paul Adams is very much the exception to this rule!). The follow-through should be a natural part of the momentum generated by both run-up and arm speed. Practising bowling at targets will help, as will ensuring that the run-up speed is correct. In order to bowl a slower ball, the arm speed need not differ (so as to fool the batsman), but the ball should slip through the fingers. If the arm action is slowed down, the batsman will spot it and invariably punish the ball – or at least he will if he is competent enough. A loose wrist and finger action will mean that the fingers are split wider and the ball will slide out. Sometimes spinning the ball when bowling quickly will have the effect of producing a slower ball.

I am sometimes asked if there is anything wrong with an open-chested action. There is not. Sylvester Clarke, the West Indian bowler who died at the tragically young age of 44, was as mean as anybody who played the game, relying as he did on short deliveries that swung into the batsman at a formidable speed. Yet he ran in off a relatively short run and had no classical sideways-on approach. He was all whirling arms with a chest-on approach. He would have found it harder to bowl the away-swinger, but the key to increasing his range was wrist and finger control.

For conventional (not reverse) swing the seam must point in the direction in which the ball should go. To swing it out, the bowler must lock the wrist back, slightly inwards towards the body. When the ball is delivered the fingers should run down the back of the ball, ensuring the seam revolves backwards, slightly angled towards the slips. The arm needs to be between eleven and twelve o'clock, and the follow-through should be across the body. For the inswinger, the wrist should be locked inwards. The seam should point towards leg slip, the arm should be vertical or just past twelve o'clock, and as the ball is delivered the arm must go towards and past the right hip. For both deliveries, the front arm and head should lead the bowler on to his target – the off stump for the outswinger and the wicketkeeper for the inswinger. The bowler should vary the width of the crease for variety and surprise.

The basic principles apply to batting just as much as they do to bowling. The batsman must be still when the ball is released. Once he has judged the length, his front shoulder should lead the way. His foot should move outside the line but his toes should keep pointing at the ball, leaving enough room for the hands to hit through it. Weight should be transferred to the front foot – front hip over front foot – thereby allowing the hands to follow the shoulder line. If the bowler is deliberately firing the ball down the leg side, or has simply lost his ability to direct his yorker properly, the batsman could stand outside leg stump or change his guard permanently to leg stump. If the ball is too wide, he should not worry too much about chasing it, for there is always the chance that he will get a tickle to the wicketkeeper. David Gower, late in his career, would be out in this way, moving too far across his stumps or relishing the challenge of going for anything bowled too wide. A leg slip would sometimes be posted for this flaw, and there was a danger, too, that he would be caught on the deep square leg boundary, flicking too casually. This happened just before lunch in a Test match on his last tour to Australia in 1990/91, the trap having already been set. Graham Gooch, his captain that day, watched aghast from the non-striker's end, and was so non-plussed that by the time he had walked off the field it was almost time to come back out again. That moment signalled the beginning of the end of Gower's Test career. He had forgotten one of the elementary basics of batting: watch the ball and do not move until you have picked the length. Even the best players are culpable.

The need to be still at the crease and to watch the ball is paramount so that the length can be judged properly. If the batsman moves his foot back as the bowler releases the ball his forward movement will be rushed and he may be caught on the crease, resulting in being out lbw. He needs to move on to the back foot just before the bowler releases the ball. Then he can judge the length and, if the ball is pitched up, move his front foot alongside the pitch of the ball and play the appropriate shot. To find out if he is moving too soon, he can ask someone to bowl at him and hold on to the ball occasionally instead of letting it go. The batsman will then be able to see if his foot movement is premature and can adjust accordingly.

When I played, there was no question of specialising in first-class or one-day cricket; everybody mucked in and tried to excel at both. Nowadays, it is all rather different. I agree with the policy of choosing so-called one-day specialists for certain games, but I would not like to see the point reached at which a country's Test and limited-overs teams are completely different. There is so much international cricket these days that more and more players are going to play, and the younger ones will probably be given their chance in the shorter game first, not least because they are likely to be better fielders than their elders. Gavin Larsen of New Zealand, for instance, played 55 one-dayers before making his Test debut.

Yet I know from experience that all cricketers see themselves as able to handle both forms of the game – and a lot can and will do so. Adam and Ben Hollioake are good examples of players suited to the one-day game, whereas at Test level they are competing with a number of specialists for batting places. More than four bowlers are required in limited-overs internationals, which means much more scope for the likes of the Hollioakes. I talk about this subject with a certain amount of authority because I was chosen initially by England as a one-day performer, someone who could bat a bit and bowl a bit. At the time, Kent, my county, were the best team in the country at instant cricket. So strong was our batting order that I was going in at number nine behind players who were batting higher for their countries. Only when I was promoted up the order in the Championship did I become a contender for Test cricket. At that stage, my batting became stronger than my bowling. The top-class all-rounder, it is said, will merit a place on the strength of either, but the reality is that few do; one can think only of Trevor Bailey, Keith Miller, Gary Sobers, Mike Procter, Kapil Dev, Ian Botham and perhaps Imran Khan and Richard Hadlee since the war. Shaun Pollock has the ability, but as

Geoff Boycott, my co-commentator for Talk Radio during England's 1999/2000 tour of South Africa, was telling him, if he wants to be recognised as a great all-rounder this millennium he has to work on his choice of shots on different pitches.

So who was, or is, the perfect cricketer? Picking the top player in the world is a familiar game, but I am going to take this a stage further. What I am after is the ultimate modern cricketer. One way of going about it is to run through the anatomy and see if we can build the perfect cricket body. 'From the feet up,' cries the coach. 'Check your position from the feet up!'

The feet should be fast and tough as we are going to aim for the perfect all-rounder. Among batsmen, I like Sachin Tendulkar's small and nimble feet, which give him excellent balance and are responsible for him moving down the wicket so smartly to attack spinners. But we need a little more beef for the bowling department. Of the bowlers that spring to mind, Allan Donald, Darren Gough and Shaun Pollock have all suffered foot problems, so I am going to go for those of Javagal Srinath, who was brought up on the rough ground of India. Walking barefoot as a kid will really have toughened him up. Visit the subcontinent and you will see an incredible number of boys playing cricket with only the most rudimentary equipment. At least in the West Indies feet can be softened by playing on the sandy beaches.

The calves, too, need to be powerful both for the spring required in the field and running between the wickets. We will come on to Jonty Rhodes later, but Michael Bevan is also tremendously quick – probably the fastest over 100 metres in world cricket. The way he runs and turns between the wickets suggests he has the calves for us. This is one of the main reasons behind his considerable success in the one-day game.

I have decided to combine knees and thighs because the thighs need to be well developed to keep the knees in place. As much as pace and power, we are looking for suppleness, since we are now dealing with hamstrings. If I can cheat a little, I shall take Allan Donald's hamstrings, because anyone who can go 24 centimetres past his feet in a hamstring stretch is going to be supple. In a tricky operation, I shall combine them with Rhodes' thighs. Jonty's ability to spring off the ground in both directions is phenomenal. We can all picture in the mind's eye a remarkable piece of fielding by him down the years. So the physical shape of this particular cricketer will be a little strange, but all the better for it.

The modern cricket itinerary makes it vital to have strength in the stomach and back. These days, many players work very hard with weights to improve their strength – Bevan, for instance, and Jacques Kallis. But I am going to choose Lance Klusener. Years of humping sugar cane on the farm has developed these areas on his body nicely. The manner in which he clumps boundaries, particularly when he is given too much width by opposing bowlers, is incredible.

The shoulders and forearms are also vital areas for both batsmen and bowlers. Viv Richards had huge forearms and could make the ball disappear to the boundary with ease. Among players of today, Graham Thorpe looks strong in the forearms and plays punchy shots all around the wicket. Darren Lehmann and Inzamam-ul-Haq both come into the reckoning too, but for our player to be an all-rounder we need him to have the versatility of a spin bowler – in this case, Shane Warne before his operation, with the extra strength of Inzamam or Lehmann.

In the wrists and hands, a definite combination of strength and suppleness is needed. I am inclined to add fingers as well. Firstly, we are looking for the feel necessary to play spin, which is sometimes known as soft hands. The dexterity to ease the ball into the gaps with supple wrists is largely the property of the subcontinent. Saeed Anwar and Sachin Tendulkar certainly have it, but so does Australia's Mark Waugh. In fact, I am going for Waugh because of his renowned catching ability, though it would be remiss of me not to mention Brian McMillan in this respect, a man known as 'buckets' for the very reason that his hands are very large and little ever came out. For the bowlers, we must have the fingers of Warne, whose ability to spin the ball prodigiously is revered worldwide. Warne also has a fantastic wrist. But for our Sobers-style all-rounder, who bowls seam-up as well as spin, we need to spread the net wider. Glenn McGrath, Shaun Pollock and Wasim Akram are all masters at keeping the seam upright with a perfect wrist position.

For the neck, we need look no further than Jacques Kallis (rugby-prop strength) and Sachin Tendulkar (the suppleness of the subcontinent) – a divine mixture for batting. Among the bowlers, I like the look of Geoff Allott. Being a Kiwi, he has probably propped a scrum or two himself. Our team, then, has an eclectic look about it.

Next, the cranial area. How important is it? Not being a brain surgeon – I have never even read about the brain; in fact, I am still hunting for most of mine! – I shall stick to individual attributes of character or intelligence. The ideal cricketer would have the guts and determination of Steve Waugh together with the calmness under pressure of Hansie Cronje, and the never-say-die attitude of both. The speed of thought of Mark Taylor would also have to come into the reckoning here, although now that he has retired he will have to be discounted.

So which cricketer comes closest to this ideal? The incomparable Gary Sobers, who was one of the finest batsmen and best left-arm swing bowlers in cricket history, could bowl both varieties of left-arm spin and was a wonderful close-to-the-wicket fielder. He was also a wonderful sportsman who never set out to play in a negative way. He was not so adept at captaincy, but then he did not always need to be when he was performing so well himself. Problems occurred when he lost his own form through tiredness, such as on the West Indies tour of England in 1969, but his was a natural talent, the like of which will probably never be seen again. He was the one exception to the rule when it comes to the impression a coach can make. In his case, he could just be sent out on to the pitch and told to perform in his own unique way. For these reasons, and more, Sobers is as close as we can probably ever get to the perfect cricketer.

*   *   *

Putting forward ideas, trying to get other people on your side (cricket is such a subjective game that everyone has ideas), fighting against the past, persuading people that earpieces and other inventions are the way forward – such is the life of a coach. In discussion one day on tour in New Zealand early in 1999 I was accused of not listening, and the point was well made. How good a listener does one need to be as a coach? Sometimes one forgets to listen. Paying attention to detail is the most vital aspect of coaching as events and people change on a daily basis.

At the same time, it is almost impossible not to react to adverse criticism. Why? Simply because you work your butt off seemingly for no reward. Few players take the trouble to remember the effort a coach puts in; of those who did in my case, I have been overwhelmed by the responses of Allan Donald and Gladstone Small in particular. But the coach acts as a buffer to all things. In my time with Andy Lloyd, Dermot Reeve, Kevin Bridgens (at Boland), Terence Lazard (at Boland) and finally Hansie Cronje, each of these captains has lost his cool in different ways. This may, of course, be an indictment of my coaching. The pressures on each of these players has been enormous, though, especially at international level. My best relationship was with Dermot, as between us we questioned the norm in the game, which was fun. But he was really upset with me when Brian Lara was at the club as I treated Brian differently owing to his nature and the burdens he was labouring under. At the time, and probably to this day, Dermot would consider that a weakness. Unfortunately, a coach has always to be impartial to a tee, and the strength of his equanimity is tested almost daily.

One of the great difficulties about Test cricket for a coach is that quotes are summarised in headlines, often in an incorrect or misleading way, and stories are hardened or sensationalised to suit the editor's requirements. If players read the newspapers or have cuttings sent to them, then things can rapidly become nightmarish. As cricketers and entertainers we need the papers to promote our sport, but we believe that they in turn should tell the true story. The true story is usually boring and not (or so we are told) what the readers want. In South Africa we have a number of cricket journalists who are very easy to get on with. Players make friends with them and they become close to the team. We are fortunate that we do not suffer the type of tabloid journalism that infiltrates the Australian and English media, the type that ensnares its victim with what the sports psychologist calls 'external focus': the player believes what the papers are saying, not what the coach has said.

I, too, have fallen into this trap. I have been as guilty of overreacting to other people's views as the next person, but I genuinely believe that players are too affected by the press and other forms of the media. Like a lot of players, I really enjoy reading the good things that are written about a team of mine; on the other hand, when things go badly, it is not nice to be told about them. But in order to succeed you have to be able to read both strands of opinion and to be able to deal with them. For example, if a journalist has a go at you and you do not agree with him, then why, when the same journalist is full of praise, do you as a player believe him? I was lucky to be influenced by Alan Knott, who never read a newspaper during his playing days. For all he knew the world could have ended and he would still have wanted a spoonful of honey in his tea. What a marvellous temperament he had, and what a shining example he set.

I found that spending part of the 1999 season in the media's midst in England was an interesting experience, to say the least. As a so-called expert, I had been asked to give forthright opinion for the *Mail on Sunday*; sitting on the fence was out of the question. I found the press box at a Test match a surreal place to be. There is a continual hum of noise as discussion goes on during the game. The fall of a wicket arrests everyone's attention as they study the replay – only a small percentage of those present having seen the real thing. The dismissal is shown by television five times from five different angles and in slow- and super slow-motion. Very rarely do the journalists decree that the dismissal has occurred as the result of a good ball. If it is not the umpire's fault, then inevitably the batsman is criticised – and, of course, the worse the shot the more likely it is he is going to cop it. I was also in awe of how the experienced journalist can turn 1,800 words into 650 and put an article into tabloid form. It is clever, and gives the article the necessary bite that catches the eye of the reader. It is unfortunate, though, that in many of the modern press boxes the game's atmosphere is lost, owing in the main to modern safety requirements. Newlands is an exception, though, and it has to be said that the new flying gherkin, as the press box at Lord's has been nicknamed, is an absolutely fantastic facility.

The media is very important for the game, but it should be remembered that without the game there would be no need for the media. In addition, players need to understand that they are going to be criticised if they behave badly or perform poorly. There is no excuse for the player if he is surly and bad-tempered and the world gets to know about it. There is a need for a coach to make them aware of this, but at the same time there is a need to make the journalist aware that the game must come first.

I found, too, that people often questioned whether or not I was doing a decent job. When I read a disparaging article about me by some journalist I barely know, I am always reminded of the young autograph hunter who wrote: 'Dear Bob, you are the best coach in the world! Can you get me the team's autographs please for my collection?' How does he know I am the best in the world, I wondered at the time? He has never even been to a practice session. I was accused by the media of not getting South Africa's top order right for the World Cup, although I know I worked hard enough with them. The journalist who wrote that had never bothered to come to a single practice. As a coach, I felt I could not win.

Often, when confronted with such words, I had to ask myself why I was doing the job. But I never found it difficult to answer that one, because I was once shown Lord Harris' monograph on the game and its sentiments made a big and lasting impression on me:

You do well to love Cricket, for it is more free from anything sordid, anything dishonourable, than any game in the world. To play it keenly, generously, self-sufficiently, is a moral lesson in itself, and the classroom is God's air and sunshine. Foster it, my brothers, so that it may attract all who find the time to play it, and protect it from anything that may try and sully it so that it may grow in favour with all men and women.

11 Final Thoughts

WHY IS THERE such a big difference between Test matches and the game at other levels? Whatever the standard, cricket is an exciting game. Just waiting to go into bat creates a special feeling, so special that I remember in one school fixture I took part in the first eight batsmen were getting ready at the same time to go in. Either we did not have confidence in the upper order or everyone wanted to have a bat. From the beginning that sense of excitement, of nervous tension, remains with you and it is the man who can contend with that who generally succeeds.

I shall always remember my first Test match. To this day I have the odd dream about it, so vivid is my recollection. I was selected for the second Test of four against Australia at Lord's in 1975. England had lost the first Test and there was much gloom about our chances even though a change of captaincy had been made and there was an air of excitement and anticipation in the crowd that watched us practise. A new-look England, a charismatic leader in Tony Greig, Lord's was abuzz. I was one of a squad of thirteen and did not dare believe that I would be picked. I was very quiet at the team dinner on the night before the match started. I listened intently to where and how we would bowl out the Aussies. I sat surrounded by players who had played fifty or more Tests.

The pleasure I was experiencing was almost uncontrollable. The side would be announced in the morning after the selectors had looked at the pitch. I went to bed early, just in case I got the nod. There were other prospective debutants as well. I wondered how they felt. After dinner my mind was working overtime with instruction. Bowl this line to Doug Walters; don't let him cut; he drives with his feet together. I showered and got into bed, then switched off the television (this was long before remote controls and satellite TV came into being) – we had BBC1, BBC2 and ITV and the controls were operated by switches by the bedside. This was the best hotel I had ever stayed in. Usually on the county circuit we would stay in a hotel with one TV room and you had to get there first if you wanted the programme of your choice! I remember vividly the rush for a Wednesday night football match.

I turned the light off. I had never had a problem sleeping before, but there is always a first time. And here it was. I must have dozed, for after an hour I woke up on the floor. I had been dumped unceremoniously by a Jeff Thomson bouncer and had ducked. I awoke with a start in a sweat, realising I had obviously picked myself to play. This pattern continued throughout the night. Four cold showers later I got up at eight in the morning. In those days we had to be at the ground only at 10.30 for an 11.30 start. Breakfast was at nine and Lord's was within walking distance. By 8.30 I had finished breakfast and my stomach was in turmoil. I somehow knew I was going to play, for I read all the papers and they had all picked me. After the night I had I was in no nick, my eyes were heavy from lack of sleep and my legs were like lead. I walked to the ground nearly two hours before the start. I was a mess. I had another shower to try and wake up, put my whites on, got my kit together and went over to the nets.

Usually one could get a bowler from the MCC groundstaff to give you a net. I had one and could hardly lay bat on ball. I felt terrible! Eventually the rest of the team came across and we warmed up. In contrast to today, this comprised ten minutes of light stretching, a quick bowl and a bat. I could see Tony Greig, our captain, in conversation with the selectors, who were chaired by Alec Bedser. I was so tired by now that I was yawning away and I was beginning to think I should tell someone my state of mind so that they wouldn't pick me.

I was busy practising some bat/pad catches when that familiar South African voice rang out. 'Bobby, you're in, well done and good luck.' I turned and accepted the firm handshake from the grinning 6ft 7in giant from Port Elizabeth and, as if someone had waved a magic wand over my body, the heavy legs and the tiredness dissipated – where to I will never know, but I had just discovered adrenalin in its neat form. From then on I played the Test match in this state. No sleep or very little of it (and that has remained constant even when coaching South Africa).

I was down to bat at seven and ended up going in at eight. We lost four wickets before lunch and I couldn't eat and brought up my breakfast. Never before had I experienced such butterflies in my stomach. Alan Knott once said to me it gets worse the more you play, but it is the reason you play. There cannot be a high like it in the world. No drug – surely – can give you this boost. Pain is forgotten, stiffness eradicated. It is unbelievable! When eventually I walked out to bat in front of that capacity crowd against the great enemy, for a moment I felt like a king. Fortunately Thomson and Dennis Lillee soon brought me down to earth and I had to concentrate like mad.

This sense of excitement, this nervous tension, afflicts cricketers to the extent that they play as if in a cocoon. They can be oblivious to what is going on around them. The batsman is intent on occupying the crease and can be indifferent to comments and events around him. This determination not to surrender his wicket is exacerbated by the rewards that are now on offer for successful Test cricketers. This has to be considered when taking into account what happened in Port Elizabeth during England's tour of South Africa in 1999/2000. There was an incident that was to be debated for weeks afterwards. When South Africa were 48 for two, Jacques Kallis played forward to Phil Tufnell and edged the ball low and quickly to Chris Adams at short gully. He swooped low and one-handed (the left) picked up the ball in his fingertips, threw it up when he realised that the ball had stuck, and whooped with joy. He was quickly surrounded by his English team-mates and there were smiles all round.

Suddenly the exuberance was dulled by the realisation that Kallis was not walking off the field. Now a batsman who is unsure whether he is out or not has every right to stand his ground. Jacques assured me that he was convinced that the ball hit the ground. Now came the drama. The England side formally appealed to the umpire, Rudi Koertzen. As luck would have it, Rudi was unsighted by the bowler's follow-through. He had to turn to his square-leg colleague, Steve Bucknor from the West Indies, who intimated that he was also unsighted, this time by the wicket-keeper. (In my day the batsman would have asked the fielder 'Did you catch it?' and he would have been taken at his word.) Today I am afraid this is not the case. Players in Test cricket very rarely walk because their financial future is at stake as well as national pride. Of course, if the fielder had said he was uncertain, then the umpires would have been called in.

Obviously the etiquette of cricket is no longer what it was. We are in the era of technology, of the third umpire and countless TV cameras on the ground. South African Broadcasting Corporation had the rights in Port Elizabeth and captured the various pictures that the third umpire had to make his decision from. Again, nothing was conclusive and after an interminable delay Kallis was given not out. The air was blue on the field.

There was more drama off it. Sky TV had another angle which everyone assured me was conclusive and that Kallis was out. Yet the third umpire, Dave Orchard, did not have the benefit of this and even if he had I am not sure he would have found it to be conclusive evidence, either. Anyway, in the Talk Radio box (with its mainly English commentators) the ball was reckoned to have been caught four inches off the ground. In the Supersport box (South African commentators) the comments suggested the opposite. The drama had embraced patriotism.

If technology is the way forward to help the beleaguered umpire then we must ensure that it is the best and the most productive available. Haphazard use of the television feed is not the fault of the TV stations that cover the cricket. The umpires should be consulted with the aid of visual experts and trial-and-error experimentation to make the best use of technology. As soon as the field is set then special pan-eye-type cameras should be put in place to pick up the low catch, aimed at an area near the slips. The stillness of the camera is essential and the zoom factor is available on all digital cameras these days. The other way, of course, is to go back to what the game is really all about: accepting the word of the fielder and for both sides to trust each other.

The difference at Port Elizabeth was that Jacques Kallis' average stood at 40.30 before the Test. He scored one in the first innings which reduced it to 39.41. If he had been given out to the Adams catch his average would have been 38.79. After his undefeated second innings, it was 41.39. A three-point difference. The public perceives you as a top-class Test match performer if you average in the forties. With all the pressure now on players to perform and stay in the team, there is no wonder that they are going to leave it to technology.

In order to help the umpire, who also is more inclined to use the technology now because he is scared to make mistakes (realising that the livelihood of the player is in his hands), administrators have to understand that they have to go all the way. Microchips in the ball, bat and stumps will quite clearly show if the batsman has hit the ball or whether he is lbw or not. Then specially operated remote cameras should be trained on the slip cordons and catchers. Positioning of these cameras can be worked out and operated by remote control from a special area through a state-of-the-art computer. The result can be almost instantaneous. This would prevent a repeat of the bizarre incident on the 1994 tour of Pakistan when, as I have detailed elsewhere in this book, the third umpire gave Dave Richardson run out and at the end of the game came into our dressing room and said, 'I am terribly sorry, I pressed the right button but the wrong light came on!'

This would then cover another aspect of the game and absolve the umpire from poor decision-making. Of course it won't stop there, as flaws will be exposed in the use of technology, but there will be no stopping progress. The scary thing is that some countries are still not using the pan-eye camera for run outs and stumpings. Scarier still is that the International Cricket Council is still deciding on which route to take with all sorts of technology. In the never-ending battle to compete with football and other sports, cricket has to keep pace.

For years the game in England had been played on the understanding that players tried to help their colleagues who had become umpires. The names of those who did not walk became mud. I remember being severely admonished by Alan Dixon, Kent's vice-captain, when I stayed at the crease after an appeal for a bat/pad catch off the bowling of Fred Titmus at Canterbury early in my career. I was given out and ticked off in the dressing room for not walking. I had not hit the ball but, suitably chastised, I promised to walk in future – always.

Needless to say it was the Australians who, brought up amid some very average umpiring, coined the phrases, 'Leave it to the umpire, mate!' and 'It evens itself out in the end.' At least there is a consistency about their attitude to walking. The reality is that this attitude has changed – among all countries – to 'Let's see if we can get away with it.' Yet even now some umpires want to have no reliance on technology whatsoever. I strongly disagree. If the game could harness the equipment properly then players would have no option but to leave the crease. Maybe technology and chivalry could then join forces.

At international, provincial and county levels, the 'win at all costs' attitude prevails. This is not least because the coach and the captain count the cost of failure. I firmly believe that children should not be inculcated in this way of thinking and that they should learn to win and be able to handle defeat with good grace.

Coaching, like teaching, is a process and it takes five years or more for a youngster to get to grips with the game before he starts to perform. What is important for parents of our aspiring young cricketers to remember is that encouragement is of more value than constant criticism. I believe firmly that the five years between ten and fifteen will determine which boys – and girls – will become decent cricketers. If, during that period, they have had opportunities to bat, bowl and catch, up and down the order, they will understand the nuances of the game: the disappointment of not batting, and the elation of scoring runs and of taking wickets.

Consider the difference in the game at grass-roots level. At schools there is a distinct lack of opportunity for aspiring youngsters. I know that what happened to my family when my elder son, Dale, was learning the game has occurred to many other parents. He was selected for the 'A' team for the under-11s, having shown genuine signs of promise. At the age of three he could bowl a tennis ball straight more often than not with a lovely side-on action. He could hit it quite cleanly and had taken to mini-cricket when very young.

As I was coaching every afternoon, I had limited opportunity to see him play. When I did have the chance I was disappointed that he never had a bowl and batted at number eight. He spent his time throwing acorns at a friend at mid-on. His team was extremely powerful and every Wednesday mashed the opposition, usually by ten wickets. More often than not the same pair opened the batting and the bowling.

Frustrated, I eventually walked up to the coach (the master in charge) and asked if my son might be given a couple of overs before I had to leave. I was embarrassed to do so, given that I was an ex-international cricketer and well-known coach and did not want to interfere. I would not have wanted others to get in the way while I was coaching. The master kindly obliged and Dale, in his two overs, actually took four wickets. Dad was pleased as punch and left the ground a happy man.

What occurred after that was even more disappointing. Dale was then left out to give him more opportunity in the under-11s 'B' team. When asked by their master in charge what he did, honesty prevailed. 'Sir, I bat at eight and field at mid-wicket,' he said, so the master promptly followed suit. Sadly, Dale has now given up the game. An opportunity was lost, it seemed to me, because of the penchant to win at all costs.

The teacher in charge invariably gives up three or four afternoons a week to introduce youngsters to the game, mostly voluntarily as it is not part of his teaching contract. There are so few individuals interested that he will have the job for life if he wants it. Often these teachers have little knowledge of cricket, hoping desperately that they are not thrown a question that will show them up. Of course they make mistakes. Don't we all? Criticising the omission of our children turns us, of course, into armchair selectors. Yet we also know that in general the teacher/coach is doing his best. The solution is for all schools to balance opportunity with winning at all costs. Then the teachers/coaches who do not understand the nuances of the game would not be under pressure from stupid parents like myself.

I was able to gain a different perspective on the game when I was asked to commentate on South Africa's series against England in 1999/2000. I have mentioned already my experience of the press box. Now, in addition to writing columns for the *Mail and Guardian* in Johannesburg and *Mail on Sunday* and *Wisden Cricket Monthly* in England, I was commentating for both Talk Radio and Supersport TV. My first question as I walked into the radio box was from Chris Cowdrey, my former team-mate, who asked me, 'What are you today, Bob? Are you English or South African?' So I said if South Africa did well I would be South African and if England did well I would be English.

Working in the two boxes was a difficult discipline, not least as at times I was doing nine half-hour sessions in a day. I found it hard making the transition from television to radio and vice versa. One form of commentary requires adding to the pictures and the other telling the whole story, but they must not be confused. Summarising is undoubtedly easier than commentating. It is a matter of saying why something happened, rather than giving the entire picture. In other words, if a ball jagged back and the batsman played and missed, I could talk about the movement of his feet and try to explain the finer points of the game. That was a lot of fun. After coaching for a long time, I try to study players in different ways to the average watcher who is viewing the overall game. I am looking to see if the non-striker is backing up properly, if fielders are in the right position to throw the ball and why things are going wrong. I am used to watching players from all sorts of different angles as opposed to sitting behind the arm in a commentary box all the while. It is much easier to watch a game with a television monitor next to you. I think we should take on board what rugby commentators do and sit at a desk with a fitted screen in front of us.

Brian Johnston and John Arlott, with his lovely slow Hampshire drawl, were the two commentators I listened to as a kid in England. When I was older and came to South Africa, I was taken with the eloquence of Charles Fortune, but I never had any pretensions that I could become a commentator or desire to be one. My first bloomer on TV was quite funny. I was trying to explain why Allan Donald's bowling action had gone wrong. His front arm was dropping away, his head pushing it out of position. Poor Mark Boucher was having to stop huge in-swingers ten yards outside leg-stump. I tried to explain to the viewer what was happening and said, 'As Allan Donald comes in, just watch how his front head falls away!'

Sharing a box with Geoffrey Boycott was quite an experience. 'Coom on, out of t'chair – you're talking too mooch rubbish,' he said. We managed to take the micky out of Geoffrey in the box when he got a little over the top. We would say to him, 'Do you remember that ball Chris Cowdrey bowled to you in the Benson and Hedges tie between Kent and Yorkshire all those years ago?' He replied: 'It hit a pebble.

It hit a bloody pebble.' Graeme Pollock was another summariser. During the millennium celebrations at the fourth Test he was presented with an award for South Africa's player of the century. He is regarded in the Republic as being only a little lower than the angels, not just for his Test average of 60.97 and the ease with which he made his runs but for the easy-going and charming way he has carried himself ever since the huge disappointment of having his Test career curtailed when he was only twenty-six – before, presumably, he had even reached his peak. 'I would have liked to have played more than twenty-three Tests,' he said, 'but one way to change the apartheid system was through isolation, so I am quite happy my career was affected in that context.' That is a magnanimous approach. Others among the ten contenders who were chosen and paraded before the crowd, played in even fewer Tests than that. The likes of Barry Richards and Mike Procter, great players both. Basil D'Oliveira did not play for South Africa at all and when he walked to the middle at Newlands during that ceremony, it was, amazingly enough, for the first time. He had never been allowed to play there and would have been allowed to watch only from a segregated part of the ground. Symbolically, he walked out on a red carpet.

Being present at these Test grounds through commentating has enabled me and other old players to keep in touch with the game and keep in touch with one another. I should like to do more of it as and when I can, especially when I am no longer coaching. It is good to learn different skills and I am looking forward to helping players deal with the media so that they can promote the game more. I do feel they need to talk to journalists, to give them information that can be put across to the general public.

Although England lost the Test series against South Africa, I was pleased I could observe them progressing under the leadership of Nasser Hussain and the coaching of Duncan Fletcher. Their body language on the field was markedly different than it was against New Zealand the previous summer when the players looked uninterested in the proceedings and wandered around in a bit of a mess. I think it showed what effect a senior official like a coach could have on the disciplines needed for Test cricket. Nasser's batting was impressive at a time when everyone was saying that once Allan Donald had removed Mike Atherton, that would be it. He and Alec Stewart played really well.

I have not been convinced as yet that Nasser is sufficiently tactically astute. I thought he made some errors in the second Test in Port Elizabeth. He did not use Andy Caddick and Phil Tufnell as a pair as well as he might have done or necessarily bowl the right bowlers at the right end. Only through watching as an outsider can one spot these details. What I do perceive about Nasser is that he will not capitulate easily and that he will learn very quickly. He will, I think, become a pretty good captain. He talks to the youngsters and involves them in decision-making, which is good to see. This is not in line with previous English thinking because on the 1995/96 tour to South Africa Mike Atherton and Ray Illingworth made all the decisions and the rest of the side were told not to demur. If they did, they were castigated, not so much by the captain as by the manager. He would not accept that one-day cricket had changed and so England went to the subsequent World Cup completely underprepared. Knowing Duncan Fletcher as I do, he will be very sharp on those details. Whether England's cricketers are skilful enough is another matter.

The story goes – and it might be apocryphal – that Fletcher could not pursue all the methods he had in mind because the level of fitness of the England players was much lower than he had anticipated. This was something he was not able to control before he went on tour. Andrew Flintoff, for example, is strong and beefy, Bothamesque in build, but not as fit as Ian was at the same age. He has a reputation of eating and drinking too much. Other all-rounders, and Ian of course was one, were regarded in much the same way, but I expect only at certain times. They were pretty disciplined during Test matches. I think Duncan will say to Andrew that if he prepares himself properly, he will become a good cricketer and important to the England side. On South Africa's tour of 1998, I thought he looked a very average performer and wondered why he was rated highly. A lot of my team felt that there must be a better all-rounder in the country than him. Now, he looks a different player – still raw, still a powerful hitter, but his bowling has taken on a new dimension.

Once on tour, England worked hard to get themselves fitter and to match the South Africans, but in the heat there was a difference between the two countries. Any side that spends a lot of time in the field, as England did in the third Test at Durban, will normally find that their performance in the next match is pretty average. So it proved in the second of the back-to-back Tests at Cape Town in the New Year. Andy Caddick was tired by then, although his success overall and the fact that Allan Donald, for all his wickets, was not quite himself, meant the two sides were reasonably well matched. Lance Klusener's ability to come in and make quick runs has, of course, had a profound effect on the balance of their side. England tried to match that by bringing in Flintoff at number seven and shortening their tail, although that did not prevent them from some collapses. Darren Gough's batting was a disappointment, for he looked to me as though he was not confident against pace. I shudder to use the word 'scared' because people react so violently against it, but the reality is that he looks as if he does not want to get into line.

South Africa were hampered by pretty poor selection policy. Their first slip-up came before the series started when they announced that Hansie Cronje was to be captain for only four Test matches, two against Zimbabwe and two against England, and this, of course, immediately raised suspicions. He had captained his country for five years and done well. Why, now, were the selectors not trusting him to continue? The reasons for that were that they felt, going on press reports, that he was not fully committing himself to South Africa. He was negotiating to coach Glamorgan in the English summers. They did not bother asking him his opinion.

Hansie and Graham Ford, my successor as coach, were not consulted over selection for South Africa's visit to Kenya for some limited-overs matches before England's tour. A young man called Botha Dippenaar, a fine player, was picked. He will probably play Test cricket in the long-term, assuming he improves, and I realise he needed to be given some experience, but opening the batting against international bowlers on the poor surfaces there was not an easy task. Daryll Cullinan was dropped for that trip – and was not informed by the selectors beforehand. A lot of mistrust built up as a result, which meant that Ali Bacher decided to go to Kenya to try to make the peace. Ultimately he couldn't do so because a chicken bone became stuck in his throat and he required an operation. So no meeting to clear the air took place until much later.

The captain and coach do not necessarily have to have a vote on selection matters but their opinions must be taken into account. They have to take responsibility for preparation and for results. If the coach does not know until the last minute who he is preparing, then his task becomes pretty difficult. South Africa, as expected, were far too strong for Zimbabwe in their two Tests. Then, having lost to India in Kenya when the ball turned square, they managed to recover and beat them in the final. That showed the character of the players involved.

Then, of course, there was the selection mistake over Jonty Rhodes. His wife was expecting their first child in March 2000, so he had asked the selectors if he could miss South Africa's tour to India. This resulted in an out-of-date recrimination: if he was not committed when he was contracted to play, the thinking went, then he should not be picked in the side against England and consequently he was left out of the third Test at Durban. The selectors should have understood that in modern society the birth of a first baby is important to a player – especially someone like Jonty, who is a Christian and has a close relationship with his wife. In my opinion they should be more comprehending of the conflicts international cricketers face. That apart, the balance of the side was wrong when Jonty was omitted against the wishes of the captain and the coach. Six front-line batsmen should always be included in a Test side, leaving numbers seven, eight and nine – you hope – to make another 150 runs. South Africa have excelled in that respect of late.

This dictatorial attitude of 'like it or lump it' largely has no place in society any more, whether it be sport or business. People like to be made to feel important, to have a say, and I think that if the captain is merely told he is not having Rhodes or any other established player in his side, it immediately puts his back up. I reckon this is one of the reasons why Hansie did not fire as a batsman during the series. He was not being treated as an important person and yet he is vital to South Africa's success. His batting has been affected because of what has happened off the field. This lack of judgement by the selectors played into the hands of England, because South Africa were not as focused on their game as they normally are.

I do not think the selection of Paul Adams for the first Test, when the pitch suited fast bowlers, was a decision born out of affirmative action. Geoffrey Boycott, my co-commentator, insisted that no-one could fool him about the cricketing politics of the country, but on that point we had to disagree. He and Herschelle Gibbs are in the side on merit, although Paul will have to be left out from time to time in certain conditions. I know that at Port Elizabeth Hansie would have liked to have included Paul instead of five seamers. In fact the only time that the make-up of a side against England was an issue was when a combined Gauteng side fielded 11 white players. From what I can gather, the Government-formed committee that oversees selection was contacted and they approved the selection. The committee includes Percy Sonn, the vice-president of the UCB, who knew all about it, although he was quoted in one of the newspapers as saying that he was not consulted.

My visit to the Nuffield Schools week during the series was instructive. The boys there were aged between 17 and 19, and 46 per cent of them were non-whites. The most amazing statistic was that 19 per cent of those were African, i.e. blacks. This is an amazing breakthrough given how few are playing cricket with a hard ball and would suggest that affirmative action will not be necessary within the game in the future. Every white child who is cricket crazy will be supported by his parents, but a black child might not have that same backing from his family and hence could be lost to the game. Twenty white children might come through the schools system, but how many will be good enough to go on and play for South Africa? One, maybe two. So if there is one black child excelling, the chances of him becoming a Test cricketer are even less.

I have written a report recommending that we have a special academy now for blacks from the age of 14 upwards. Eventually, when we have identified 18 or 20 players, we would put them in a team that will be captained by an experienced former Test player and coached off the field by Jimmy Cook, who since retiring from the game has become involved in development. As they improve through exposure and experience, so they can join the provincial sides with which they are associated.

All credit to Hansie Cronje for his declaration on the final day of the fifth Test that prevented the match from being totally forgotten after three days without any play. The fact that England won by two wickets in the very last over did not mean that his captaincy should have been criticised. Indeed, South Africa would in all probability have won had Paul Adams been fit to bowl. Those observers who felt that Hansie was too dour a captain would have had to re-assess their opinions, even though probably he would not have left Nasser Hussain such an enticing target had England still been in a position to square the series.

It was suggested that the ICC was not too happy with both captains forfeiting an innings – the first time this had happened in the history of Test cricket. If that was the case, then its outlook was too parochial. Hansie himself said that if there was criticism of his declaration then the time had come for him to get out of the game. In the Talk Radio box we all concurred that he was the best captain South Africa could have and that this last day's play in the series made for a stirring finale.

At the outset of the series between England and South Africa, the two key cricketers were forecast to be Allan Donald and Mike Atherton. Why they are rated so highly, not least by their opponents?

I first came across Allan Donald when I was coaching Kent in 1987. I had been away with the second XI when I turned up at Canterbury and was told he had decimated our batting line-up. It was the first indication I had that this was someone special. As a batsman myself, I always thought that unless the bowler was black – in other words West Indian black – then he might be quick, but only quick in terms of how white people bowled. On seeing Allan, I suddenly realised that this guy was really quick.

It was not for another four years that I was to meet Allan for the first time, when I joined Warwickshire. I was really looking forward to working with him. Unfortunately he could not come to Trinidad for pre-season training in 1991 because he was South African and hence considered a pariah in the Caribbean. This was before his country's re-admittance to world cricket. So it was not until I got back that we were able to work together.

My immediate impressions were of a really nice guy with a terrific physique. He made me feel at home straight away in Birmingham, where he was living, having just married. There seemed little chance then of South Africa playing Test cricket, so Allan playing for Warwickshire carried more significance than it would have done for most overseas players. In county cricket, the permitted allocation had just been reduced to one per club. In 1990 Allan had been sharing first-team duties with Tom Moody, the Australian who subsequently captained Worcestershire, and before that with Tony Merrick, the West Indian fast bowler. Before I arrived, Warwickshire had to make a difficult decision over who to retain.

By all accounts Bob Cottam, my predecessor as coach, had plumped for Moody and Andy Lloyd, the captain, wanted

Donald. Cottam had also disagreed with Lloyd on one or two other matters and the chairman, Bob Evans, had created some ill-feeling over the running of the club. The upshot was a huge bust-up resulting in the resignations of both Cottam and Evans. A new era had just started when I arrived, so Allan was keen to see where I stood. He need not have worried. Having been an opener, I very much appreciated the worth of extra pace.

He had a beautiful action with a wonderful run-up. It was important for me to find out early on how receptive he was to advice, so I started by timing his run-up. I immediately saw a man whose pace was conditioned by this. The smoothness of his run-up was so important to his bowling and after much conversation and watching him bowl, I felt I needed to gauge an optimum pace profile which would help me to see if there was any difference when it went wrong. When Allan bowled badly the ball would veer down the leg-side with a breaking of his wrist action. He did not really move the ball away from the right-handed batsman but had a wicked yorker and a very quick bouncer. He was a little wild at times and used to break the fingers of our poor wicketkeeper, Keith Piper, seemingly at will.

At team meetings he contributed little and had the annoying habit of tapping his pencil when we were talking. So he was still a pretty naive cricketer when I first came across him. Over the years Allan became one of the best pros any county could ask for and he was never shy to take responsibility with the ball. He says he learnt that from Alan Jones, the Australian rugby coach, and as he grew older he assimilated information from all sources. In a way I was fortunate that Allan was at his most receptive stage in terms of listening to advice.

My first step with him was to get him to concentrate on moving the ball away from the bat. Then we needed to work on a slower ball for one-day cricket, and over the years we worked on shortening his run-up to help cope with the demands of fast bowling. That sounds straightforward enough but in reality it was a difficult period for Allan. The key, of course, was to ensure that his action was smooth at the crease and that he did not try to bowl too quickly. The shorter the run-up the more likely one is to force oneself at the crease and lose one's action. As long as Allan knew this then he would always be able to handle himself.

My big task was to make Allan aware of his body, of what he could do and what he could not. He is now in my opinion a complete cricketer, for he has proved beyond doubt that he can bowl out the best batsmen in the world. Certainly he would be on my list of all-time great fast bowlers. He is fortunate that South Africa returned to international sport when he was reasonably young – twenty-five – and he can now take his rightful place amongst the Lindwalls, Truemans, Lillees, Holdings and Marshalls. He won't beat the world record of Test wickets owing to his age and because he will want to spend time with his family, but he will always be remembered.

There is something beautiful in watching a quick bowler run in and destroy a batsman's stumps. Donald's tussles with Michael Atherton have been quite something and I have never seen a man more motivated to do well than when he bowled against Brian Lara in South Africa. He is an honest person who in his autobiography told the truth. He would love to finish his career with Warwickshire and I know he will act as a wonderful bowling coach when his playing career ends.

For South Africa he has, of course, been their main strike bowler for several years. His performance at Old Trafford in 1998 when Pollock and then Klusener suffered injuries was described as superhuman. Hansie Cronje always turned to Allan for a wicket and he responded brilliantly. On occasions when he has broken down, captains have become frustrated that he cannot bowl and this has led to the odd flare-up, but he is a cricketer with a huge heart and someone who cannot let a team down. His emotional breakdown after South Africa had lost the semi-final of the World Cup in 1999 was typical of him. He had bowled magnificently earlier when he had destroyed the Australian lower order. The fact is that however good you are or however hard you try, you cannot be successful every day. It takes a strong man to rebound from defeat. Recently, injuries have plagued Allan as his body has been worn down from the continual beating it receives.

His English wife, Tina, daughter Hannah and son Oliver are so important in his life that he will, I expect, settle in Birmingham once he has achieved his goal of becoming the first South African to take 300 Test wickets, although I am sure the sunshine of Bloemfontein, his home city, will draw him over to South Africa. Like all fast bowlers he has an aggressive streak in him and yet he always lifts his team when they need it. He has been accused of poor body language on the field and showing too much disappointment. When this was pointed out to him, he immediately made a conscious effort to change his attitude.

I am more fortunate than most in that I have had the honour and privilege to work with Colin Cowdrey on batting, Alan Knott on wicket-keeping, John Snow and now Allan Donald on fast bowling. The basic principles of the game are what these great players adhered to with almost consummate ease.

I have mentioned Allan's tussles with Mike Atherton. Athers does not walk, as he showed when Donald had him caught at the wicket in that famous incident at Trent Bridge in 1998, and then at Cape Town in the fourth Test on the 1999/2000 tour. On England's last tour of Australia, Mike was told by a fielder after an appeal was turned down: 'I thought you Pommies always walked.' He replied: 'When in Rome . . .' He is strong enough to put these incidents behind him, carry on and score runs, whereas a lot of batsmen develop a guilt complex and then throw their wicket away. One has to admire him for that, but I suppose one should beware when the time comes for him to go into business. He always walks off without a fuss when he is out through a bad decision.

One of the reasons why South Africa beat England in 1999/2000 was that Atherton was out for a pair in the first Test at Johannesburg. Anyone who averages around 38 as a batsman has to be a fine player. Known as 'Captain Grumpy' on England's previous tour in 1995/96, he did not endear himself to press or public by the way he behaved. He would have his feet up on the desk at press conferences and the incident when he called a Pakistani reporter 'a buffoon' in Pakistan was an example of poor public relations. I thought that for all his class and sound technique, he needed to be far more in tune with the reasons he was playing the game of cricket.

It was nice to see him, four years on, relieved of the pressures of captaincy and with a smile on his face. We all knew he could defend, but it was good that he played some beautiful shots at Cape Town. Indeed, Alec Stewart said that he had never seen him bat more fluently in Test cricket. If there is a flaw in his technique, I would think it is when facing the ball that comes in at him from outside off-stump. He uses a unique front foot shuffle movement which, if utilised at the wrong time, means he struggles to move his foot out of the way. He ends up being bowled or lbw, simply because that timing has to be so much in sync with the person who is bowling to him. I imagine that in his latter years he has wanted to be a slightly more attacking batsman and anyone who has scored as many runs as he has should have the confidence to attack any bowling, be it at Test match level or otherwise. A measure of his ability is that every side that has played against England has reckoned that if they dismiss him quickly then they have England in trouble, and that includes the South Africans.

As a captain, I think he was pretty sound. He understood the game and led England well, although I do not know what he was like as a motivator. To compare him with someone like Hansie Cronje, his opposite number in Tests against South Africa, Mike would be a better player of quick bowling technically but lacked the same flair in one-day cricket. He always represented an obstacle to us when I was South Africa's coach and so it was important that we tried to upset him. Jonty Rhodes was asked to try to unsettle him with a few words and on occasion it was clear he had done that. The whole point was to get to the batsman's psychological state of mind and affect his ability to concentrate – which is considerable, as is the case with all great batsmen. It has been written in the media that Mike actually hated Jonty, but I find that difficult to believe. Certainly, though, he would have found Jonty an irritant on the field and that might have brought about his dismissal on one or two occasions. When Jonty dropped him in the covers on the opening day of the fourth Test at Cape Town, looking to hurl the ball up in the air in over-exuberance before he had properly caught it, the English supporters seated directly in line gave Jonty some fearful stick.

Mike has his detractors. The main reason for that, I think, is his body language. This can be understood because he is always on the defensive. He has played in an England side that has been quite close to winning various matches and yet not quite done so. He has played in a very difficult era for England, when they were losing for much of the time, and yet he personally did markedly well in spite of all that pressure. He was earmarked, and appointed to the captaincy, too soon in my opinion. Maybe he should have played under someone else for longer to improve his feel for the game. Latterly, of course, his back injury has been an impediment. He has had to change his stance, holding his bat off the ground so as not to stoop at the crease. He would be happy, I guess, that he has been able to bat as well as he has in this new style almost immediately.

I would like to see a change made in the registration of players. I feel that countries like Zimbabwe could benefit from fielding native players who have been registered for another country that no longer wants them. I am thinking of Graeme Hick, despite his call-up for England's triangular series in early 2000, and of Trevor Penney, the Warwickshire batsman. Both would have been decidedly useful to Zimbabwe, as would Steve Elworthy, who might well not play for South Africa again. I feel it would be nice to encourage players to take part at the highest level, regardless of where they live or whether they have been involved in Test cricket for another country. The ICC wants to move the game around the world and this would help. In addition to this, there ought to be a transfer system replacing the benefit system in county cricket, so that players can move around a bit more at will. Obviously this would be to the advantage of the richer counties, but it would also mean that players would be able to collect a slice of a transfer fee that would not be as exorbitant as in football because there is not so much money around.

There is an argument that this would bankrupt some of the eighteen county clubs – but there is also an argument that there are too many clubs. Cricket is having to face some of the problems that have afflicted football. Problems like Roy Keane's wage demands, which were such that he is now earning £50,000 a week from Manchester United. That doesn't even cover a season's salary for around 90 per cent of professional cricketers in England and has to be something that the game must address, otherwise another TV mogul will buy up players as Kerry Packer once did. There is clearly plenty of money around in sport and if cricket is deemed still to be worth watching, then it is ripe for a takeover. When I joined World Series Cricket, I was earning £2000–£3000 a year before tax and I was suddenly being offered £15,000 for two months work. In 1977 that was too much to turn down.

Having said that, I don't know where the game will obtain that kind of money, but it is probably possible to increase the earnings of the players quite considerably, particularly in one-day cricket, which has taken off to a huge degree. Administrators have to be very astute in attracting talented sportsmen towards cricket as opposed to football. If I was a talented sportsmen now in England, I would head only one way, even though I love cricket. I would take the chance of getting on to the books of Liverpool, Manchester United or Tottenham if I could. I have heard of two or three kids being paid retainers of £100,000 a year to prevent them from joining other football clubs. I find that unbelievable. If I was offered that now, why would I want to go and play cricket? E.W. Swanton said shortly before his death that cricketers are paid a reasonable salary, and they are. But by whose standards? The game is in the business of attracting people to watch it, so it must be very careful in what it does.

At the start of the new millennium I decided that I would not be deterred by the International Cricket Council's refusal to allow me to use earpieces for communication to batsmen, captain or fielders and that I would utilise another technological innovation as soon as I could. I asked Tony Kirkbride, a scientist at the Council for Scientific and Industrial Research in Pretoria, to investigate what kind of watches could be used by cricketers that would receive emails sent from my laptop in the pavilion.

Tony it was who had looked into the use of earpieces as a means of communication in sport. Technological advancement has been such that these will soon be outdated. Nokia are developing a watch that can receive emails, photographs and moving pictures and Swatch are hoping to bring out a watch that can develop as a telephone. The cost of this would be around £20,000 so the likelihood is that the captain would be the only person to wear one initially. I believe it is possible to coach more effectively this way.

The reaction from the England and Wales Cricket Board was that I would not be allowed to use earpieces in county cricket and that its cricket advisory committee had concluded that the importance of the role of the captain should not be affected by electronic gadgetry. I do not see how it is possible to prevent players from wearing watches, as they have been worn in the past, not least as a means of sponsorship. Spaceships are not banned by science, so why should watches be?

For instance, before Alec Stewart was out hooking rashly with only six overs to go before close of play in the fourth Test, an email could have been sent by the coach to tell him to calm down. The batsman at the other end could have done that, but the email message would have had more effect. I would not impose technology on any player who did not want to use it and would talk to any side I coached about the implications without forcing it upon them. I don't agree with the viewpoint that this is against the spirit of the game and would impede the development of captains and have asked the ICC if I can submit a report on technology in the game. Half the problems in cricket are caused by lack of communication and the game spurns science at its peril.